The Gambi

By W.G. Davis

PROLOGUE

The Gambino Crime Family is known worldwide as the "First Family" in organized crime. The names may have changed over the years but today's Gambino Family is still structured and controlled very similar to the earliest days back in Sicily.

The Gambino Crime Family is the most well-known and storied of New York's five Families. Their lineage traces back to the beginning of the 20th century.

The current structure of the Gambino Crime Family took centuries to develop. It all began on the island of Sicily, just below Italy. Although there are other organized crime groups from other parts of Italy, the Sicilian Mafia is considered to be the blueprint for all other Mafia organizations.

Several factors contributed to the development of organized crime on Sicily. The island is located at an easily accessible and strategically place in the Mediterranean Sea. And because of this, Sicily was invaded, conquered, and occupied by hostile forces many times. The local people were often enslaved by the conquering party and were often treated very inhumanely by the foreign overlords. This led to an overall distrust of central authority and organized legal systems.

The family, rather than the state, became the focus of Sicilian life, and disputes were settled through a system in which punishment was dealt quickly and justice was received through personal vengeance and vendetta, beyond the limits of the law.

In the 19th century, the European government system finally collapsed in Sicily. With no real government or functioning authority of any kind, the island quickly descended into lawlessness. Some of the local landowners and other powerful men began to build reputations and eventually came to be seen as local leaders. They were soon to be known as capos.

The capos used their power to extract tributes (a form of a tax) from farmers under their authority (much like the feudal lords before them). Their authority was enforced through the threat and use of violence. Their criminal activities were never reported to the authorities, even by the victims, because of the fear of reprisal.

This was the beginning of today's Sicilian Mafia.

Today the word "Mafia" is used to refer to almost all groups or gangs involved in organized crime. Originally, the word "Mafia" meant an organized criminal organization of Italian, predominantly Sicilian heritage.

In fact, the word "Mafia" is a literary creation. The real name is believed to be "Cosa Nostra" meaning "our thing". The phrase was used to describe the lifestyle of a Mafioso in Sicily.

The shroud of secrecy that surrounded Mafia activities in Sicily became known as Omerta, "the code of silence". Omerta is the Code of silence when dealing with the government. It means "manhood" and refers to the idea that a man deals with his own problems without the help of a law-body. Mafia bosses still use this code to protect themselves from the activities of the criminals below them in the organization.

The people of Sicily believed that the government was there not to help them out, but to make things even more difficult. As a result, the Mafia's golden rule of Omerta was born.

Also, the practice of recruiting young boys into the Mafia, culminating with a final test, "making their bones" also stems from Sicily.

In Sicily, many people regarded the Mafia not as law-breaking criminals but as role-models and protectors of the weak and the poor, as the government offered no protection to the lower classes.

At one time, the Mafia had been more like an attitude of pride, honor, and high social responsibility and had commanded great respect and adoration; rather than a criminal organization interested only in monetary benefits.

Unfortunately, the Mafia didn't stay like this for long.

Sicilians and other Italians began immigrating to the United States at the start of the twentieth century.

While the vast majority of them worked hard at building a new life for their family through legal means, some of them sadly brought the ways of the Sicilian Mafia with them.

From 1890 to 1900, 655,888 Italian immigrants arrived in the United States, of whom two-thirds were men.

Many Italians arrived in the United States hoping to earn enough money to return to Italy and buy land. Coming especially from the poorer rural villages in Southern Italy, including Sicily and Campania, most arrived with very little cash or education; since most had been peasant farmers in Italy, they lacked craft skills and, therefore, generally performed manual labor.

Some would say that New York was built from the ground up by the blood and sweat of Italian and Irish immigrants.

The immigrants populated various US cities, forming what is known now as 'Little Italy', where they could easily establish an Italian cultural presence.

Italian neighborhoods typically grew in the older areas of the cities, suffering from overcrowded tenements and poor sanitation.

Living together in such small communities created little more than a miniature version of the society they had left back in Italy.

Some of their own people exploited this fact and began to extort the more prosperous Italians in their neighborhood.

The extortions were done anonymously by delivering threatening letters demanding money.

The letters were written in a mixture of dialects, by people originating from different regions throughout Italy, and the Black Hand symbols varied greatly in design. Some designs were a knife or a skull, an open hand, others a closed fist, while others showed a hand holding a knife.

This became a crime that would eventually become a criminal epidemic known only as, 'The Black Hand'.

The Black Hand was a highly disorganized version of the real Italian Mafia.

People paid the Black Hand extortionists in the fear that the American law had no understanding, or power, to help them.

The myth of the Black Hand spread through every Little Italy in America. This caused a strong fear in the communities, and even the mention of 'La Mano Nera' would cause people to cross themselves with the hope of protection.

While the Black Hand was operating in America, the Honored Society was active in Sicily.

The Honored Society was slightly more complicated than the Black Hand of the United States.

The main organizer of the American Mafia, Salvatore Lucania, who would later be known worldwide as, Charles "Lucky" Luciano was born on November 24, 1897, in Lercara Friddi, a small town located about 45 kilometers (28 mi) southeast of Palermo.

Luciano wasn't the only future Mafia leader born in the area around Palermo at that time.

Just five-years later, Carlo Gambino, the future ruler of the Gambino crime family, was born in the city of Palermo, Sicily, on August 24, 1902, to a family that belonged to the Honored Society.

Part One
The Birth of the American Mafia

Ignazio 'the Wolf' Lupo

On March 19th, 1877, Ignazio Lupo was born to parents Rocco Lupo and Onofria Saietta, a middle-class family in Palermo Sicily. He had three brothers and one sister.

The word "Lupo" means wolf in Italian. This gave Lupo the nickname 'Lupo the Wolf'.

Which translates to, "Wolf the Wolf".

Ignazio Lupo has sometimes been referred to by his mother's maiden name as Ignazio Saietta.

From about the age of ten, he worked in a dry goods store in Palermo.

In October 1898, twenty-one-year-old Lupo shot and killed a business rival named Salvatore Morello.

We will note that Salvatore Morello is no relationship to Giuseppe Morello.

Lupo said that he had shot Morello in self-defense after Morello attacked him with a knife during an argument in Lupo's store. Lupo went into hiding after the killing and on the advice of his parents eventually fled Italy to avoid prosecution.

After leaving Sicily he made his way to Liverpool, Montreal, and eventually arriving in Buffalo New York.

Proceedings were held in Italy on March 12, 1899, against Lupo.

Just two days later, on March 14, 1899, Lupo was convicted in absentia of 'willful and deliberate murder'.

He was convicted reportedly due to the testimony of the other clerks who worked in his store at the time of the killing.

Once Lupo had settled in New York, he opened a store on E72nd Street with his cousin, but after the two had a disagreement he moved his business to Brooklyn.

Shortly after moving his business to Brooklyn, he moved back to what is now the "little Italy" area of Manhattan in 1901.

Lupo opened a small import store at 9 Prince Street, and also ran the saloon across the street at 8 Prince Street. the saloon would become a known base for the Morello gang over the following years, with Giuseppe Morello owning the restaurant at the rear of the premises.

It was around this time, Lupo began preying on his fellow Italian immigrants, using the extortion tactics of the Black Hand to extort money from them.

Giuseppe Morello arrived in New York City around September of 1892.

He was joined there roughly six months later by the rest of the Morello-Terranova family, including Morello's first wife Maria Rosa Morello.

The Morello's had two children: a daughter, Angela who died in infancy before arriving in America. And one son, Calogero "Charles" Morell who was born in 1892 and died at the age of ten.

In the mid-1890s, the family decided to relocate to Louisiana, where some of their relatives and friends from Corleone resided.

In Louisiana, they worked on a sugar cane plantation. The next year, they moved to Bryan, Texas to pursue cotton farming.

Members of the family became seriously ill with malaria while in Texas. His first wife Rosa died while in Texas.

Giuseppe Morello remarried the following year to another Corleone native, Lena Salemi. Giuseppe and his family moved back to New York, where he and his brothers were involved in several businesses.

This included coal, saloons, date factory, restaurant, oil, lathing, and plastering.

However, the family primarily earned their living through underworld rackets, such as extortion and counterfeiting.

Just as Morello and his family were returning to New York City, Mafia bosses Candelero Bettini and Nicholas Taranto were sent to prison for wholesaling counterfeit bills to associates who passed them in the community.

Morello and an associate named Meggiore were arrested in 1900 on charges of passing counterfeit $5 U.S. notes.

Meggiore was sentenced to six years in prison but Morello's charges were dismissed.

Vito Cascio Ferro

In 1901, influential Sicilian Mafioso Vito Cascio Ferro visited New York City and assisted in uniting the Mafia families in the U.S. into a national network.

Ferro appointed Morello as Capo di tutti Capi (translated to "Boss of Bosses") to oversee operations and resolve any disputes.

Giuseppe Morello was the first known, Capo di tutti Capi, "Boss of Bosses" of the Mafia. While he was a unifying force initially, he later became a central figure in underworld conflicts between families.

At the end of 1902, Morello founded the Ignatz Florio Co-op.

The Ignatz Florio Co-operative was chartered at the end of 1902, it was a successful, and by all accounts legitimate, business until the financial panic in the summer of 1907.

At the time, Italians were a powerful workforce in the City. Over two million Italians came to New York between 1900 and 1910.

Morello was not a builder in the literal sense, but his Co-op was one of the earliest developers of the Italian neighborhoods in East Harlem and the Bronx.

Giuseppe Morello was the Co-op's first treasurer, and Lupo was also a partner in the business.

Their mission was to build housing for the Italian community in New York City.

Initially, the Ignatz Florio Co-Operative Association sold inexpensive shares, of two or five dollars, to Italian immigrants. Upon the completion of a building, shareholders earned dividends, which they could either take in cash payment or reinvest the money in the Co-op's next construction venture.

What appeared at first to be a legitimate business venture, eventually took on the familiar tones of more recent Mafia involvement in construction.

Within nine years from arriving in America, Giuseppe founded a gang known as the 107th Street Mob, which would evolve into the

Morello Crime family with the help of Morello's half-brothers Ciro, Vincenzo, and Nicholas Terranova.

The Morello family is considered to be the first "organized" Mafia family of New York, with its leader, Giuseppe Morello often tagged the 'Boss of Bosses'.

However, by way of lineage, Lupo was the first boss of what would evolve into the Gambino Crime Family. Lupo was one of the first prominent Sicilian Mafia members to come to America.

Like Lupo, Giuseppe Morello's lineage would lead to another of the Five Mafia Families of New York, the Genovese Crime Family. Which is the oldest of the Five Families in New York City. Giuseppe Morello was also known as "The Clutch Hand," because a birth defect left Morello with a badly disfigured right hand.

The only identifiable digit on that hand was the fourth finger; the others were curled together into what appeared as a small knot.

Giuseppe Morello

It was the eventual merger between Lupo in Little Italy and Morello's Italian Harlem crew that put Italian organized crime on the map in New York City. Their mass numbers of criminals made intimidation and extortion of businesses easy money and it served as a deterrent to any potential competition to make their way into their territory.

By 1902 Lupo is regarded as the leader of the Manhattan Mafia. He is just an enforcer for Giuseppe Morello at this time.

Morello's half-brothers Ciro, Vincenzo, and Nicholas Terranova, are also considered as "top lieutenants".

The Morello Gang was known to stuff victims' bodies into barrels and then leave them out in the public on local street corners. The message to the community was clear and that led to less resistance.

But it wasn't just people in the community that the Morello Gang had to deal with.

On the evening of July 23rd, 1902 four boys went swimming near 73rd Street in Bay Ridge Brooklyn. One of the boys spotted a potato sack a few yards from the bank.

Inside they discovered a badly bruised corpse of thirty-year-old Giuseppe Catania, a Brooklyn grocer, with his throat cut from ear to ear.

Detectives later found another sack close by that contained the victim's blood-soaked clothes, they believed that the body had been tossed from a moving cart down onto the river's bank.

At first, the police thought that Catania had been the victim of a twenty-year vendetta from back in Sicily.

Catania had been a witness at a murder trial in Sicily, resulting in the conviction of two defendants. The police arrested one of the men, but no charges were filed and he was eventually deported back to Sicily.

At the time, the Secret Service believed that Catania had been a member of the Morello gang.

They suspected the gang had murdered him due to his habit of drinking and talking too much about the gang's criminal activities.

Just before Catania's death, he traveled with Lupo to Manhattan together to get some stock out of bond from the importer's office.

However, after a thorough and painstaking investigation, the police were never able to gather enough evidence to warrant any arrests in the case.

Salvatore Clemente, of the rival Frauto gang, later stated that Giuseppe Morello and Domenico Pecoraro were behind the slaying of Catania. But this information could never be confirmed.

After the murder of Joseph Catania, in Brooklyn, Chief Inspector Flynn, of the Eastern Section of the Secret Service, learned that Catania had been a member of the Mafia and was associated with a gang of counterfeiters whom the Bureau had long had under surveillance.

Meanwhile back in Calabria, Italy on February September 26, 1902, the future New York crime boss Albert Anastasia is born.

Shortly after the death of Giuseppe Catania, Lupo's father arrived in New York. And together they opened a retail grocery store.

Lupo imported Italian goods from his brother-in-law, Francesco Gambino, via an import company.

In February 1903, a shipment of empty olive oil cans labeled 'Rocco Lupo & Sons' was sent by Francesco to the 'Lupo Brothers'.

The cans were discovered and impounded for inspection by the Secret Service, after a telegram sent by Vito Cascio Ferro, led them to believe the gang was smuggling counterfeit currency into the city.

At the retail grocery store, he worked along with his brother, Giovanni Lupo who went by the alias, John Lupo.

Lupo worked as a presser for six years before leaving to work for his brother at his retail grocery store on Mott Street.

John worked with Ignazio for just less than two years, he then left in October 1908 to start a wholesale grocery store in Hoboken named, 'Lupo & Lo Presti'.

Just one year later in May 1909, a gunfight broke out in Hoboken. One of the trucks belonging to Giovanni's business had killed the four-year-old son of an Italian Banker. The accident caused a riot in which 'forty to fifty shots were fired at members of the Lupo faction'.

On Thursday, April 16, 1903, Lupo, was arrested in connection with a killing after a body was found on East 11th Street in what would come to be known as the 'Barrel Murder' case.

Two days earlier, on Tuesday, April 14, 1903, at 5:30 a.m. in front of the building at 743 East 11th Street, a barrel was discovered with a man's body stuffed inside.

The victim was thought to have been from a fairly wealthy background, due to his 'clean person, good clothes and newly manicured nails'. The police found a piece of paper in his pocket, upon it was written 'Vieni Subito!' which was 'Come at Once!' in Italian.

The victim's throat had been cut from ear to ear, and eighteen stab wounds in the neck. The wounds to the neck were noted as being inflicted before the fatal cut to the jugular vein, which meant the man was either attacked in his sleep or restrained as he was tortured. As the police determined that the victim did not fight off his assailant.

The body had been forcibly pushed into the barrel with the head resting between the knees.

The local Police believed that the barrel, that had once been used for shipping sugar, was dumped from a wagon in the early hours. On the bottom of the barrel was stenciled the letters, 'W.T', and on the side, 'G 228'.

The police located where they thought the murder had been committed. It was a pastry shop on 226 Elizabeth Street — Dolceria Pasticceria, which was right around the corner from Lupo's small import store at 9 Prince Street.

It was there they found an identical barrel to the one used in the murder, even bearing the same inscriptions.

Sawdust, and some burlap, on the floor of the shop, had also been found in the base of the murder barrel. The barrel was eventually traced to Wallace & Thompson bakery, where their record books showed an entry of a sugar order, by Pietro Inzerillo, just two months earlier in February.

The following day, Secret Service agents, who had been tracking the Morello gang for over a year in connection with counterfeiting, claimed to have seen the victim with various members of the gang in a butcher's shop on Stanton Street on the evening of Monday 13th.

On Wednesday the 15th, eight members of the Morello gang were arrested. Each member of the gang was found to be armed, with either a knife or a pistol.

One of the gang members arrested was Giuseppe Morello. It was later learned that he held a gun permit, granted by the Deputy Commissioner, under the authorization of the local police captain.

On Thursday the 16th, four more of Morello's gang members were arrested in connection with the murder.

The police also went to Lupo's apartment where they forcibly entered the apartment while he was asleep. Lupo acted as if he was sick and a physician was called from the Roosevelt Hospital.

After the physician checked on him, he was deemed healthy and taken into custody. In his apartment, the police found a dagger and three revolvers.

That afternoon three patrol wagons carried the prisoners to the Jefferson Market Court to be arraigned. The court held the men on a charge of 'suspicion of homicide' and remanded them to police custody for forty-eight hours.

On Friday the 17th, the prisoners were re-arraigned at Jefferson Market Court. The men were again remanded to the jail for an additional 48 hours until Sunday morning.

The police were still trying to identify the murder victim found in the barrel.

While being held in the Jefferson Market Court, Lupo was questioned by the police about the murder case he had fled from in Sicily just four years earlier.

The Secret Service told Lupo that they planned to re-arrest him on counterfeiting charges if they could not secure a conviction for the 'Barrel Murder' case.

They informed Lupo that they also planned to pin another murder on him based on evidence found during the raid on his apartment.

Lupo was the last man seen with Giuseppe Catania, the Brooklyn grocer who had been murdered in 1902. Catania was believed to have been involved in counterfeiting with the Morello gang before they killed him.

On Sunday, April 19th, the prisoners were arraigned for the third time. Assistant District Attorney Garvan was present for the people, and five lawyers represented the prisoners.

The lawyers all argued against the holding of their clients in jail as no charges had been presented against them. One of the lawyers produced a writ of habeas corpus signed by a Justice of the Supreme Court. The Jefferson court magistrate decided to adjourn the hearing until the next morning.

By this day the barrel victim still has not been identified, and the gang's lawyers fighting for their immediate release due to the lack of evidence against them.

That changed when the police received an anonymous letter. The letter claimed that the dead man was related to Giuseppe Di Primo,(the surname is sometimes written *De Priema* or *De Primo*) a member of the Morello gang from Buffalo who had been jailed three months earlier and sent to Sing Sing prison to serve four years for a counterfeiting case based around Morristown NJ currency.

Lt. Joseph "Joe" Petrosino who was a New York City police officer who was a pioneer in the fight against organized crime visited Giuseppe Di Primo in Sing Sing prison.

Giuseppe Di Primo had been in New York since 1891. His position was what was known as a "*Queer Pusher or just Pusher*," the low-ranking men in the counterfeiting organization who circulated Morello's bad counterfeit bills. Di Primo also owned a grocery store and was married with four children.

Di Primo told the police the victim in the barrel was his brother-in-law, Benedetto Madonia.

He also told the police that he was a father of five children and worked as a stonemason in Buffalo.

Di Primo left out the fact that Madonia was already a high-ranking member of Giuseppe Morello's counterfeiting gang.

Benedetto Madonia

Di Primo told the warden of Sing Sing that he was sent to prison before the money from the counterfeiting crime was split up.

He said that not everyone was caught by the police and that he was entitled to his share. He sent his brother-in-law to get his share of the money from the Morello gang.

He believed that they must have argued over the money that was owed to him.

Detective Petrosino also traveled to Buffalo to visit Madonia's wife, Lucy, and stepson, Salvatore.

They told Petrosino about a pocket watch that Madonia had carried with him to New York. Petrosino telegraphed the description of the watch to the police inspector in New York, where his men traced a pawn ticket found on Tommaso Petto, a criminal associate of Morello's who was called "The Ox" when he was arrested on the 15th.

When Petto was arrested, he had been found in possession of pawn ticket number 27696 from P. Fry Collateral Loan Office 276–278 Bowery, dated April 14.

The ticket had been traced to a watch that had belonged to the murder victim and had been described to Petrosino by the victim's step-son Salvatore.

Petrosino returned to New York with Salvatore, as a witness for the court.

The authorities also learned more information about the days leading to Madonia's murder.

Madonia had left Buffalo for New York City around Sunday, April 3rd. On Thursday, he was taken by Giuseppe Fanaro to meet Peter P. Acritelli, who worked for Connell & O'Connor, the law firm that had represented his brother-in-law Giuseppe Di Primo who was currently in Sing-Sing prison.

Two days later Madonia traveled to Sing-Sing to see visit his brother-in-law. He was not seen again until Monday morning where he was seen in a barbershop on East Houston Street. It was learned that he had been using the barbershop to send mail and telegrams to his wife in Buffalo.

Later that afternoon he was recorded on the Secret Service files as being in the company of the Morello gang at 16 Stanton Street, and later that night he was murdered.

On Monday, the police had run out of time to hold the prisoners in jail.

They were once again brought before the judge at Jefferson Market Court.

The charges against Lupo were dismissed due to a lack of evidence.

Unfortunately, he was immediately rearrested on a counterfeiting charge and held on $2500 bail. (About $72,750.00 at today's dollar value) Lupo was immediately taken to the Ludlow Street jail where he was held awaiting trial for the counterfeiting charges.

The other men were held on the original charge of 'suspicion of homicide' and returned to Jefferson Market jail.

On Wednesday, April 22, the men were taken before the Magistrate of the Tombs court. After being dismissed due to lack of evidence, the men were taken before the Coroner, who held them on bail of varying amounts.

Vito Laduca, Giuseppe Morello, and Antonio Genova were each held on $5000 bail. (about $140,500 at today's dollar value)

Pietro Inzerillo, Joseph Fanaro and Domenico Pecoraro were held on $2000. (about $56,000 at today's dollar value)

Lorenzo LoBido was held on $1000. (about $28,000 at today's dollar value)

Tommaso Petto, Giuseppe Monti and Nicola Testa on $500. (about $14,000 at today's dollar value)

Giuseppe Lalamia and Vito LoBido were held on $100 bail. ($2,810.72 at today's dollar value)

All of the men were held at the House of Detention, where that night the detectives took Morello from his cell to see Madonia's body, but he denied knowing who the man was.

The police also learned that Giuseppe "Joseph" Fanaro, had been arrested on the same night of the murder.

Giuseppe "Joseph" Fanaro was the man Madonia met with to meet Peter P. Acritelli, who worked for Connell & O'Connor, the law firm that had represented his brother-in-law Giuseppe Di Primo who was currently in Sing-Sing prison.

Fanaro had been involved in an argument outside of the saloon at 8 Prince Street when the police intervened.

The police found a pistol on him and he produced a firearms license to explain the pistol but was arrested for disorderly conduct.

About fifteen minutes after Fanaro was locked up he was bailed out, and fined $10 (about $280.00 at today's dollar value) the following morning in court.

Secret service agents learned that Madonia was a member of the Morello gang when a letter was found addressed to Madonia, written by Morello.

The letter asked Madonia to travel to Pittsburgh along with Vito Laduca and to secure the release of two men who had been arrested there while trying to pass the gangs counterfeit money.

A second letter was found penned by Madonia. Sent on March 23rd from Pittsburgh, it accused Morello of sending him on an impossible mission and charged Morello with indifference towards his own gang members. Madonia claimed he had done all he could, threatening to return to his home in Buffalo instead of finishing the job that Morello sent him to do.

On Saturday, April 25, Tommaso Petto was formally charged with committing the Benedetto Madonia murder.

Petto was removed from the House of Detention and taken to the Criminal Courts building and arraigned before Coroner Scholer where he was committed to the Tombs pending an inquest.

In the meantime, the police were trying to learn Petto's true address to search for new evidence against him.

An associate of Lupo's, Pietro Inzerillo, who owned the bakery where the barrel used in the Benedetto Madonia murder to dispose of the body was reported to come from was released on bail.

Across New York's Italian communities, there was a forced collection to help pay the gang's defense and bail costs. Many Italian families had armed themselves, after a collection in New Jersey having poor results caused the Mafia to threaten revenge against the Italian communities.

Coroner Scholer was having difficulties finding a jury for the inquest that was due to be held on Friday, May 1. Most of the people subpoenaed to be on the jury began to make excuses when they learned they would be dealing with a trial of a Mafia member.

On Thursday, April 30, the District attorney announced that the man currently held for the murder was not named Petto as he claimed, but was named Giovanni "Domenico" Pecoraro.

When Pecoraro was arrested he had Petto's gun permit with him and had falsely given his name to the police as Tomasso Petto.

The Secret Service discovered this fact when one of their agents spoke to Petto and noted him as 'cursing Pecoraro for assuming his name'.

Later the same day, Lupo was officially charged by the Grand Jury concerning the counterfeiting case and held on a $5000 bail. (about $140,500 at today's dollar value)

On Friday, May 1, 1903, the coroner's inquest into the 'Barrel Murder' began. (A coroner's inquest is an inquest held by a coroner to determine the cause of any violent, sudden, or mysterious death.)

One of the men to testify was nineteen-year-old Nicola Testa who worked in the Stanton Street butcher shop where the wagon that was suspected of carrying the murder barrel was believed to come from.

He said that he was the nephew of Giuseppe Catania, the Brooklyn grocer, who was found murdered and stuffed in a potato sack in 1902.

The other members of the gang who were questioned as witnesses at the inquest gave little information that could be beneficial.

it was feared that the jury would be unable to fix responsibility for the murder.

Giuseppe Di Primo was reluctant to give any evidence against the gang, even though he had given the District Attorney a statement.

When he was questioned, he laughed and now stated that Petto was a close friend of his.

Morello took to the stand and denied knowing Madonia even when presented with the letters found in his home.

Peter Acritelli was also questioned during the inquest.

Peter Acritelli was the lawyer that Madonia with Giuseppe "Joseph" Fanaro was to meet, who worked for Connell & O'Connor, the law firm that had represented Madonia's brother-in-law.

Acritelli said that Fanaro came to him at his father's bank on April 9th accompanied by Madonia. They explained Madonia wanted to see Di Primo in Sign-Sing about some property and didn't want to wait until the regular visitor's day.

They wanted a letter to the warden of the prison and he told Madonia to come by the Connel & O'Conner's office the next day.

The following day Madonia went to the Connel & O'Conner's office alone.

And was seen by Acritelli, Mr. O'Connor, and Mr. De Ville.

Madonia said that when his brother-in-law was sent to prison, he had a good deal of property. This property he turned over to his friends.

Madonia had come down to get this property and keep it for his brother-in-law but had been unable to get any of his brother-in-law's associates to give him anything.

Madonia then made up his mind to try and see Di Primo, find out who had his property, and begin some legal action against him.

Acritelli told the inquest that Mr. O'Conner gave Madonia the letter to give to the warden at the prison, and he left the office.

Acritelli said that the following morning, April 11, he met Madonia on the Street. He said Madonia was on his way to take the train to Sing Sing.

That was the last he saw of him.

Pietro Inzerillo, who owned the bakery where the barrel used in the Benedetto Madonia murder to dispose of the body was reported to come from also testified.

His testimony, like the other members of the gang who were questioned as witnesses at the inquest, gave little information that could be beneficial.

After Inzerillo gave his testimony he was excused then rearrested on a bench warrant from the US District Court.

He was indicted along with Lupo on a counterfeiting charge. The charge dated back to September 1902, when Lupo had mailed a letter containing a single five-dollar counterfeit note to Salvatore Matise aka Andrea Polora in Canada.

On Friday, May 8th, one week after the inquest began; the coroner's jury returned the verdict that the crime had been committed by some person or persons unknown to them.

This was a favorable decision for the State, and they called for the detention of six men already in custody, Morello, 'Petto', Fanaro, Laduca, Inzerillo, and Genova.

Also, based on the evidence of Nicola Testa, Giovanni Zarcone, the owner of the Stanton Street butcher shop and owner of the wagon that was suspected of carrying the murder barrel, was arrested at his home in Brooklyn.

The seven men were immediately taken to the Tombs to await a Grand Jury.

Domenico Pecoraro, Lorenzo and Vito LoBido, Giuseppe Lalamia, Nicola Testa and Giuseppe Monti were all released without being charged with any crime.

Giuseppe Fanaro was re-arrested for perjury. He had claimed in court to not know Benedetto Madonia, but the Secret Service had records of him with Madonia in the days leading up to the murder. He was given bail at $3,000. (About $84,000 at today's dollar value)

Madonia's links to the gang are certain, the paperwork that was discovered in Morello's homes mentioned him concerning the gang's previous crimes.

Madonia's wife had also stated that he had spent time in a Sicilian jail and that he had mentioned to her about being a member of a secret society.

At the end of the inquest, the general consensus of the press was that Madonia was killed for making demands to the Morello gang, with regards to his brother-in-law. Either to demand money owed or to seek the missing money that was raised to help Di Primo's legal case.

It was believed that when Morello's Queer Pushers were arrested passing the gang's money in Pittsburgh, Madonia was sent to intervene, leading him to argue with Morello over the leader's apparent lack of concern for his men.

The arrests of Morello's men go back to 1901, when Chief Wilkie, of the Secret Service, noticed the appearance of multiple counterfeit five-dollar bills that resembled currency issued by the National Iron Bank in Morristown New Jersey.

The counterfeit five-dollar bills known as 'Morristown Fives', had been manufactured in Italy and then shipped in empty olive oil containers to Manhattan.

A man named Giuseppe Boscarino was suspected of being in charge of controlling the distribution of the Morristown notes for Morello.

When Morello's pushers were arrested later, this time in Yonkers, Madonia's brother-in-law Giuseppe Di Primo was one of the men who went to prison.

Although Di Primo didn't talk to the police, his associate, Isadore Crocevera, was told by the detectives that he had. In hopes that this ploy would make the man cooperate with the police. However, their plan failed and Crocevera did not share anything with them.

However, Crocevera believed the detective and told Morello that Di Primo had talked to the police.

Many believe that Morello killed Madonia to send a message to Di Primo. But others believe that Madonia was killed because he and Morello had their own quarrel, which was now coming to a head. ($28,000 at today's dollar value)

It was believed that Madonia had sent $1000 (about $28,000 at today's dollar value) to Morello for his brother-in-law's defense, but Morello pocketed the cash and did nothing to help Di Primo.

It was also believed that Morello would help to get Di Primo moved to a prison closer to the Buffalo area, which did not happen either.

So, on the weekend of Easter, Benedetto Madonia left Buffalo and went to New York City. He told Morello he was coming and demanded the return of the money he sent to help his brother-in-law.

When he arrived in New York City, Benedetto went first to Sing-Sing prison to see his brother-in-law Giuseppe.

After leaving the prison, the exact circumstances surrounding the remainder of his trip are not fully known.

In total, twelve men were arrested, but when the trial was finished none were convicted of Madonia's murder. Di Primo, who was once the criminal accomplice of the defendants, swore he would eventually avenge his brother-in-law's death.

After the completion of the 'Barrel Trial' against the gang, Secret Service records noted a conversation between Pietro Inzerillo and one of their undercover agents.

During this conversation, Inzerillo claimed that his release from the trial was due to the actions of New York Congressman Timothy Sullivan, who controlled Manhattan's Bowery and Lower East Side districts.

Just over a month later, Pietro Inzerillo and Lupo were finally released on bail from the counterfeiting charge in June 1903. They would later forfeit this bail, and the charges were eventually dropped.

The Morello gang was heavily involved with counterfeiting. The Secret Service had been building a case against the gang concerning the counterfeit 'Morristown Fives' for some time before the murder of Benedetto Madonia occurred.

However, as Chief Wilkie of the Secret Service explained in his 1903 Annual Report, the government's case was dropped so that the gang could be tried for the more serious crime of the 'Barrel Murder'.

the Secret Service gave the police all of the material that was gathered by their agents, who pointed out and identified the various members of the gang.

With this information, the local authorities were able to secure the indictments of most of the Morello gang members involved in Madonia's murder.

And this put the Morristown's National bank notes case temporarily on hold.

However, once the 'Barrel Murder' case collapsed and no convictions were made. The Secret Service lost their ability to use their strategies against the gang, who now knew that they were being followed regularly.

After the trial in 1903, the gang moved away from counterfeiting and concentrated more with Morello's construction business and Lupo's wholesale grocery network.

Lupo became part of Morello's immediate family when he married Nicholas Morello's sister, Salvatrice Terranova on December 23rd, 1903.

Lupo maintained his leadership over his Little Italy-based interests and kept his base of operations in Little Italy, but shared the overall leadership of the crime family with Giuseppe Morello from his base in East Harlem.

Lupo demanded absolute obedience from the members of his crew.

It was said that he killed one of his own relatives because he suspected that he was a traitor.

Lupo's reputation became so fearsome that it was common for Italian immigrants to cross themselves at the mere mention of his name.

Following the 'Barrel Murder' trials, Lupo expandsed his import business and opened a new store at 210–214 Mott St. just a block away from the small import store at 9 Prince Street.

It was said to be 'one the most impressive stores in the neighborhood, many of the locals could only dream of shopping there'.

Years later, in 1914, William Flynn, chief of the Secret Service described how Lupo used his network of businesses.

He said that the small Italian grocers in the area were forced to buy their supplies from Lupo's store. If they did not their establishments were in danger of being destroyed by bombs or burned.

They even threatened that their children might be kidnapped or themselves killed if they did not purchase their supplies from him.

By intimidating the local grocery store owners into buying only at their wholesale store, Lupo and Morello accomplished a double purpose. They increased their so-called legitimate profits and were able to dispose of some of the counterfeit money.

At this time, twenty-nine-year-old Salvatore D'Aquila immigrated to America from Palermo, Sicily, and was already heavily involved with organized crime.

Salvatore D'Aquila

Before leaving Sicily, D'Aquila was known as a "Mustache Pete", which unlike the younger Sicilian-Americans known as the "Young Turks", the Mustache Pete's' had usually committed their first killings in Italy, not America.

When D'Aquila arrived in New York, he joined some of the other Sicilians working in the cheese importing business.

Salvatore D'Aquila moved to Brooklyn and quickly aligned himself with Giuseppe Morello where it was believed that he worked alongside Morello as his caporegime under Morello's brother-in-law Ignazio Lupo.

A caporegime, usually shortened to just a capo, is a rank used in the Mafia for a made member of the family who heads a "crew" of soldiers and has major social status and influence in the family.

Lupo was arrested on March 7, 1906, after being identified by an Italian boy who had been kidnapped and held on 59th Street.

The kidnapped boy was the son of a wealthy Italian banker who had helped the Morello gang in the past by filing their incorporation certificate for the Ignatz Florio Co-Operative Association.

Lupo was sent to the tombs in default of $1000 bail. However, the victim failed to identify Lupo once they were in court.

Lupo was sent to the tombs in default of $1000 bail. However, the victim failed to identify Lupo once they were in court.

While Giuseppe Morello was the head of the gang, the press would often incorrectly name them in the newspaper as 'The Lupo Gang' or the 'Lupo-Morello Band'.

The fact that Ignazio Lupo had been labeled with the street name, 'Lupo the Wolf', would often receive more column space when the gang appeared in the newspapers.

Nearly 900,000 immigrants pour into New York City In 1906.

Among them, was a nine-year-old Sicilian named Salvatore Lucania.

Salvatore, his four siblings, and his parents, Antonio and Rosalia Capporelli-Lucania arrive from Lercara Friddi, Sicily with hopes of a better life.

Unfortunately, what they found was nothing like what they had expected.

What they found in New York City was, over four million people living in highly segregated blocks of rundown apartments.

Most of these neighborhoods consisted of Jewish, Irish, or Italian immigrants.

Most of the people in these crowded neighborhoods work an honest job while others turn to crime to make a living.

They victimized their own people.

They shook down storekeepers for protection money.

If a shopkeeper didn't pay the gang money, they would face being beaten or having their shops vandalized.

Across New York City, hundreds of unorganized gangs terrorize entire blocks in a chaotic turf war.

In the borough of Manhattan on its Lower East Side, Salvatore Lucania's family struggles to survive.

And as Salvatore's father struggles to find work, he tries to deal with the pressures of providing for his family. He eventually turns to alcohol and takes his frustrations out on his family.

Salvatore eventually dropped out of school by the age of 15 and started working a fulltime job to help support his family.

However, after winning money in a dice game, Salvatore quit his job and began earning money on the street illegally.

That same year, Salvatore's parents sent him to the Brooklyn Truant School.

It was about this time that Salvatore decided to Americanize his first name. He chose to go by "Charles" instead of Salvatore. He did this to avoid the nickname of "Sally," which was a nickname for his birth name "Salvatore."

Eventually, he chose to also change his surname.

"Lucania" became "Luciano" and Charles Luciano, the future leader of the American Mafia was now created.

Back in Italy in February 1908, a large group of Italians held a mass meeting at the office of an Italian newspaper named, *Bollettino Della Sera*.

They ridiculed the Black Hand, saying it only existed in Sicily and was a mild form of the Mafia.

The group petitioned the Italian Government that all prefects and priests in Italy, and Royal Commissioners on the immigrant boats, be instructed to tell the people to not carry guns when coming to America.

The 'Bollettino Della Sera' was very critical of the American press and its willingness to publicize Black Hand crimes, which seemed merely to increase the epidemic.

Two columns in the Bollettino (Jan 1908) called on Italians to rise up and put a stop to the crimes which are tarnishing the Italian name ... An editorial headed "*The Cry of Alarm*" warned that the doors of this country would be closed to Italians ...

The Bollettino printed a notice, "*Against the Black Hand*" advising all honest Italians to aid Commissioner Bingham by sending him all threatening letters, and information about Black Handers and idle Italians, with a description of individuals

After the formation of the *'The Italian Vigilance Protective Association'*, the New York City Police Commissioner Theodore Bingham was asked of his plans to eradicate the Black Hand in New York City.

He claimed his request for $25,000 to establish a secret detective service had been turned down by the city's aldermen.

He also stated that Lt. Joseph "Joe" Petrosino who was a New York City police officer who was a pioneer in the fight against organized crime and his squad was too well known in the Italian quarter to be of any real assistance.

In 1908, Lupo disappeared from New York and in November claimed bankruptcy against his import business owing his creditors up to $100,000. This would later be known as 'The Grocery Conspiracy'.

On Monday 30th November 1908, Lupo's Mott Street store was closed under the order of the US Court. The suppliers inventoried the store and only reached $1,500.

Other Italian owned stores in the city began to fail at the same time.

The New York Times reported that a dozen other Italian dealers had also disappeared, resulting in total liabilities close to $500,000.

The authorities soon realized that they were facing an organized conspiracy, with combined liabilities across Brooklyn and Manhattan estimated at over $500,000.

Twelve warrants were issued for, Fraudulent Disposition of Property, and with Conspiracy to Defraud Merchants.

The attorneys for Lupo's suppliers discovered that he had made around $50,000 worth of purchases in the week leading up to his disappearance.

Goods totaling over $45,000 were tracked down to a Jersey City pier and a Manhattan pier, ready to be transported back to Italy in early December.

In an attempt to disguise the source of the goods, company and product names had been removed from the barrels and crates, but workers for the suppliers identify the barrels and crates.

A storeroom and another warehouse on Washington Street were raided.

During the warehouse raid, the authorities found more produce, a hundred barrels of wine, and almost one hundred bags of beans was found in a warehouse on Washington Street.

The bankruptcy courts auctioned off the reclaimed merchandise, along with other assets from Lupo's store.

An auction was announced to sell Lupo's grocery goods that had been found on the pier on Monday, December 21, 1908.

In the matter of IGNAZIO LUPO, Bankrupt.-Chas. Shongood, U. S. Auctioneer for the Southern District of New York in Bankruptcy, sells this day, Monday, Dec. 21, 1908, by order of the court at 10:30 A.M at 113 Leonard St, Borough of Manhattan, assets of the above bankrupt, consisting of a large stock of Italian wines, liquors. groceries, barrels of claret, port and other wines, vinegar, barrels of soda, bags of beans, peas, nuts, salt, bales of stockfish, cases of soap, starch, washing powder, macaroni, bologna; also, fixtures, consisting of safe, revolving chairs, desks, sealer, letter press ...

After the failure of 'The Ignatz Florio Co-Operative' and Lupo's bankruptcy, they returned to the counterfeiting trade. They set up a base in Highland NY, with a plan to print hundreds of thousands of counterfeit bills.

Lupo stayed just under two hours north of Little Italy in Ardonia New York, with a family that ran a cheese farm.

Lupo stayed there under the alias of Joe La Presti as he was avoiding his creditors from his failed Mott Street business.

While staying at the farm Lupo travelled regularly to Highland New York to check on the counterfeit business. In November, Giuseppe Morello and several of his conspirators are arrested for counterfeiting after the police raid the Highland, New York home.

In July 1909 Lupo was summoned by the NY Supreme Court in connection with his mortgage foreclosure on 630 138th Street. Others listed in the summons were: Salvatrice Lupo — his wife, The Ignatz Florio Co-operative, Antonio Rizzo, Joseph DiGiorgio, The Stone Hill Wine Company, and Giuseppe Morello.

The building was eventually sold by public auction in October to pay off the creditors.

On November 1, 1909, Lupo moved to the Bath Beach area of Brooklyn and rented a house, again using the alias of Joe La Presti.

On November 12, a year filing bankruptcy, Lupo returned to New York. He walked into his supplier's office with his lawyer.

Lupo told his suppliers that the reason he fled the city, and his bankrupt business, was that he was being blackmailed for $10,000 by the Black Hand.

And this left him broke and caused him to flee to Baltimore and Buffalo.

Less than one week later, Lupo was arrested in connection with the extortion of Salvatore Manzella.

Manzella was an importer of wine and Italian produce. He was also forced to file bankruptcy.

Manzella told the court that for over three years he had been a victim of extortion from Lupo, and as a result, he had lost his business.

He was arraigned on November 22, on the charge.

When Manzella failed to appear in court Lupo was released.

He was immediately rearrested by a Deputy Marshall regarding a counterfeiting charge from September 1902, he was later released on $5,000 bail.

On January 8, 1910, Secret Service agents gathered at Lupo's home in Bath Beach, Brooklyn. A search of the upstairs rooms revealed a revolver, letters, passports, and a bank book containing the names John Lupo, Joseph La Presti, and Giuseppe La Presti. They arrested Lupo in connection with the Highland counterfeiting case.

Lupo was formally charged the following day with extortion and counterfeiting on January 9, 1910. His trial began on January 26th.

The first witness for the prosecution and probably the most damaging is, Antonio Comito, who says that he unwillingly assisted in the printing of counterfeit currency for the gang.

For almost five days, Comito continues his testimony regarding the printing of counterfeit currency at Salvatore Cina's home in Highland NY.

He testified that the gang had plans called for the counterfeit currency to be circulated in Chicago, Pittsburgh and Buffalo.

And in return for his testimony, Antonio Comito was paid $150 (about $4,000 at today's dollar value) in June the following year.

He was given this money only on the condition that he leave the country.

The trial's security was high after Judge Ray had received death threats in the style of the Black Hand.

Judge Ray received a Black Hand threat through the mail at the start of the counterfeiting trial. The letter was translated: "If the counterfeiters are not liberated, you will die like a dog. We have killed better men than you or Smith or Flynn."

It was later learned that a knife had been found in the US Marshal's office.

A few years after the trial ended, news reports indicate in July 1912, that Lupo intended to assassinate Detective William J. Flynn and others who had a hand in his conviction on counterfeiting.

In the middle of his counterfeiting trial, U.S. officials consider deporting Ignazio Lupo back to Italy, to face a lengthy sentence for murder in Italy.

After nearly a month's long trial, Judge Ray of the U.S. Circuit Court issued a two hour and thirty-five-minute jury instruction to aid them in their deliberations.

They were sent to decide the fate of the accused on February 19th, at 2:00 p.m.

The jury took just an hour and fifteen minutes to decide guilty for each of the defendants.

Before the sentences were announced, the courtroom was emptied of relatives and onlookers.

The court was secured and the corridors were cleared.

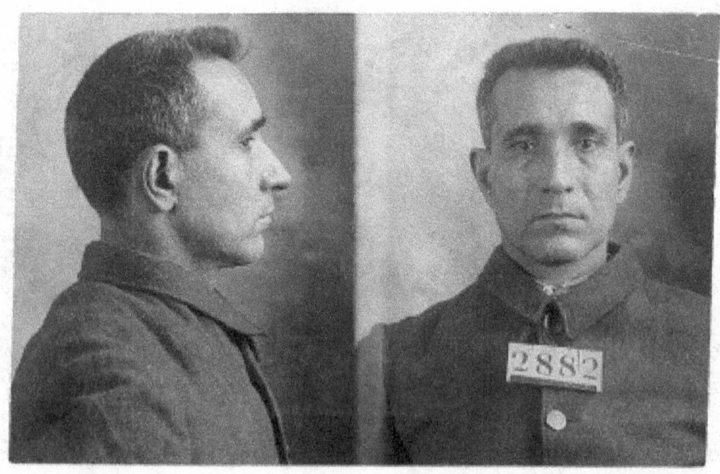

Giuseppe Morello

Giuseppe Morello was sentenced on the first count to 15 years hard labor and a $500 fine. On the second count, he was sentenced to 10 years of hard labor and a $500 fine.

He pleaded with the judge for a suspended sentence and to be allowed to return to Italy. The judge denied his request and he was carried screaming from the courtroom by the police.

After the trial, Giuseppe Morello and Ignazio Lupo were both sent to the United States Penitentiary at Atlanta, Georgia on February 20.

Giuseppe Morello as inmate #2882.

Ignazio Lupo as inmate #2883.

Morello's sentence was eventually commuted to 15-years and he was released in 1920.

Ignazio Lupo was sentenced on the first count to 15 years of hard labor and a $500 fine. On the second count, 15 years of hard labor and a $500 fine.

In total, Lupo was sentenced to 30-years but would get out in 10 when he received a conditional commutation and was released in 1920.

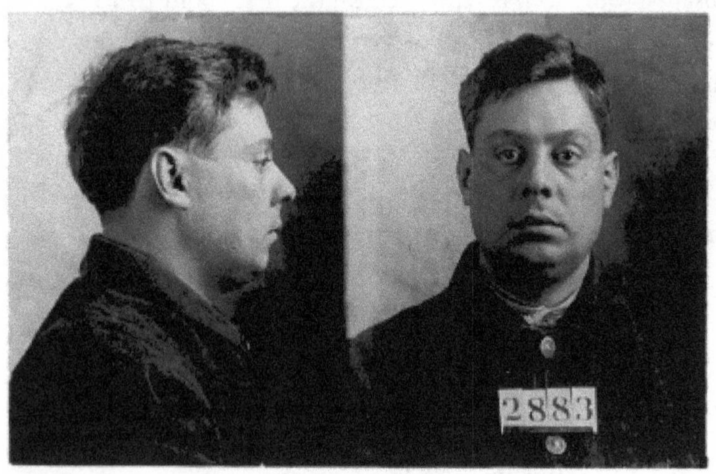

Ignazio Lupo

After Lupo was convicted, his brother John was heavily involved in trying to secure his release. He gave many interviews to the press, and it was estimated he spent almost $65,000 on his efforts to free his brother.

Giuseppe would later get out of prison and lead his gang again but Lupo never regained his status after getting out.

He was later forced to retire by Luciano, who was redefining the New York underworld.

It's widely believed in 1910 that D'Aquila took over as the leader of the Morello family after the incarceration of Morello and Lupo.

But it was quickly learned that was not the fact.

It was later discovered that Morello was having problems with an up-and-coming Mafioso and former capo of the Morello's Giuseppe Masseria before he was imprisoned.

Giuseppe Masseria

D'Aquila didn't have the backing of the other family members to battle Masseria, so D'Aquila decided that this was the right time to separate from the Morello Crime Family and create his own family and was able to take with him several of Morello's men.

Future Boss, Frank "Don Cheech" Scalice, served as a Capo in D'Aquila's gang.

D'Aquila's new crime family operated from East Harlem and the Bronx, where his family's power was just as equal to the Morellos.

Salvatore D'Aquila immediately emerged as the new chief Mafia power in New York City, mostly in East Harlem and Little Italy (in southern Manhattan), but he also led a faction in Brooklyn that was headed locally by his future Underboss Manfredi "Al" or "Alfred" Mineo.

D'Aquila had assumed the title from Morello of Capo di tutti Capi or "Boss of Bosses".

D'Aquila's family, with Mineo's Brooklyn faction included, reigned supreme through the 1910s.

This would be the birth of what we know today as the Gambino Crime Family.

Morello's half-brothers, the Terranovas, Vincenzo, Ciro, and Nicholas Morello took over Morello's crime family.

Vincenzo and Nicola often used their half-brother's name "Morello", even though they were legally Terranovas.

They now controlled Harlem and most of the area of northern Manhattan.

D'Aquila wanted to unite all the Mafia gangs in New York. His goal was to kill off several of the low-ranking gang leaders in East Harlem.

He sought to dominate the Mafia organizations previously loyal to Morello and Lupo.

D'Aquila had one of his men, Umberto Valente, kill East Harlem Mafia leader Fortunato "Charles" Lomonte to gain control of East Harlem.

Within five years D'Aquila seized control of several ports around New York City.

With all the potential money to be made in the early years of prohibition, D'Aquila's family grew.

Many up and coming criminals seen the opportunity to make good money and quickly joined the family with the potential to make money on their minds.

The fight over the control of the New York rackets started to heat up after the undisputed " King of Little Italy " Giosue Gallucci is shot along with his son Lucca at Lucca's coffeehouse, 336 E. 109th Street on May 17th.

Gallucci, who was born in Naples Italy, had previously led a band of Sicilian and Neapolitan racketeers in East Harlem.

Recent shootings seem to indicate that the Sicilian and Neapolitan factions have split and are now warring.

The following day Lucca Gallucci dies at Bellevue Hospital of his gunshot wounds. Followed three days later on May 21, by his father Giosue Gallucci, who also dies at Bellevue Hospital of his gunshot wounds.

This would become the start of The Mafia–Camorra War.

Just over one month later, on June 26, 1915, future Gambino Family crime boss, Constantino Paul Castellano, was born in Brooklyn, New York.

Castellano's parents Giuseppe and Concetta (née Casatu) were immigrants from Sicily. His father was a butcher and a member of the Mangano crime family.

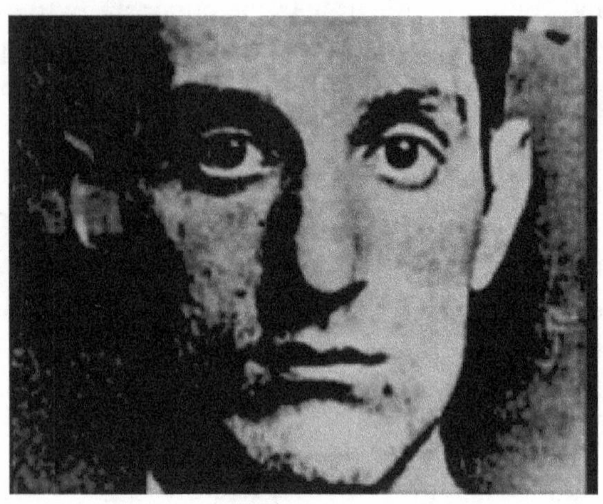

Young Paul Castellano

Castellano would later follow in his father's footsteps when he dropped out of school in the 8th grade to learn how to be a butcher from his father, as well as collecting numbers game receipts for the mob.

At the time Brooklyn was considered as the middle class among the immigrants from Italy.

On one side of The Mafia–Camorra War was the Morello crime family of Manhattan; on the other side were gangs originally from Naples and the surrounding Campania region of Italy.

These rival gangs were based on the areas of Navy Street in Brooklyn and Coney Island referred to as the Camorra.

Before this conflict started, relations between the two sides were relatively amicable; in fact, each year the Morellos would attend a 'smoker' held by the Camorra boss Andrea Ricci in Brooklyn.

The Mafia-Camorra war started due to greed.

The Morellos goal was to control all of the gambling in Manhattan. The Morello's first target was the Del Gaudio brothers, who controlled gambling operations in East Harlem.

The Morellos killed Nicolo Del Gaudio and forced his brother Gaetano to submit to them by intimidation.

The Morello's next target was Joe DeMarco who ran a restaurant and several gambling locations on Mulberry Street in Lower Manhattan.

DeMarco had already survived two assassination attempts in 1913-1914.

DeMarco had unsuccessfully tried to murder Nicholas Terranova in November of 1915.

Nicholas Terranova (known as Nicholas Morello) was shot from behind by a sawed-off shotgun. Nicholas was seriously injured but eventually recovered from his wounds.

After the two attempts on his life, DeMarco opened a restaurant at 163 West 49th Street and then opened two gambling rooms.

One was located on Mulberry Street and another at 54 James Street.

As the battle between Joe DeMarco and The Morello family grew to a boiling point, Charles Luciano joined the deadly Five Points Gang and began dealing heroin.

The Five Points Gang operated in the run-down Manhattan neighborhood called the Five Points.

It was a cheap slum that consisted of the poorest and least fortunate of Manhattan.

It was home for many poor immigrants who were mostly sweatshop workers, and newly-freed slaves from the southern states that had made their way north and settled in New York.

His journey in the world of crime would soon change after he was arrested and he spent six months in jail for selling heroin.

Once Luciano was released from jail, he and his friend Gaetano "Tommy" Lucchese formed the 107th Street gang.

Lucchese had only three fingers on his right hand after an industrial accident amputated his right thumb and forefinger the previous year.

The gang made their money by stealing wallets, burglarizing stores, and extorting protection money from youngsters from Italian and Irish gangs for 10 cents per week.

The 107th Street gang operated under the protection of Bronx-East Harlem family boss Gaetano "Tom" Reina.

And it was at this time that Meyer Lansky met Luciano on the streets of New York.

Meyer Lansky is a Russian immigrant, whose parents came to America to avoid religious persecution.

Luciano attempted to extort Lansky for protection money as he walked home from school.

Lansky told Luciano, "I'm not giving you any money; you'll have to fight me for it."

It was at this point that Myer Lansky earned Luciano's respect and the two formed a lasting partnership thereafter.

Luciano later said that Lansky was the bravest man he ever met.

After his run-in with Luciano, Lansky saw a need for the Jewish boys of his Brooklyn neighborhood to organize in the same manner as the Italians and Irish gangs did.

The first person he recruited for his newly formed gang was an intimidating Jewish kid from Brooklyn, known for his charm, and also his violent outbursts named Benjamin "Bugsy" Siegel.

Bugsy Siegel got his nickname because when you were considered "bugs", you were thought to be crazy.

Bugsy Siegel was from a poor Jewish family that immigrated to the United States from the Galicia region of what was then the Austro-Hungarian Empire.

And just like Luciano, Bugsy dropped out of school and joined a gang.

Bugsy also developed a protection racket in which he threatened to burn pushcart owners' merchandise unless they paid him a dollar.

Bugsy had a criminal record, dating from his teenage years that included violent crimes like, armed robbery, rape, and murder.

It was through his friendship with Lansky that Luciano became acquainted with Lansky's close associate, Benjamin "Bugsy" Siegel, and together they became the "Bugs and Meyer Gang."

Luciano, Lansky, and Siegel begin to establish themselves as an up and coming criminal force on the lower east side.

As his crew starts to have small-time success, Luciano sets his sights on joining the ranks of the much bigger operation of Joe Masseria.

Masseria is now asserting his dominance in Luciano's neighborhood.

And Luciano knows that working for Masseria would be a way to make a bigger name for him and in turn earn more money.

But, to get in with the Masseria, Luciano knows he'll need an opportunity to prove his worth.

One of the newest criminals in Masseria's gang is a 20-year-old Italian immigrant named Frank Costello.

While working for the Masseria, Costello met Luciano, Lansky, and Segal

The men immediately became friends and partners and became involved in robbery, theft, extortion, gambling, and dealing narcotics.

Over the next few years, they run successful rackets for Costello under Joe Masseria.

As Luciana was making his way up the ranks, The Morello family decided to ask for help from the Navy Street and Coney Island gangs to eliminate Joe DeMarco once and for all.

The Morellos met with the Navy Street and Coney Island gangs in Coney Island at the end of June 1916.

They met at Coney Island to divide up all illegal activities in New York, including gambling in lower Manhattan, drugs, and extortion.

Nick Morello and his associate Eugene "Charles" Ubriaco, Steve LaSalle, explained that Joe DeMarco would have to be killed before they could expand gambling in the lower Manhattan area.

They discussed the idea of killing Joe DeMarco. The two Brooklyn gangs agreed and Lauritano Leopoldo, the Navy Street boss, set up a meeting at his Brooklyn coffeehouse to plan the hit.

Lauritano was a Brooklyn-based Camorra leader who ran a coffeehouse/saloon at 113 Navy Street and also conducted a profitable murder-for-hire business.

Three weeks later, Nick Morello and his associates Steve LaSalle, Ciro Terranova, and Giuseppe Verizzano met at Lauritano's coffeehouse.

One problem that they faced was that DeMarco knew all of Morello's men and wouldn't let them get anywhere near him.

However, Giuseppe Verizzano was a very close friend of Joe DeMarco's.

He agreed to set up the trap to kill DeMarco.

The first attempt at killing DeMarco failed when a Navy Street hitman named Fetto, arrived late at the gambling house, by that point, DeMarco had already left.

Complicating the planning for a second attempt, a friend of DeMarco, Joe "Chuck" Nazzaro would accompany DeMarco that afternoon.

Joe Nazzaro had been chased out of Harlem by the Morello gang.

The plan now was for Verizzano to sneak a Navy Street hitman, Johnny "Lefty" Esposito into DeMarco's gambling location, and point out DeMarco.

They would then carry out the mission to kill DeMarco.

On July 20, Esposito and Fetto waited at a saloon on Elizabeth Street to await a signal from Verizzano.

At around five o'clock, Verizzano arrived at the saloon and told the two gunmen that DeMarco had arrived at the gambling house.

Verizzano and the two hitmen left the saloon and made their way to the James Street gambling house.

A DeMarco employee, who was a Navy Street sympathizer, got the three men past the doorman and inside the house.

The men went straight to the back bedroom where the card games were going on.

Inside the back bedroom, Joe DeMarco and Charles Lombardi sat next to each other playing cards with several other men in the room.

It was later learned by the hitmen that; Charles Lombardi was a close friend of Lauritano.

To identify the target for Esposito and Fetto, Verizzano sat down opposite of Joe DeMarco.

Outside the room, Sassi and Rocco Valente from the Navy Street gang were standing watch to make sure everyone had a clear escape route after the killing.

Just after Verizzano sat down, Johnny Esposito pulled out his gun and fatally shot Lombardi.

Esposito had misread the signals from Verizzano and thought that he was shooting Joe DeMarco. Total chaos broke out in the room when Lombardi was shot. Through all of the commotion, Verizzano managed to shoot and kill Joe DeMarco himself.

After both DeMarco and Lombardi were shot dead, the gunmen then crawled out the bedroom window on to Oliver Street and quickly made their escape.

When the police arrived at the James Street gambling house, they found the lifeless bodies of Joseph DeMarco and his friend Charles "Nine-Fingered" Lombardi seated at the card table next to each other.

The room was empty except for the two dead men.

Ten other chairs were scattered about the room. Ten hats were hung on wall hooks behind the table.

At first, the authorities believed that DeMarco had been killed for trying to secure for himself the position of East Harlem's top Mafia boss of Little Italy, which had recently been vacated by the murder of Giosue Gallucci.

They learned much later that DeMarco's death was secretly agreed upon by the Sicilian Mafia and Neapolitan Camorra leaders who wanted to divide the Manhattan territories between them.

That evening Nick and Vincent Morello, LaSalle, Terranova, and Verizzano all returned to Lauritano's coffeehouse.

They told Lauritano that Joe DeMarco was now dead.

Nick Morello gave Lauritano $50 (about $1,175 at today's dollar value) to give to his gunmen for the job.

With the death of Joe DeMarco, the Morello's were able to open more gambling operations in Lower Manhattan.

However, the Camorra organization also used the opportunity to open gambling houses in Lower Manhattan also.

Since the Morello goal had been to be the only gambling racket in Lower Manhattan, the stage was set for a major conflict between the Morellos and the Camorra.

The head Camorra bosses took offense at the Morello-Terranova actions to kill DeMarco.

One of the top Navy Street leaders had never been happy with cooperating with the Morellos on the DeMarco hit and decided to dissolve their partnership and eliminate as much of the Sicilian Mafia leadership in New York as possible.

This would give them full power and put the Camorra in full control of all of the gambling rackets in New York.

A meeting was held in Philadelphia between Navy Gang representatives and the Camorra leadership about hitting the Morellos and taking full control of all of Manhattan.

After discussing the Morello issues with the Camorra boss, Andrea Ricci, the two groups agreed to form an alliance to take down the Morellos.

The Navy Gang and the Camorra planned to lure the leaders of the Morello gang to another meeting in Brooklyn, only to murder them to avenge the earlier 1916 killing of Nicholas DelGaudio in Manhattan.

On September 7, 1916, Nick Morello and his associate and personal bodyguard, Charles Ubriaco met with the Navy Street Gang.

Once they arrived at the meeting, they were served drinks. Morello and Ubriaco were then told that the Navy Street people were waiting for them instead, at Vollero's Cafe in Brooklyn.

Morano was deeply disappointed when Morello showed up accompanied only by his personal bodyguard.

Morano had hoped Morello would bring his top lieutenants with him to the meeting. As soon as Morello and Ubriaco stepped from their car, they were ambushed and killed by Johnny "Lefty" Esposito, Anthony "Shoemaker" Paretti, James "Mike the Fixer" Notaro, and Alfonso "Butch" Sgroia. Killing them both in broad daylight on Johnson Street, between Fleet Place and Hudson Avenue, Brooklyn.

Morello is hit by six bullets, Ubriaco by two. Police identify Ubriaco from fingerprints from when he had been arrested in June 1915 for carrying a revolver.

Ciro Terranova identifies Nicholas as his brother.

Following the murders, the Vollero gang celebrated with a dinner at the San Lucia Restaurant at Coney Island.

When the police searched Morello's body; they found a bank book for NY Produce Exchange Bank in Harlem, with a balance of $1,865 (about $43,826 at today's dollar value).

Subsequently, the gang went after other East Harlem gang leaders, killing Giuseppe Verrazano at the Italian Gardens in Manhattan.

However, they were unable to reach the other Morello gang leaders who stayed close to their house in East 116th Street.

Joe DeMarco's younger brother, Salvatore "Toto" DeMarco disappeared following the death of his older brother.

He was not seen again until days after the murders of Nick Morello and associate Charles Ubriaco.

Perhaps fearing he would also be targeted by a Morello vendetta, he reportedly decided to meet with New York Police Detective Frederick Franklin on Oct. 14, 1916, and tell him all he knew about the war between the Mafia and the Camorra.

Salvatore DeMarco never made it to the meeting with Detective Frederick Franklin.

On the morning of October 13, Salvatore's mutilated corpse was found by a street cleaner on the Astoria side of the Queensboro Bridge.

His head had been cracked open with an ax-like instrument. A razor slice across the throat had nearly severed his head from his body.

Detective Franklin remarked, "He'll never tell who killed his brother now."

Many assassinations and attempts happened after this, making neither side safe. Since the Camorra could not kill all of the new Mafia leaders, their plot for destruction would have to be executed indirectly.

The Camorra tried but failed, to take over many of the Mafia's profitable business.

Even though Lupo is now in Federal prison his involvement in murder had not ceased.

In December 1916, Deputy Warden Brock of the Atlanta Federal Prison is murdered as Lupo stood just six feet away.

Lupo claimed to know nothing about the murder.

However, another prisoner claimed that Lupo knew of the deputy warden's murder before it happened and positioned himself where he could watch it happen, because "he wanted to see this thing come off."

The man who played the biggest part in the victory of the Mafia was Ralph 'The Barber' Daniello who belonged to the Brooklyn Navy Street Gang and testified against Navy Street's criminal activities.

After being acquitted on robbery and abduction charges, Daniello decided with the wars between the Camorra and the Mafia, it was no longer safe in New York.

In May 1917, following the May 7th murder of Louis DeMarro in Brooklyn, Daniello, and his girlfriend fled to Reno, Nevada to get as far away from New York as they could.

The following month, the New York City Police issued an arrest warrant for Daniello for the murder of DeMarro.

Meanwhile, Daniello and his girlfriend were running low on money in Reno. He decided to reach out to the Camorra gang and ask for help.

To Daniello's surprise, they ignored his requests. Daniello was eventually arrested in Nevada and then quickly extradited back to New York to face the murder charge.

Daniello was now facing indictments on murder, grand larceny, and perjury.

Daniello was still mad that the Camorra had ignored his requests when he needed it the most, so he began to tell the police about the Navy Street crew and its connection to the Morello and Ubriaco murders.

In total Daniello provided evidence about twenty-three murders.

With this information, several Grand Juries issued a total of twenty-one indictments in November 1917.

Daniello's confession causes police to arrest ten gangsters around New York. Daniello tells of the Mafia-Camorra war and provides details related to twenty-three killings.

New York prosecutors offered Daniello a deal if he would testify against Alessandro Vollero and Pellegrino Morano the current Camorra leader.

Daniello, who had been present for several high-level meetings with both Morano and Vollero, agreed to the deal with the prosecutors.

Daniello explains to prosecutors that there are three major areas of Italian criminal operations in New York. They are Brooklyn, East Harlem, and Downtown Manhattan.

He explains that there are ten different bosses in those areas, Brooklyn has four bosses and three each in the other territories.

July 31st, in a bid to get out of federal prison early, Giuseppe Morello's Lawyer files a petition for executive clemency on his behalf.

The following week, the prison physician reported that Morello developed an "organic heart lesion" and has lost weight and is in "rather poor condition" and suffers with "organize heart trouble."

By November the prison physician reports that Morello's condition has become "very poor" and he has lost 12 pounds in just under two months and is now down to 163 pounds.

After this information is made public President Woodrow Wilson writes to Attorney General T.W. Gregory in late November to ask about the Morello case.

In his letter he states; "I would be very much obliged if you would be kind enough to have a memorandum sent me about the pardon case of Giuseppe Morello. I have been very much interested by what I have heard of it and would like to have a report on it."

Also, in 1917, Alessandro Vollero was extradited to New York and indicted in the murders of Morello, Ubriaco, and a Manhattan gambler named George Verrizano.

Daniello's testimony, along with that of former hitman Johnny "Left" Esposito, and other Navy Street and Coney Island gang members, led to both Morano and Vollero's conviction in 1918. And also lead to the indictment of seventeen men for murder. The defendants include the Terranova brothers.

On January 8th, Giuseppe Morello Morello's counterfeiting sentence is commuted to 15 years by President Woodrow Wilson.

On January 14th, the Federal Prison Warden contacted Morello's attorney and tells him that the commutation document had been received, but he explained that Morello will not be eligible for parole until he has served at least one-third of his original sentence.

Giuseppe Morello was sentenced on the first count to 15 years hard labor and a $500 fine. On the second count, he was sentenced to 10 years of hard labor and a $500 fine. Which totaled to 25 years of hard labor and a $1000 fine. He would have to serve eight years and four months in prison before being eligible for parole. His eligibility date will be June 20, 1918.

Ignazio Lupo had also applied for executive clemency.

And in January 1918, Former Secret Service Agent William Flynn supported Lupo's application for executive clemency by writing a letter to the president in Lupo's defense.

He wrote; "I believe this defendant has been sufficiently punished by his present imprisonment of eight years and I, therefore, beg to recommend the granting of executive clemency in this case."

Just two weeks later Former Secret Service Agent William Flynn writes a second letter to the President on Lupo's behalf. He writes that he believed the relative guilt of Morello and Lupo was the same and notes that Lupo's punishment has been greater than Morello's

On May 15, 1918, Pellegrino Morano was convicted of murder in the case of Terranova and Ubriaco and sentenced to twenty years to life at Sing-Sing prison.

His associate, Alessandro Vollero, was sentenced to death at Sing-Sing Prison on June 20, 1918.

On May 20th, the Atlanta Federal Prison records clerk sends a letter to Morello's lawyer, noting that Morello's application for parole is denied.

One-week later Giuseppe Morello is moved to the prison's hospital wing. Though Morello is confined to the prison hospital, the physician reports that Morello is not seriously ill.

In May of the following year, Giuseppe's daughter Angelina Morello, writes to the Atlanta Prison warden, asking him to help with the release of her father.

It wasn't until mid-December before the Atlanta Prison warden writes to the Superintendent of Prisons D.S. Dickerson. He explains to the Superintendent that President Wilson's Presidential commutation wiped out the $1,000 fine against Morello and set his prison term at fifteen years.

The warden notes that good conduct allowance would permit Morello's release on March 18, 1920.

On June 6, 1918, assassin Johnny "Lefty" Esposito testifies against Terranova as Terranova stands trial for ordering the murder of Joseph DeMarco and also killing his friend Charles "Nine-Fingered" Lombardi (Charles Lombardi was accidentally killed). Esposito says he was paid by and took orders from a Brooklyn saloonkeeper.

On June 7, Johnny "Lefty" Esposito, James "Mike the Fixer" Notaro, and Alfonso "Butch" Sgroia plead guilty to first-degree manslaughter in connection with the killings of Terranova and Ubriaco.

Terranova was eventually acquitted because the witnesses against him, were also technically accomplices in the crimes and no outside corroboration was offered to prove his guilt.

On June 20th, Ralph Daniello pleads guilty to second-degree manslaughter and is given a suspended sentence due to his cooperation with the prosecutor.

However, Vollero's sentence was later reduced to life imprisonment with a minimum of twenty years. On April 28, 1933, after serving just fourteen-years in prison, Vollero was released and sent back to his birth town, Gragnano Italy.

The convictions of Pellegrino Morano and Alessandro Vollero and their criminal associates marked the end of both the Navy Street Gang and the Brooklyn Camorra organization.

Daniello received a suspended sentence in consideration of his testimony against Alessandro Vollero.

However, shortly after being released from jail, he was arrested again for assaulting a man in Coney Island.

Daniello shot the man thinking that he had been sent by his former associates of the Navy Street gang to kill him.

He was sentenced to five years in prison where he lived in fear of retaliation for his testimony that put the leader of the Camorra away.

He was eventually released from prison in 1925.

Ralph 'The Barber' Daniello was shot and killed in his saloon, near Metuchen, New Jersey.

Johnny "Lefty" Esposito was also sentenced in June 1918 for his involvement in the ambush of Nick Terranova and Eugene “Charles” Ubriaco for which he received a six to ten-year sentence.

He was later killed in 1924 while on parole in New Jersey

In 1918, Lauritano Leopoldo was arrested for his involvement in the 1916 murder of Giuseppe Verrazano in Manhattan.

While held for that crime, he was tried and convicted of manslaughter in connection with another killing.

He was sentenced to serve twenty years in state prison. The 1920 Census found him at the Clinton State Prison in Dannemora.

By 1919, Luciano and Costello's crew was nothing more than a group of petty criminals, making money through small-time gambling rings and protection shakedowns.

Seeing an opportunity to strengthen their crew, Frank Costello brings in a new soldier named Vito Genovese.

Genovese is known as a low-level Sicilian thug and has earned a reputation as a lethal enforcer.

With Vito Genovese, they're ready to transform themselves from low-level street thugs into a legitimate gang.

Meyer Lansky is very smart mathematically and becomes the money man.

Bugsy Siegel is a charmer with ruthless instincts.

Frank Costello has all the connections in the city's underworld and knows how to play the system.

And Charles Luciano is the visionary of the group with relentless ambition.

All they need now is the right opportunity. This comes when The Eighteenth Amendment, commonly referred to as the Volstead Act, prohibited "the manufacture, sale, or transportation of intoxicating liquors" goes into effect.

However, it did allow consumption, private possession, or production for one's own consumption.

Unlike earlier amendments to the Constitution, the 18th Amendment set a one-year time delay before it would go into effect and set a time limit of seven years for its ratification by the states.

Its ratification was certified on January 16, 1919.

The 18th Amendment took effect on January 16, 1920, making it illegal to manufacture, transport, or sell intoxicating liquor was added to the United States Constitution.

The government's theory was, the prohibition would decrease alcoholism, and it would increase the morals and the moral fiber of Americans.

The whole concept backfired because of supply and demand.

The demand was that people wanted to drink and there was no supply.

Across the country, there was very little federal funding for law enforcement to enforce Prohibition and many local governments were unable to quickly adapt to it.

Instead of cleaning up America as they predicted, prohibition plays into the hands of the gangsters, creating a billion-dollar industry virtually overnight.

Unfortunately, prohibition was one of the best things the government ever did for the Mob.

Up until now, Joe Masseria has been running gambling rackets, but he changes his entire business plan to take advantage of prohibition.

Masseria creates an underground network of bootlegging distilleries in warehouses, selling his own product.

However, once the Mafia saw the weakness of the law and the weakness in its enforcement, they moved in to exploit it.

Prohibition opened the door for the Mafia to take advantage of one of the most lucrative industries in the United States.

It was the institution of the 18th Amendment that constitutes as a major turning point in the American Mafia.

There were millions of dollars to be made in bootlegging and so the Mafia assimilated themselves into the alcohol industry. And in doing so, organizing themselves into one of the largest most influential criminal syndicates in America.

While the reformers rejoiced across the country, the Mafia capitalized and profited from the illegal alcohol market.

The Mafia supplied underground establishments with beer and liquor. These bootlegging operations used rivers and waterways to smuggle alcohol across state lines.

As the Mafia grew throughout the Prohibition era, territorial disputes often transformed America's cities into violent battlegrounds.

Across America, homicides, assaults, and burglaries increased significantly between 1920 and 1933.

Law enforcement struggled to keep up with the growing crimes. Only three Federal agencies were tasked with enforcing the Volstead Act, bootleggers, and smugglers operated with relative freedom from any consequences of getting caught.

On the state and local levels in New York, police were similarly overwhelmed by the power and influence of the Mafia's involvement in the bootlegging trade.

In 1920 Luciano joined crime boss, Joe Masseria, and by 1925 he had become Masseria's chief lieutenant.

In this position, he oversaw Masseria's bootlegging, narcotics distribution, and prostitution rackets.

In the 1920s, Luciano was also working on bringing together some of New York's biggest Italian and Jewish mobsters to run the city's lucrative bootlegging business.

Boats ran out into the ocean and lakes to buy liquor from Great Britain and Canada, leading to the term "rum-running."

Bootlegging operations that served New York were mostly imported from Canada through the Great Lakes.

Shipments of illegal alcohol were transported through Lake Ontario, over to the Hudson River, and down into New York City.

The demand for liquor was so great during the Prohibition that the Mafia was earning as much as $100 million a year in the mid-1920s (about $1.3 billion at today's dollar value) and spending a half-million dollars a month in bribes to federal Prohibition investigators, local police, and even politicians.

The Mafia paid people throughout New York City to operate stills in their homes to make bad-tasting liquor.

They sold illegal beer, watered-down whiskey, and sometimes-poisonous "rotgut" booze in Mob-owned illegal bars known as "speakeasies."

Often, to screen for potential law enforcement officers at these speakeasies, a bouncer would look through a small peephole in the door before refusing or letting a customer inside.

It is believed that there were as many as 100,000 speakeasies in New York, and thousands of them sold Masseria's bootleg liquor. Masseria's empire expands, and now covers half of Manhattan.

Prohibition reversed Joe Masseria's fortunes more than anybody else in the underworld.

He goes from being petty bootlegger to the king of the mob's underworld.

It was these "bad-tasting liquors" that gave birth to the mixed drinks that we know of today. Many people had to mix something fruity or sweet with the liquor to make it drinkable. And that is how the "Mixed drink" came to be.

The new alcohol trafficking gangs during Prohibition also crossed ethnic lines, with Italians, Irish, Jews, and Poles working with each other to make money on the illegal liquor market.

However, the inter-gang rivalries, shootings, bombings, and killings would ultimately shape the 1920s and early '30s.

By 1933, more than 1,000 people were killed in New York alone in Mob battles during Prohibition.

The 1920s sparked a revolution in organized crime, generating frameworks and plenty of cash for the crime families that still exist to this day, though far less powerful.

The modern-day syndicates born out of Prohibition were based in New York and Chicago, as they were both port cities with considerable populations of immigrants from Italy, Ireland, Poland, and other areas throughout Europe.

Many of these mobsters were part of a generation born in the 1890s and early 1900s that came of age with Prohibition.

The infamous Italian-American "Five Mafia Families" of New York (Gambino, Bonanno, Genovese, Lucchese, and Colombo) would emerge from the Prohibition era.

In early 1920, as Prohibition was in its infancy, the Mafia-Camorra war was coming to an end.

Due to Prohibition, Salvatore D'Aquila was building close relationships with many New York gang leaders and Mafia bosses across the country.

D'Aquila also had several top Mafioso working for him who had once worked with several other top Mafia bosses like Al Capone and Bugsy Siegel.

By this time, D'Aquila made Manfredi "Al" Mineo his Underboss.

In the early 1920s, remnants of the Morello family tried to reassert their authority under the leadership of Peter Morello, while others followed Valenti, Salvatore Mauro, and Joe Masseria.

Joe Masseria intended to take over the entire Italian underworld in New York.

By late 1920, Masseria was unknown outside of the Mafia underworld. That all changed in late 1920, when Salvatore Mauro, attempted ambushed Masseria on Chrystie Street.

However, it was Mauro who was killed in the ambush. Masseria was immediately arrested but claimed that he had killed Mauro in self-defense. He was eventually released from custody.

At the time of the killing, Mauro was a partner in a speakeasy, on Grand Street, with Umberto "Rocco" Valenti. Valenti, who lived on Mulberry Street, was a gunman and ally of Salvatore D'Aquila.

In March of 1920, Giuseppe Morello was released from federal prison and rejoined the now struggling Morello crime family and tried to retake control of his Mafia Empire.

When D'Aquila learned of Morello's plan to retake his position back as Boss, he decided to have him and his top captains murdered to stop his comeback.

In late October 1921, Morello and Lupo, along with several others learned that they were now under orders of death by D'Aquila, fled to Sicily for a short while, seeking support from underworld figures in Sicily.

In November 1921, future Gambino family boss and namesake, Carlo Gambino illegally boarded the ship SS *Vincenzo Florio* and headed for the United States.

After a month-long journey where he ate nothing but anchovies and wine. He entered the United States on December 23, 1921, in Norfolk, Virginia.

He immediately goes to work for his cousins, the Castellano bootlegging family in New York City.

The Castellanos was already associated with the D'Aquila gang and quickly introduced Carlo as a new member.

Carlo also became close with the "Young Turks" in New York City. The Turks were led by Charles Luciano, the future creator of the Mafia Commission.

By the end of 1921 at the age of 19, Carlo Gambino became a "made man" of the American Mafia and begins his journey to the eventual position of Boss of the family named after him; The Gambino Crime Family.

Carlo had two brothers, Gaspare and Paolo. Gaspare was never involved in any the Mafia's activities.

However, Paolo worked alongside his brother in the American Mafia.

Though temporarily rid of Morello and Lupo, D'Aquila found in 1922 that he faced a new opposition in Manhattan.

Former capo of the Morello's, Giuseppe Masseria was gaining power in Manhattan and had united D'Aquila's enemies.

D'Aquila knew that he had to deal with Masseria if he wanted to keep his power and position in the criminal underworld.

D'Aquila also wanted to rid himself of one of his own associates, Umberto "Rocco" Valenti.

Valenti was considered one of the top gunmen in New York. It was believed that he was responsible for at least twenty murders.

By this time, Valenti wanted control of the Mafia of Manhattan and waged war against rival Giuseppe Masseria with the permission of Morello.

D'Aquila believed that Valenti was becoming too powerful and he also questioned Valenti's loyalty to his own family.

When Valenti learned of D'Aquila's plan to kill him, he talked the boss into giving him one more chance to prove his loyalty.

D'Aquila told Valenti to prove his loyalty; he would have to kill the Morello leadership.

Valenti set out to prove his loyalty in early May 1922 when he and his gunmen murdered Giuseppe Morello's cousin Vincent Terranova at East 116th Street and Second Avenue.

Later that day, they attempted to kill Joe Masseria at Grand Street near Mulberry in lower Manhattan but failed to do so.

When Morello's ally, Masseria, heard about the shooting, he supposedly set an ambush for Valenti outside the Liquor Exchange, a curbside liquor exchange, where bootleggers meet to swap surpluses in downtown Manhattan.

Other accounts suggest that it was Umberto "Rocco" Valenti, not Masseria, who actually set up the ambush.

During the ambush, Masseria shot and wounded Valenti's bodyguard Silva Tagliagamba. Both Valenti and Tagliagamba escaped the scene while Masseria was apprehended while fleeing from the scene.

That night, Tagliagamba was brought by ambulance to Bellevue Hospital with serious bullet wounds.

Even though Tagliagamba would not answer police questions, it was soon determined that he was part of the gunfight at Grand Street near Mulberry in lower Manhattan.

In May 1922, as Masseria sat in jail for shooting Tagliagamba, Ignazio Lupo tries to re-enter the U.S.

Immigration officials attempt to deport him back to Sicily. He is held three weeks on Ellis Island as this case is processed.

After Lupo's case is processed the government decides rather than deport him, the U.S. government orders that Lupo be readmitted into the U.S. on June 12th.

Upon his return to the U.S., Lupo works in a bakery business and operating a wholesale fruit operation with his son in Manhattan.

In the summer of 1925, Thirty-nine-year-old Salvatore "Little Caesar" Maranzano, arrived in New York from the small town of Castellammare del Golfo, Sicily.

Maranzano has been sent to New York by the Mafia bosses in Sicily to establish a foothold for the Sicilian Mafia in America.

The Mafia's power was being crushed by the rise of a tyrannical young dictator named Benito Mussolini.

The Sicilian Mafia has dominated Italy for the past century and Mussolini saw the Mafia as one of his biggest problems.

The main issue that he had was that the Mafia wouldn't bend to his will.

His way of dealing with the Mafia was to round up what he considered suspected Mafiosos and imprison them.

And this is what led to one of the largest exoduses of future Mafia members in America.

Many people today believe that Mussolini was unintentionally responsible for helping to create the American Mafia.

Maranzano started with a legitimate business as a real estate broker.

However, on the side, he also maintained a growing bootlegging business, using the real estate company as a front for his illegal operations.

Maranzano eventually took over the leadership of the Castellammare family and soon became a mentor to a young Joseph Bonanno. (Maranzano's crime empire would later become the Bonanno crime family)

At the time, the Castellammare family was the second oldest mafia family that operated out of the Williamsburg section of Brooklyn and was led by Nicolo "Cola" Schirò.

In June 1922, Tagliagamba died from his gunshot wounds. Masseria was indicted and Masseria was charged with homicide. He was free on $15,000(about $229,000.00 at today's dollar value) bail in August, just three months later.

However, the case never went to trial.

Valenti once again attempted to kill Joe Masseria when Masseria was released on bail in early August.

When Masseria stepped out of his home at 80 Second Avenue alone shots rang out. Masseria ran inside Heiney's Millinery.

Valenti chased Masseria into a local millinery store where Masseria managed to once again escape.

Masseria gained the reputation for ducking bullets as every shot missed him, only one bullet passed through his hat.

This time Valenti had exceeded his authority; he had never asked Morello's permission to hit Masseria the second time and Morello now turned against Valenti. Morello and Masseria soon made a deal to kill Valenti.

It was during this quest to kill Masseria that Valenti began to see a shift in power within the gang.

Valenti now realized that he may never get a chance to kill Masseria and would himself become a target.

Charles Luciano and his crew are bringing in money for Masseria, but not enough to get noticed.

So Luciano begins to devise a plan that he believes will get the Masseria's attention.

Luciano decides to hijack a rival gang's truck, filled with illegal booze, and deliver it to Masseria.

If he can pull it off, he'll have a chance to move up in Masseria's organization and finally earn some big money.

Luciano and his crew have just pulled off a huge heist.

The only problem is, they've robbed a truck belonging to their own boss.

To make a name for themselves, Charles Luciano and his gang have pulled off a daring heist, only to learn they've inadvertently stolen from their own boss, Joe Masseria.

Luciano knows that he and his crew can't just return what they've stolen, as Masseria will make a brutal example of anyone who crosses him.

Luciano decides to go and talk to Masseria and explain to the boss what they had done. Luciano tells Masseria that he didn't know the truck was his.

Luciano and Masseria agree that Luciano would kill Umberto Valenti in exchange for Masseria sparing Luciano and his crew.

Charles Luciano has never killed a man before.

And now he must kill one of the most dangerous mobsters in New York who nearly killed Joe Masseria just days earlier.

For weeks, Luciano and his crew plan the hit on Valenti, waiting for the perfect opportunity to make their move.

Finally, their opportunity came when a meeting to settle the dispute between both gangs was set up for August 11, 1922, by Morello and Masseria at a restaurant near 233 East 12th Street and 2nd Avenue.

Valenti and Masseria, plus one bodyguard each, met at the restaurant on East 12th Street.

After the meal, and talk, the men walked along East 12th Street, towards 2nd Avenue.

However, Masseria had stationed more of his men at the corner of East 12th Street and 2nd Avenue.

Valenti ran when he saw the gunmen, one of which was Luciano.

Valenti dodged bullets as he ran, and tried to jump onto a moving taxi to escape. Valente ran out into the intersection, as the three gunmen drew handguns and shot at him.

A bullet hit Valenti in the spine. He fell mortally wounded into the street.

A street cleaner and an eight-year-old girl were wounded during the ensuing shootout.

With Umberto "Rocco" Valenti now dead, the war in lower Manhattan was effectively won by the Masseria faction. Masseria's position as top Mafioso in Prohibition Era Manhattan dramatically increased his wealth and influence.

Twenty Five-year-old Charles Luciano has committed his first murder.

He saves himself and his crew, but he's now under Masseria's control.

Masseria sees Luciano's potential and promotes him within his crew.

Salvatore D'Aquila also lost much of his influence throughout New York.

Mineo understood at this time that the new power in New York was Joe Masseria, so Mineo secretly began to align himself with Masseria.

This alliance would later cause a conflict between Mineo and Frank Scalice.

Several of D'Aquila's closest associates began to defect. This included a close friend named Saverio "Sam" Pollaccia, who became a personal adviser to Masseria.

In 1925 Salvatore D'Aquila was forced to move to the Bronx where he purchased a home directly across from the entrance to the Bronx zoo.

Giuseppe Masseria was now battling with D'Aquila for control of New York's organized crime.

In 1924, the United States Congress banned the sale, importation, or manufacture of Heroin.

That opened a new door for Joe Masseria to make money.

Now in Masseria's inner circle, Luciano was ordered to run a high stakes racket, selling heroin.

And with the help of Luciano, Heroin becomes Joe Masseria's biggest business. And Luciano quickly becomes one of Masseria's top earners.

Luciano and his crew devise ways of smuggling heroin to their clients.

One of their most popular ways was to disguising their deliveries in hatboxes.

Their main customers at the time are prostitutes, who are not only addicts but can also sell Luciano's drug out of the local brothels.

Luciano was soon arrested for dealing heroin and sentenced to six months in jail.

While Luciano sits in jail, Masseria continues to rake in the profits.

Luciano soon realizes that if he truly wants to succeed in the criminal underworld, he'll have to find a way to become his own boss.

Meanwhile, Meyer Lansky made an important new contact with another Major bootlegger in New York City at a bar mitzvah names Arnold Rothstein.

Rothstein was known to fix horse races, operate illegal casinos, and it was believed that he had planned the most notorious sports betting scandal of all time; the fixing of the 1919 World Series.

It was believed that in 1919, Rothstein's men paid players on the Chicago White Sox to deliberately lose the World Series to the Cincinnati Reds.

He bet against them and made millions in what was called the "Black Sox Scandal".

Meyer Lansky knows that working for a gangster like Arnold Rothstein is the opportunity that he and Luciano have been waiting for.

After serving his six-month jail sentence, Charles Luciano was a free man,

And he was determined to find a better way to succeed in crime.

Lansky introduced Luciano to Rothstein and even though Luciano was still part of Masseria's gang, he begins distributing alcohol for Rothstein on the side.

Rothstein becomes a role model for Luciano.

He was like the father he always wanted, but never had and he looked up to him.

And Rothstein was teaching Luciano that there's a smarter way to do business and shows him how to organize his criminal rackets like a well-organized corporation.

Luciano and his crew following Rothstein's bootlegging advice and soon making a fortune.

However, because Luciano still technically works for Masseria, they still have to give a huge cut of everything they make to him.

Masseria wanted as much as $10,000 from each person who worked for another gang.

He believed that he deserved it because he was so important and so vital to Italian gangsters in New York City at the time.

By 1925, Rothstein was one of the most powerful criminals in the country, with a reported wealth of over $10 million (about $150 million today)

Meanwhile, Carlo Gambino fell in love and married his first cousin, Catherine Castellano, on December 5, 1926.

This marriage now made his cousin Paul, his brother in law.

Carlo and Catherine raised four children. Three sons; Thomas, Joseph, and Carlo, and a daughter named Phyllis.

Carlo Gambino quickly became one of the family's top earners and controlled several of the family's illegal rackets including loansharking and gambling.

Masseria began backing challenges to D'Aquila-supported crime families across the country, most notably in Cleveland.

Much of Masseria's extended family lived in Cleveland and Masseria's brother was involved in the Mayfield Road Mob, so he had an interest in the city of Cleveland.

Through his domination of the corn sugar and corn whiskey industries and with the support of the D'Aquila crime family, Salvatore "Black Sam" Todaro, and the Porrello brothers, Joseph "Big Joe" Lonardo became the first known boss of the Cleveland crime family which he organized from a competing number of organized crime gangs.

Lonardo was regarded as an effective boss. He overcame resistance to his criminal activities by maintaining good relationships with the organized crime outlets in Little Italy (the area most affected by his bootlegging), helping to resolve their disputes, and donating money to those in need.

In 1927 Giuseppe Masseria encouraged Salvatore "Black Sam" Todaro to murder Joseph Lonardo and take over the Cleveland crime family in a move to embarrass Salvatore D'Aquila.

Todaro likely ordered the murder of Joseph Lonardo, and most likely arranged the meeting at which Lonardo was killed.

On October 13, 1927, D'Aquila lost another ally, Joseph "Big Joe" Lonardo, when he was shot and killed.

Lonardo's death ignited what the press called the "Corn Sugar War", a series of power-grabs and retaliatory blood feuds around the Cleveland area that left another Lonardo family member and seven Porrellos dead.

Masseria did not have immediate family with Mafia ties, so he had to rely on alliances, and he had to be practical, rather than traditional, in those alliances.

At the time, Little Italy's population was a mixture of Sicilians, Neapolitans, and Calabrians. And he knew that he had to build his power through alliances with these people.

He made allies among most of the non-Sicilian gangs.

The most important of these allies that he made was with Frank Ioele Yale, a Calabrian and the most powerful Mafioso in South Brooklyn.

His longstanding alliance with Ciro Terranova led to further allies among Gaetano Tommy Reina's faction in the Bronx.

And then there were the younger, Americanized gangsters, like Luciano and his associates Genovese and Costello.

With these allies on his side, Masseria grew in power.

By 1928, Masseria posed a serious threat to D'Aquila's position as Head of the New York City Mafia.

Masseria was already making plans to take down D'Aquila and was in contact with disgruntled members of D'Aquila's Family.

In July 1928, Brooklyn crime boss, and a close D'Aquila ally, Frankie Yale, was slain.

Although D'Aquila was still considered very powerful, Masseria and Morello were still determined to end his reign.

Although Frankie Yale's murder was most likely ordered by Al Capone in Chicago, rather than his local Sicilian enemies, it was the spark that set off several conflicts within the Mafia.

With the death of Brooklyn crime boss, Frankie Yale, D'Aquila saw an opportunity to move into Yale's territory.

However, D'Aquila was met with opposition from Yale's men.

D'Aquila ordered the murder of Michele "Mike Schatz" Abbatemarco, a top lieutenant in the Frank Yale organization.

By September, Arnold Rothstein's luck is starting to run bad.

He's been losing at the track, cards, and his marriage is also starting to fall apart.

Rothstein was losing money at every turn. And he thought he found a way to redeem his luck when he was invited to a card game with high rolling betters.

Rothstein plays cards for three days, and just like his luck on the horses, he's steadily losing money.

On the third day, he believes that the game is fixed and tells the other players that he's not paying.

He gets up and leaves the game. Not realizing that he had just sealed his own fate which would play out in the coming months.

On the evening of October 5, 1928, Abbatemarco played poker at a coffeehouse, at Union Street and Fourth Avenue.

Abbatemarco left the card game to go home after 3:00 a.m.

Abbatemarco was next seen at 4:15 a.m. in front of 2421 83rd Street in Bensonhurst, Brooklyn.

Abbatemarco was slumped dead in the front seat of his still-running car, with bullet holes in his neck, forehead, right cheek, and chest.

After Abbatemarco's murder, the new leader of Yale's old gang, Anthony Carfano, also known as "Little Augie Pisano" went to Masseria for support.

Anthony Carfano later became a caporegime, in the Luciano crime family under mob bosses Charles Luciano and Frank Costello.

Frank Costello

Later Frank Costello earned the nicknamed "The Prime Minister of the Underworld," and eventually became one of the most powerful and influential mafia bosses in American history.

He eventually became the leader of the Luciano crime family (later called the Genovese crime family).

With the alliance with Anthony Carfano, Masseria had an opportunity to eliminate his main rival and gain a stronger position in Brooklyn.

Masseria contacted his ally in D'Aquila's Family, Underboss Manfredi "Al" Mineo who was most likely given an ultimatum; either set up D'Aquila or be killed with him.

Together they organized a strategy to take out D'Aquila.

On October 10, 1928, just days after Abbatemarco's murder, Salvatore D'Aquila left his home for a doctor's appointment. As he walked down Avenue A in Manhattan, D'Aquila was approached by three of his own men.

After a violent argument, one of the men pulled out a pistol and shot D'Aquila two times in the chest.

Fifty-four-year-old D'Aquila fell to the ground where the hitman fired another seven bullets into his body.

Mineo declared his allegiance to Masseria and showing his distorted loyalty by betraying his former boss, Mineo's place at the top of the D'Aquila crime family leadership was secured.

Soon after D'Aquila's murder, Manfredi Mineo was given control of the D'Aquila family where through a series of successions would one day become known as the Gambino crime family; The most powerful crime family in New York.

Carlo Gambino also aligned with Masseria. Half of the Young Turks joined Masseria as well, with the others aligning with Maranzano.

At the time, the Castellammarese Clan included Joe Bonanno, Stefano Magaddino, and the Profaci crime family.

Former Masseria allies Tommy Lucchese and boss of the Reina family Gaetano Reina, joined the Castellammarese and Maranzano.

Mineo had secured his Brooklyn interests and would now command one of the larger Manhattan-based Mafia groups in New York.

With Steve Ferrigno as his Underboss based in the Bronx, the Mineo crime family would control several rackets: bootlegging, gambling, and extortion.

After the murder of D'Aquila, the power in New York shifted to Joe Masseria's Manhattan-based gang.

With Abbatemarco and D'Aquila now out of the way, Masseria moved in and Anthony Carfano ('Little Augie Pisano') was appointed as the head of the Yale family.

Carfano's organization retained control of Yale's gambling and bootlegging interests.

However, it may have been at this time that the Waterfront racket was reallocated and came under the control of Manfredi "Al" Mineo and the D'Aquila family.

Giuseppe Masseria was now known as, "Joe the Boss" Masseria, head of the largest Mafia family in New York City.

Morello, now sensing his time to rule had passed and the power of Masseria was on the rise, became consigliere to Masseria, and prospered under him throughout the Prohibition years of the 1920s.

Other Sicilian gangsters in the New York area, who were not yet part of his empire, took note of what had happened to D'Aquila and soon began to pay homage to "Joe the Boss" Masseria.

One of those who were paying homage was Tommy Reina who allied with Giuseppe "Joe the Boss" Masseria in the late 1920s.

Twenty-five-years earlier, Tommy Reina had been a captain in the Morello family.

As the Morello family dealt with the imprisonment of its leader during the 1910s, Reina, along with Salvatore D'Aquila and Joe Masseria, chose to split off and form their own families.

By 1920, Reina ruled as the boss of his own crime family, which would later be known as the Lucchese crime family.

Reina's family was controlling criminal operations in parts of East Harlem and The Bronx. Reina's crime family was in control of the icebox distribution in The Bronx.

Reina's underboss was Tommy Galliano, who was also a former Morello gang member.

Then on November 4, less than one month after the murder of D'Aquila, Rothstein was assassinated.

Rothstein was shot and died two days later at a hospital in Manhattan.

On his deathbed, Rothstein refused to identify his killer.

Gambler George "Hump" McManus was arrested for the murder but was later acquitted for lack of evidence.

With Rothstein gone Luciano decides to put his plans to take out Joe Masseria on hold.

But while Luciano plans out his next move, an even bigger problem is brewing by the actions of a notorious gangster over 800 miles away named Al Capone.

Al Capone is a Brooklyn gangster who fled from New York to Chicago.

On February 14, 1929, Capone orders the brutal execution of rival Chicago gangsters.

More than 150 shots are fired, in what becomes known as "The Saint Valentine's Day massacre", one of the bloodiest days in Mafia history.

The Saint Valentine's Day massacre brings unwanted attention to the mob.

Soon, special Government task forces begin raiding speakeasies and Mob headquarters throughout New York to take down mobsters triggered by the actions of Al Capone.

Joe Masseria knows that he has to act fast to take the heat off of his own operation.

He knows that he needs to get Capone under control quickly.

Knowing that Luciano and Capone were part of the same New York gangs as teenagers, Masseria is convinced that Luciano is the only one in his organization that can get close to Capone.

Joe Masseria orders Charles Luciano to take care of Al Capone.

In May, Luciano organizes a Mob conference at the Ritz-Carlton, in Atlantic City.

Jewish, Irish, and Italian gangsters from across the country are invited, including Chicago's Al Capone.

They discuss the impact that the St. Valentine's Day massacre has had on the mob and they encourage Capone to turn himself in.

At first, he refuses, however after Luciano talks to him he agrees.

And Luciano tells Capone that he would only have to plead to a minor charge. And Luciano would personally look after his business in Chicago until he returns.

And with Luciano's connections, Al Capone is sentenced to just a year in prison.

Following in Arnold Rothstein's footsteps, Luciano has proven himself to be a skillful leader and a very effective negotiator.

Luciano earned a great deal of respect from gangsters around the country, but his criminal abilities are about to be put to the ultimate test.

When Reina switched sides and allied with Maranzano and the Castellammarese Family.

The Castellammare Family came from the Sicilian seaside town of Castellammare del Golfo, a small town just forty miles west of Palermo Sicily.

The Castellammarese Family rose to prominence during Prohibition and became extremely independent and opposed the dominance of Joe "The Boss" Masseria and his supporters.

When Joe Masseria learned of Reina's betrayal, he approached Luciano to arrange Reina's murder.

Reina's alliance with Maranzano and the Castellammarese Family caused a heated rivalry between Masseria's crime family and Nicolo "Cola" Schirò's, Brooklyn-based Castellammarese clan.

Masseria began to put pressure on the Castellammarese clan and Schirò paid Masseria $10,000 and then "went into hiding", and was never heard from again in New York.

It was widely believed in New York that Schirò had been killed by Masseria.

However, Schirò was alive and well and had returned to Italy; settling in his old hometown of Camporeale in Sicily.

In 1949, Schirò renounced his U.S. citizenship at the American consulate in Palermo and died in Camporeale on April 29, 1957.

After the disappearance of Schirò, Masseria attempted to appoint Joe Parrino as the new leader Castellammarese clan.

However, Parrino was soon shot to death in a restaurant.

Instead of Joe Parrino, Schirò's place as the leader was taken by Salvatore Maranzano.

Masseria was not happy with Maranzano leading The Castellammarese clan and soon ordered the death of Maranzano.

The rivalries between Joe "The Boss" Masseria and Salvatore Maranzano would eventually turn into a war within the Italian underworld and drag every Mafia crime family and faction in New York into what would become known as the Castellammarese War.

The Castellammarese War began in late 1929 and dragged on for the better part of two years, as New York Mafia leaders Joe Masseria and Salvatore Maranzano fought for dominance over the New York rackets.

In May 1929, a conference was held in Atlantic City, attended by leading Mafia figures from around the country to organize what would become to be known in the media as The National Crime Syndicate.

This was the idea of Chicago mob boss, Johnny Torrio.

Torrio was the boss of the Chicago Mafia outfit that would eventually be led by Capone.

Torrio later became an unofficial adviser to Luciano.

The National Crime Syndicate mostly consisted of the Italian-American Mafia and Jewish mob.

However, it also included various lesser groups such as Irish-American criminal organizations and other ethnic crime groups.

Some of the well-known Mafia figures of the day that attended the conference were, Johnny Torrio, Al Capone, "Bugsy" Siegel, Luciano, Vincent Mangano, Frank Costello, Frank “Don Cheech” Scalice, and Albert "the Mad Hatter" Anastasia.

Just five months after The National Crime Syndicate conference ended Luciano would take a trip that he would not soon forget.

As The Castellammarese War rages on the streets of New York, Luciano is kidnapped and is now in the hands of Maranzano.

And for the next eight hours, Luciano is beaten and tortured to send a message to Masseria and his crew.

After the beating, Luciano was taken to a remote area in Staten Island, where he's dumped and left for dead.

However, Luciano somehow survives.

Just after one o'clock in the morning on October 17, 1929, a bloodied Luciano, was found staggering along Hylan Boulevard, near Cornelia Boulevard and The Terra Marine Inn, at Huguenot Beach on the southern end of Staten Island,

Luciano had been beaten and his throat slashed and left for dead in a nearby wooded field.

Luciano staggered from the woods and asked the first person he saw, who turned out to be a police officer, to get him a taxi so he could get back to Manhattan.

Instead of taking Luciano to Manhattan as he requested, the officer took Luciano to the 123rd Precinct stationhouse. There, a surgeon from the local Hospital treated Luciano's wounds.

When questioned, Luciano told the police that he'd been abducted at the corners of 50th Street and Third Avenue in Manhattan, and then he was beaten and dumped off in the field.

He stated that he didn't know his attackers and he had no idea he'd been taken to Staten Island.

He thought that he was being taken to New Jersey.

Luciano appeared before a grand jury at Richmond County Court House in St. George twelve days later.

When questioned about his attackers Luciano said he couldn't remember how he got the wounds on his neck.

Luciano said that he was knocked out by his abductors, and that's all he could remember until he eventually woke up in the woods on Staten Island.

As word spread of the attack, conflicting accounts of the episode quickly grew.

Some people believed that the beating was inflicted by cops after Luciano refused to give up information about another mobster.

It was also rumored that it was Luciano's surviving this attack that gave him the nickname, "Lucky".

On October 28th, the U.S. stock market crashes, losing billions of dollars in just one day.

It's the worst economic disaster the country has ever experienced.

Thousands of banks fail, and one in four Americans are now suddenly unemployed.

Most people at the time see the great depression as a time of hopelessness, however, Luciano and the mob sees it as a great financial opportunity.

Together, with Meyer Lansky, Luciano develops a new racket, designed to take advantage of the depression.

Luciano begins providing loans to businesses on the verge of bankruptcy, at extremely high interest rates.

With Meyer Lansky in charge of the money, Luciano and his crew are using the depression to make a fortune.

Banks were not lending money so people would turn to "loan sharks," and the interest from a loan shark was 20%.

While America is in financial ruin, Luciano and his crew are making a fortune.

The Mob owns a stake in businesses across New York, and Luciano is earning 20% interest, every week on money that he loaned to these companies.

Luciano is still obligated to pay a portion of his earnings to Joe Masseria.

Luciano believes the time has finally come to remove the only person standing his way of getting to the top of the New York underworld.

On the evening of February 26, 1930, Tommy Reina was ambushed and shot in the head with a double-barreled shotgun, instantly killing him as he left an apartment in the Claremont section of the Bronx.

With Tommy Reina now dead, Tommy Gagliano took over the position as boss of the Reina family, with Lucchese as his underboss.

In May of 1930, one of Masseria's warehouses comes under attack by Salvatore Maranzano.

By this time Al Mineo felt secure being aligned with Joe "The Boss" Masseria, as the Masseria-Mineo alliance quickly gained the upper hand in The Castellammarese War as their forces began to move on Castellammarese-controlled territories and eliminating their rivals at every opportunity.

However, on August 15, 1930, the tide began to change when Giuseppe Morello, Masseria's top strategic adviser and "war chief", was killed while collecting cash receipts in his East Harlem office.

Joseph Valachi, who was a soldier in the Reina family, and the first made man in the American Mafia to turn state's evidence, identified Morello's killer as a Castellammarese gunman he identified only as "Buster from Chicago".

Many believed that "Buster from Chicago" was invented by Valachi to hide the fact that he was Morello's real killer, while others believe that Luciano orchestrated Morello's murder himself.

Al Mineo was quickly named Masseria's new "war chief" and strategist and quickly suspected that the Castellammarese were gaining more support and more ground as the war dragged on.

Mineo felt the only way to win this war was to find and kill Maranzano before he could kill Masseria.

Mineo knew that this would be the only sensible solution to ending the war and Masseria re-establishing dominance over the New York Mafia.

For the next three months, the Castellammarese War dragged on.

In the first week of November 1930, several Maranzano gunmen had rented a first-floor apartment in a building on the Pelham Parkway in the Bronx.

Joe Masseria had been observed entering the building earlier in the week.

However, when the gunmen saw Mineo and Ferrigno alone in the courtyard of the apartment building, they seized the opportunity and shot both of them from their apartment window.

After Al Mineo's death, Francesco "Frank" Scalice was promoted to the position of Boss in Mineo's crime family.

Nobody has ever been charged in Al Moneo's murder.

Scalice immediately switched allegiance from Joe Masseria to Maranzano, who was at the time, emerging as the winner in the Castellammarese War.

In December 1930, eight months after Giuseppe Morello's murdered, the Castellammarese War would take a drastic new direction.

Some of the leaders from other mafia gangs not involved in the Castellammarese War called a meeting of representatives in December 1930 in Boston.

They were upset that the war between Masseria and Maranzano was cutting into their business.

It was decided that Masseria would be stripped of his Capo di tutti capi, "Boss of Bosses" title and the title would be given to Boston mafia chief, Gaspare Messina.

They also tried to broker peace between Masseria and Maranzano.

Maranzano refused as long as Masseria was still alive.

Maranzano also encouraged Masseria's gang members to defect and kill their boss. Maranzano got his wish just four months later.

The Castellammarese War went on for nearly four years. It was the height of prohibition where profits were large; however, the war almost completely wiped out many of the New York crime family's criminal rackets.

Luciano and members of the Young Turks from both sides began to realize that the war was pointless and prevented other Mafia gangs from making money.

Many of the Jewish and Irish crime families became the dominant families in New York During the war.

Meyer Lansky felt that Maranzano and Masseria were old-school Mafioso who was too greedy to see the riches that could be had by working together with non-Italians.

Carlo Gambino and the Young Turks agreed and decided to end the war and work with Luciano to form a national syndicate.

Luciano realized that neither Masseria nor Maranzano was going to give in and end the war.

And he also knew that there wasn't going be a peace treaty between these two gangs because they hated each other.

And Luciano decided that Masseria had to be removed from power.

He knew that the time has finally come to kill Joe Masseria.

And Luciano sees potential in allying with the man who had him kidnapped and beat him to within an inch of his life.

Luciano makes a deal with Maranzano to kill Joe Masseria.

Luciano's overall goal was to create an organized crime syndicate that would limit violence and make it easier for everyone to make money.

Luciano knew that if he eliminates Joe "The Boss" Masseria, he will be one step closer to ending the war, and seizing his own power in the criminal underworld.

At the beginning of 1931, Luciano and Vito Genovese formulate a plan to kill Mob boss, Joe Masseria.

But, first, they have to get close enough to him to pull off the hit.

Luciano knows that Masseria is always surrounded by bodyguards; Luciano also knows that their loyalty can be bought for the right price.

And it does not take him long before the bodyguards are paid off and Luciano is ready to make his move.

Luciano was willing to betray his own boss in exchange for peace.

Joe Masseria, Lucky Luciano, and Salvatore Maranzano

Over the years, the story of the killing of Joe "The Boss" Masseria has been told many different ways.

What we do know is that, on April 15, Masseria went to his favorite restaurant called Nuova Villa Tammaro, a seafood restaurant on West 15th Street in Coney Island, Brooklyn.

Masseria arrived at the restaurant in his armored steel car with plate glass an inch thick in the company of three other men shortly before three o'clock that afternoon.

The restaurant was owned by Gerardo Scarpato and named for the owner's mother-in-law, Anna Tammaro.

Gerado Scarpato, (some report shows his first name as Gerardo) who lived in the apartment above the restaurant with his wife Alvira and his mother-in-law.

Many versions of the story say that Masseria dined with Luciano that day and played cards before his death.

However, two other major newspapers of that time, the *New York Times* and the *New York Herald Tribune*, never mention Luciano being present, although Luciano was brought in for questioning by the police.

Many stories have also been said that Masseria 'pigged out' before his death, however, his autopsy showed hardly any food content in his stomach - only two ounces of bile.

There are different versions of what happened in the restaurant. Many versions of the story say that Lucky Luciano arranged the meeting to set up Masseria to be killed.

It has also been said that, while they played cards, Luciano excused himself to use the bathroom; this was believed to be the signal for the hitmen to come in.

That is when two men and, in some reports, four men, arrived while Masseria and his friends were playing cards and shot and killed Masseria.

This story, however, turns out to be untrue.

Masseria was known to be having lunch that day with Sam Pollaccia, who by that time might have risen to underboss or consigliere in Masseria's organization.

Other Masseria lieutenants might have been present, including Lucky Luciano, and no reliable account of the tale of Luciano's conveniently timed trip to the bathroom has ever been proven.

Over the years, eight men have been identified as the ones who killed Masseria after his bodyguards mysteriously disappeared: Bugsy Siegel, Vito Genovese, Albert Anastasia, Meyer Lansky, Vito Genovese, Mike Coppola, Frank Livorsi, and Joe Adonis.

Livorsi, Stracci, and Coppola were all part of the Masseria family that was run out of East Harlem under the supervision of Ciro Terranova.

It was later determined that it was highly unlikely that Albert Anastasia was one of Masseria's killers.

A young lawyer named Samuel S. Leibowitz who later became a judge in Brooklyn's King County Court, in 1931 had an office at 66 Court Street in downtown Brooklyn.

At noon on that day, Albert Anastasia walked into the lawyer's office and demanded that the receptionist check the time on the office clock.

She did and confirmed the clock was correct.

He then asked to see Leibowitz and was told he would be in court until later in the day.

Anastasia then told the receptionist he would stay and wait for Leibowitz, thereby creating for himself the perfect alibi.

The mob informer Joseph Valachi later named Lucky Luciano, Vito Genovese, Frank Livorsi, and Joe Stracci as the hitmen.

However, eyewitnesses told the police that only two well-dressed young men drove up and parked their car at the curb.

They said that the men, *strolled leisurely into the restaurant, and the shooting began immediately*.

As Masseria lay dying, the two gunmen calmly walked out of the restaurant, entered a waiting car, and drove off.

Despite Masseria's reputation for dodging bullets, he was hit with four bullets in the back and one in the back of the head.

Two of the four back shots were through and through as was the shot to his head.

The bullet to the head entered from the rear and exited through Masseria's eye socket.

Two of the shots to the back had smudged Masseria's coat jacket with gunpowder, indicating the shooter was only inches away when the shot was fired.

Masseria's heart, liver, and lungs were torn apart by the bullets and his brain was shredded.

Two lead bullets were recovered during the autopsy, both .38 caliber.

Although the autopsy does not indicate it, Masseria was most certainly dead by the time that he hit the floor.

It is also very likely that the owner of the restaurant, Gerardo Scarpato, was also in on the hit.

Scarpato had taken over the extortion ring previously run by Giuseppe 'Clutching Hand' Piraino, (a close associate of Anthony Carfano,) who had been killed the previous August.

A man who owned a small business arrived unexpectedly at the restaurant sometime before the hit to pay money that he owed to Scarpato.

The businessman later recalled that Scarpato ran over and asked him what he was doing there.

He told Scarpato that he was there to pay the money he owed to him.

Scarpato told him to leave the restaurant right away and not mention to anyone that he had been there that day.

Later that night, the man said that he had read that Joe Masseria had been shot at the Villa Tammaro.

When the police arrived on the scene, they found Mrs. Tammaro bending over Joe Masseria's body.

Playing cards were strewed around the room. A photographer snapped an image of Masseria with the ace of spades clutched in his right hand.

The next day, The *New York Daily News* reported that the boss died "with the ace of spades, the death card, clutched in a bejeweled paw."

Masseria with the ace of spades clutched in his right hand

It has long been rumored that the photographer placed the legendary "death card" in Masseria's hand before taking the picture.

As Brooklyn detectives brought Sam Pollaccia in for questioning. Pollaccia denied any knowledge of or involvement in the killing of Masseria.

Four hours after the shooting the automobile in which Masseria's murderers escaped was found abandoned near Kings Highway, at West First Street, about two miles from the Nuova Villa Tammaro restaurant.

The police found three pistols on the back seat.

One lacked two bullets; another had fired one bullet recently, and the third was still fully loaded.

Masseria was shot with a .32 and .38 caliber handgun. The police recovered two revolvers in the alley that runs along one side of the restaurant.

The Detectives also found three overcoats left hanging up in the restaurant where Masseria was killed. Two of the overcoats bear numbers that are used by cleaners to identify the garment's owners. These numbers are known as cleaners' marks.

Detectives checked these against the codes used in the city's dry-cleaning establishments and tailor shops and determined that one of the owners was a man called Johnny 'Silk Stocking' Giustra who according to some sources was part of the crew of Vincenzo Mangano.

Mangano was a capo in the Mineo crime family, operating the family's businesses on the South Brooklyn Piers around Red Hook.

Other information implies that Giustra was part of the Masseria crime family and possible rival to the organization of Vincent Mangano and Albert Anastasia at the Brooklyn waterfront.

Even the police questioned why someone would walk into a room, take off your coat, kill a man, and then walk out leaving behind evidence that would prove that you were there.

Others believe that Giustra may well have fled the scene in panic when the shooting started, with obviously no thought for his coat.

The Kings County district attorney's office probed the Murder, Inc., organization some years later.

They discovered a report that Pollaccia and a small group of men were with Masseria on the day of the murder.

They also discovered that "Johnny Silk Stockings" Giustra entered the restaurant behind Masseria and shot and killed him.

Just three weeks after Masseria's killing, Giustra was shot numerous times in the head and chest and died in the hallway of a dingy apartment building at 75 Monroe Street on the Lower East Side on May 10th.

If Giustra's killing was related to Masseria's death rather than to a rivalry between Vincent Mangano and Albert Anastasia, it could be interpreted as an effort to remove an individual who could link other Mafia leaders with the Masseria's assassination.

The owner of the restaurant, Mr. Scarpato, said that he had been out for a long walk that afternoon and returned to learn of Masseria's murder.

Fearing reprisals, Mr. Scarpato, asked the police to take his fingerprints and to keep them on file, so that his body could be identified if he were killed.

He was so certain he was to be killed; he had his full name tattooed on the inside of his right forearm.

Scarpato believed that Masseria's men would think that he was somehow in on the hit and seek revenge.

Soon after the killing of Joe Masseria, Gerardo Scarpato and his wife left New York and traveled back to Italy where they stayed for a year.

With Masseria now dead and out of the way, Salvatore "Little Caesar" Maranzano, was the ultimate victor of the Castellammarese War and the most powerful Mafioso in New York.

Two weeks after Masseria's murder, Maranzano called together several hundred Mafiosi to a banquet hall in Upstate New York.

At this meeting, Maranzano confirmed and anointed the four other bosses of the crime families who had survived the Castellammarese War.

The four bosses were Charles "Lucky" Luciano, Tommy Gagliano, Joe Profaci, and Vincent Mangano was promoted and took over Masseria's Mineo family. Young Turk, Albert Anastasia became his underboss, and Carlo Gambino was promoted to Capo.

He also assigned himself to the position of, Capo di tutti capi, "Boss of Bosses" of the American Mafia.

This announcement came as a total surprise to the other Mafiosi bosses since Maranzano himself had claimed that he wanted to end "boss rule".

However, Salvatore "Little Caesar" Maranzano's attempt to model the organization after Caesar's military chain of command did not sit well with Luciano, Vito Genovese, Frank Costello, and others.

And just like Julius Caesar, Maranzano was scheming and was arrogant towards his subordinates.

And to satisfy the older Mafiosos, he made the rule that only full-blooded Italians would be allowed to officially join a family or become a "made man". However, there would be exceptions for trusted non-Italians and they would be known as associate members.

Despite his ideas for more modern methods of organization, including crews of soldiers doing the bulk of a family's illegal work under the supervision of a caporegime he was openly opposed to

Luciano's partnership with Jewish gangsters such as "Bugsy" Siegel and Meyer Lansky.

With these new revelations, it wasn't long before Luciano and his colleagues decided that it was time to eliminate Maranzano as well.

The other four family leaders came to believe that Maranzano was, in his own way, even more power-hungry than Masseria had ever been.

Maranzano quickly realized that the others despised his way of leading the Mafia and suspected Luciano of wanting to kill him and seize power for himself.

Maranzano began planning the murders of Luciano, Genovese, and others to protect his position in the Mafia.

Maranzano knew that it would be impossible to hire an Italian hitman to kill Luciano, so he turned to Irish born hitman, Vincent "Mad Dog" Coll.

Maranzano met with Coll and the two agreed that Coll would murder Luciano for $50,000 (about $845,000 at today's dollar value).

They agreed that Coll would receive a $25,000 payment upfront and the second $25,000 payment on the completion of the hit.

Frank Costello informs Luciano that Maranzano has a contract out to kill him.

Luciano knows that he has to kill Maranzano before Maranzano kills him.

On September 10, 1931, less than five months after the murder of Masseria, Maranzano put his plan to kill Luciano into action.

He invited Luciano to visit his office and once he arrived, Coll would show up and kill Luciano.

However, what Maranzano did not know was that Luciano had received a tip and knew about this plan.

Luciano knows the Federal Government has begun investigating high-level mobsters for tax evasion.

And he also learned that in the past few months, the IRS has been planning to audit Maranzano.

Knowing that Maranzano is a target for the IRS, Luciano orchestrates a lethal plan with Meyer Lansky, and his enforcer, Bugsy Siegel, to carry out the plan to kill Maranzano.

Instead of going to Maranzano's office himself, he instead sent over his own hitmen Bugsy Siegel and his men disguised as IRS agents to Maranzano's office to kill him.

When they entered Maranzano's office on the 9th floor of The Helmsley Building, they disarmed Maranzano's guards and shot and stabbed Maranzano.

The body of Salvatore Maranzano after Charles "Lucky" Luciano's men left his office

According to the 1963 testimony of government witness Joseph Valachi, Vincent "Mad Dog" Coll arrived at Maranzano's office to kill Luciano, only to meet Luciano's hitmen fleeing the crime scene.

In less than five months, Luciano has taken out the two biggest Mob bosses of New York City. And Charles "Lucky" Luciano sets in motion the next phase of his plan: to seize control of the New York Mafia.

Luciano sends out an army of hitmen to eliminate any remaining loyalists of the New York underworld's old regimes.

Over the next few days, gangsters all across the country are killed off in the biggest purge the Mafia has ever seen.

Luciano spares a select few who he feels are more valuable as allies rather than corpses.

With his power secured, Luciano now decides to make his next move, calling a meeting with Maranzano's former underboss Joe Bonanno.

Luciano sees potential in Joe Bonanno, a man not tied to the old-school Sicilian ways, and decides to offer him the opportunity to head his own gang.

Bonanno was awarded most of Maranzano's rackets. Twenty-six-year-old Joseph Bonanno was now the youngest Mafia leader in the nation.

Bonanno embraced the Old Mafia traditions of "honor", "tradition", "respect" and "dignity" as principles for ruling his family.

He was more steeped in these traditions than other mobsters of his generation. The Bonanno family was considered the closest knit of the Five Families because Bonanno tried to restrict membership to only Castellammarese Sicilians.

He strongly believed that blood relations and strict Sicilian upbringing were the only way to uphold the traditional values of the Old World Mafia.

Joe Bonanno owned garment-centered operations on 34th Street.

He was a man of wealth, a man of influence, and a man of reason.

With Joe Bonanno as an ally, Luciano has eliminated his competition, establishing order in his operation.

Soon after the death of Maranzano, Sam Pollaccia Maranzano's consigliere suddenly disappeared.

It wasn't until years later that we learned that Lucky Luciano's underboss and Masseria family's hitman, Vito Genovese, was responsible for his disappearance.

Shortly after Maranzano's death, Genovese arranged to visit Chicago with Pollaccia, and there he arranged with a member of Al Capone's gang to kill Pollaccia.

Pollaccia's body was never found. He left behind a wife and five children.

Many people today believe that Luciano knew of the killing of Pollaccia, as a family consigliere could not be killed without the approval of Luciano himself.

After they left New York en route to Chicago, the two men stopped off in Pittsburgh to meet with local boss John Bazzano.

It is believed that during the visit, Genovese confided in Bazzano that Pollaccia would soon be killed and disposed of with the help of a member of Al Capone's gang in Chicago.

Bazzano subsequently relayed that information to one of his close friends who shared the information many years later.

Shortly after this meeting with Genovese, Bazzano and two other men were summoned to New York City by Luciano's recently formed Mafia Commission, a group of Mafia Family leaders whose job it was to arbitrate disputes and, when needed, punish those who had gone against the new set rules of the Mafia.

It's unclear exactly what occurred at the Commission meeting.

The Press later reported that Bazzano was the guest of honor at a banquet, where fellow gangsters toasted him for the July 29, 1932 slaying of Pittsburgh crime family member John Volpe.

It was reported that after the celebration, Bazzano was offered a ride back to his hotel. Other reports said Bazzano was brought before Lucian's commission and asked to defend his actions, which were unsanctioned by the Mafia Family leaders.

In August 1932, Bazzano's corpse was found in a large sack in Brooklyn.

An autopsy would reveal that Bazzano had been tied up and stabbed up to 20 times with an ice pick. Some have reported that his tongue was also cut out.

No one was ever prosecuted for the crime.

However, it was believed to have been carried out by, Joe Volpi's relative Scranton mob boss Santo Volpi, and Luciano's enforcer, Albert Anastasia.

With Maranzano dead and Sam Pollaccia gone, Luciano became the recognized leader of the former Masseria crime family and de facto Capo di tutti Capi or "Boss of Bosses" of the American Mafia.

Luciano then named, Vito Genovese as his underboss.

Vincent "The Executioner" Mangano and Albert "the Mad Hatter" Anastasia

Frank Scalice was forced to resign as head of the D'Aquila/Mineo gang to make way for the new boss, Vincent "The Executioner" Mangano of what 26 years later would be called the Gambino family.

Luciano's enforcer, Albert Anastasia was appointed as Mangano's underboss.

Vincent Mangano who would go on to lead the family for the next twenty years while his brother Philip Mangano would also become a family leader.

Once Luciano was in control, he stuck to his vision for the Mafia as a multi-ethnic and nation-wide organization.

Luciano soon rearranged New York's organized crime and established the basis of the "Five Families" of New York.

Part Two

The Lucky Luciano Years

In 1931, a meeting was held in Chicago by all of the Mafia families.

Until this time, there really is no organized Mafia in America.

You have individual gangs operating under their own rules and regulations.

Luciano saw that this had to be changed if the Mafia was to be successful for years to come.

The purpose of the meeting was to replace the old Sicilian Mafia regime of Capo di tutti Capi, "Boss of Bosses" of the Mafia, and established a Mafia board of directors.

This board was created by Charlie "Lucky" Luciano and would be known as, "The Commission" to serve as the governing body for organized crime and to oversee all Mafia activities in the United States and mediate conflicts between families and establish a rule of consensus among all of the crime families.

Conflicts between families would get reported to the Commission, and most of them would get settled.

Of course, when they didn't get settled, then a murder might have to take place.

The Commission was originally composed of representatives of the Five Mafia Families of New York City and Buffalo, and the Chicago Outfit of Al Capone.

To gain the support of the other bosses, Luciano keeps Mafia membership limited to only Italians.

But seeing that Meyer Lansky is not Italian, he will remain Luciano's most trusted advisor from outside the Mafia's ranks.

At the time many didn't realize that Luciano's goal with the Commission was to quietly maintain his own power over all of the crime families and to prevent future Gang wars.

Charlie "Lucky" Luciano was appointed as the chairman of the Commission and each Commission member was supposed to retain the same power as the next, with decisions made by a majority vote.

The Commission has been called Lucky Luciano's greatest innovation.

The Commission agreed to hold meetings every five years or when they needed to discuss important family issues.

Luciano's goal for the Mafia was going to be profit before anything else.

This would be the start of the modern era of the Cosa Nostra.

Luciano's Five-Family system allowed the Mafia to thrive over the next few decades into the period known as the "Golden Age of the Mafia."

The leaders nominated Luciano, Joe Bonanno, Joe Profaci, Tommy Gagliano, and Vincent Mangano as its inaugural governing board members.

With Vincent Mangano's position on the Commission, he set out to become one of the most powerful Mafia families in the country.

It was around this time that Vito Genovese falls in love with his fourth cousin, Giovaninna "Anna" Petillo.

Anna Petillo

After dating Anna for only a few months, Genovese and Anna decide to get married.

But to be together, Genovese will have to take care of the only thing that stands in his way: Anna's current husband Gerard "Gerry" Vernotico who was a baker at a bakery in Little Italy.

Genovese orders the death of Anna's husband and just two weeks after the murder in March 1932, Vito Genovese marries Anna Petillo.

At the time of the wedding, Anna was six months pregnant.

On June 5, 1931, the leader of the Chicago Outfit Al Capone was indicted on twenty-two counts of federal income-tax evasion. Then just one week later, Capone and others were charged with conspiracy to violate Prohibition laws.

In October Capone went to trial and was found guilty on three of the 23 counts brought against him.

He was sentenced to serve eleven years in prison and pay $50,000 in fines and court costs.

He was initially sent to the Atlanta penitentiary in May 1932.

In June 1932, six months after Maranzano's death, Gerardo Scarpato and his wife Alvira returned to New York.

Alvira then went for another vacation in September, apparently on her own, to Acra, just west of Cairo in the Catskills.

Alvira returned from the vacation late on Friday, September 9 to find that her husband, Gerardo was not in the restaurant or their apartment above it.

She became worried when he had not returned home on Saturday either.

A man who owned a small business arrived unexpectedly at the restaurant sometime before the hit to pay money that he owed to Scarpato.

The businessman later recalled that Scarpato ran over and asked him what he was doing there.

He told Scarpato that he was there to pay the money he owed to him.

Scarpato told him to leave the restaurant right away and not mention to anyone that he had been there that day.

The unknown man who owned a small business and arrived unexpectedly at the restaurant on the day that Masseria was killed to pay Scarpato money he owed him, claimed he met with Scarpato to hand over money on the night that Scarpato was murdered.

Scarpato left, promising to return soon after the man gave the money to him.

An hour later, Anthony Carfano appeared and told the man, "Listen, no matter what happens you never knew Scarpato. Get the hell out of here and keep your mouth shut."

This was between eight and nine o'clock in the evening, on the corner of Fourth Avenue and Union Street in Brooklyn.

Scarpato was later seen, at a small café he owned.

The bartender told the police Scarpato left the small café West 15th Street at about 1:00 a.m.

Five hours later, someone reported a car parked under a tree at 216 Windsor Place, two blocks south of Prospect Park.

When the police arrived, they discovered Scarpato's body in the back seat of the black sedan, wrapped in a burlap sack.

He had been knocked unconscious then tied up with a rope in such a way that as he awoke and started to struggle, the rope tightened around his neck and slowly strangled him. Scarpato died in a way that was surely designed to send a message.

However, the police believe he had been murdered in the Bath Beach area.

After Scarpato's death, a modern warehouse for a smoked-fish company was later built on the site of his restaurant.

One of the first things that Vincent Mangano did after being assigned to the position of the Boss was to establish the City Democratic Club, supposedly to promote American values.

However, the Club was a cover for a gang of hitmen founded by New York Jewish American mobsters Meyer Lansky and "Bugsy" Siegel in the early 1920s that was known first as the Bugs and Meyer gang.

Soon after Charles "Lucky" Luciano created the Commission, Meyer Lansky and "Bugsy" Siegel disbanded the Bugs and Meyer gang and formed Murder, Incorporated, or known simply as, Murder Inc.

Murder Inc. quickly became an extension of Lucky Luciano's American National Crime Syndicate.

Murder Inc. was a notorious band of mainly Jewish hitmen who performed contract murders for the Italian American Mafia nationwide.

The operating head of the Murder Inc. was headed by Vincent Mangano's underboss Albert Anastasia, who was known as the "Lord High Executioner".

The other members of Murder Inc. were, Bugsy Siegel, Abe Reles, and Louis "Lepke" Buchalter—the nickname Lepke means "Little Louis" in Yiddish.

In just ten years, Murder, Inc. killed more than 1,000 people, averaging one murder every three days.

And because no ties to Murder, Inc. are left behind, hundreds of murders remain unsolved for years.

By the 1930s, it had become clear that Prohibition had become a failure. With the mafia speakeasies and bootleggers, the 18th Amendment to the U.S. Constitution had done very little to curb the sale, production, and consumption of intoxicating liquors.

By the mid-1930s the United States was still in the financial struggle of the Great Depression.

In February 1933, Congress passed a proposed 21st Amendment that would repeal the 18th Amendment, which legalized national Prohibition.

The change in federal law in April 1933 had already legalized beer and wine with up to 3.2 percent alcohol.

However, the 21st Amendment made it harder, not easier, for people to get a drink because along with legalization came regulations on closing hours, age limits, and even limiting Sunday sales.

To compensate for the loss of massive revenues with the end of Prohibition, Vincent Mangano moved his criminal family into the money-making scams of extortion, union racketeering, and illegal gambling such as horse betting, running numbers, and illegal lotteries.

In August 1934, while the mafia was generating its wealth, Chicago's Al Capone was being transferred to the new federal prison in San Francisco Bay named, Alcatraz prison.

Capone would remain at Alcatraz for almost five years before being released to a Baltimore hospital in November 1939. He was suffering from the general deterioration of paresis (a late stage of syphilis).

Later he moved to his estate in the Palm Island neighborhood of South Beach Florida, where he died in 1947, a powerless recluse.

It is believed that in mid-1934, a fellow Mafioso named Ferdinand Boccia introduced Vito Genovese to a wealthy gambler who the two gangsters conspired to cheat out of over $150,000 in a high-stakes card game.

After the card game, Boccia demanded a $35,000 cut of the money because he had introduced the wealthy gambler to Genovese.

Rather than pay Boccia his portion of the money, Genovese decided to murder him instead.

On September 19, 1934, Vito Genovese, mobster Ernest "The Hawk" Rupolo, and four other associates allegedly ambushed Boccia in a coffee shop in Brooklyn where they shot and killed him.

This decision would come back to haunt Genovese a few years later.

Paul Castellano was arrested for the first time in 1934 at age 19, for robbing a men's clothing store in Hartford, Connecticut.

He refused to identify any of his accomplices when he was arrested and served a 3-month jail sentence.

When he was released, his actions of not ratting on his partners earned him a reputation for mob loyalty.

He remained in the meat-cutting business but also continued his association with the Mangano crime family.

Luciano and The Commission faced its first real test by a German-Jewish-American mobster named Dutch Schultz.

Schultz, whose real name was Arthur Flegenheimer, made his fortune in organized crime-related activities, including bootlegging and the numbers racket.

Dutch Schultz ran a very powerful gang in New York.

In the 1930s Dutch Schultz is known in New York as the Beer Baron of the Bronx. It was believed that Schultz was selling around $2 million a year in alcohol to speakeasies in upper Manhattan and the Bronx.

Schultz has been building relationships with politicians in New York for years by fixing their elections.

Schultz fixes elections by paying off voters and bringing them to the polls so they can vote for his candidates.

Schultz has one politician in New York that he can't pay off.

A 32-year-old assistant U.S. attorney who came from Michigan named Thomas E. Dewey.

Dewey had been a poll-watcher at one point and had seen the corruption by men like Schultz.

Dewey firmly believes in the rule of law and also wants to make a name for himself in New York.

Dewey went after Lucky Luciano; he went after him because he was a major organized crime figure in the United States and saw this as a stepping stone for his career.

Dewey felt that this would boost his ability to run for political office.

Dewey would go on to become the governor of New York State and he would later run for president losing one of the most famous elections in American history.

With Luciano protected by corruption, Dewey knows he'll have to start by going after Luciano's known associates.

With approval from U.S. attorney William Dodge, Thomas Dewey is about to declare an all-out war on the Mob.

Dewey chose to start his journey to prosecuting Luciano by first prosecuting the man helping to fix local elections, Dutch Schultz.

But unfortunately for Dewey, Schultz has been paying off judges and politicians for years. And this would bring forth challenges to get a court to prosecute Schultz.

To bring down Schultz, and ultimately Lucky Luciano and the Mafia, Dewey is going to have to find a way to prosecute them.

And a trial from a year earlier may give Dewey the answer he has been looking for.

Al Capone has ruled the violent Chicago underworld for a decade.

Tom Dewey followed the lead of the prosecutors in Chicago who convicted Al Capone for tax offenses.

Thomas Dewey sees his opportunity to do the same and goes after Dutch Schultz on tax evasion charges.

Dewey has an arrest warrant issued for Schultz, but first, they have to find him.

While the law is searching for Schultz, he is seen partying at Manhattan bars and nightclubs.

And while he was on the run, Schultz's exploits start making headlines in the national newspapers.

And all this time he manages to stay one step ahead of Dewey and his investigators.

Months pass without Schultz being arrested.

Dewey's inability to capture Schultz soon turns from a local tabloid story into a national embarrassment that eventually landed on the desk of the director of the FBI, J. Edgar Hoover.

Hoover has made his reputation by taking down some of the most notorious criminals in the country at the time, but he's refused to let the FBI investigate organized crime in New York.

For most of his time in office, Hoover ignored the Mafia and claimed it didn't even exist.

And many people today believe that he had reasons for not pursuing the Mafia.

In the 1930s, nearly all of Hoover's agents are clean-cut men who had no idea about the Mafia culture.

This made it impossible for the FBI to infiltrate the Mafia.

Some believe that Hoover may also have another, more personal reason for not going after the Mafia.

The theory is that Hoover never wanted to take on the Mafia because they had a file of him with pictures of him dressed as a woman.

Despite this theory, Hoover decides that He can longer let Dutch Schultz make a mockery of law enforcement.

For the first time in FBI history, Hoover names a New York gangster as Public Enemy Number One.

Luciano has spent years building the perfect criminal organization. Dutch Schultz is threatening to tear it all down by drawing the attention of the F.B.I to the Mafia,

Dutch Schultz was violating Luciano's rule of, "Don't put a spotlight on the Mob."

Luciano reaches out to Schultz and promises him that if he turned himself in the Mafia would assist him in his court case.

After nearly two years of successfully eluding the authorities, the FBI's Public Enemy Number One is turning himself in.

Dutch Schultz

With Schultz in custody, Thomas Dewey is now closer than ever to clinching his first victory over the New York Mafia and one step closer to taking down Luciano and the Mafia.

But what Thomas Dewey doesn't know is that Luciano has already put a plan in motion to make sure Schultz goes free.

Schultz was released on bail while his case went to trial.

Schultz was initially convicted in a Manhattan court; however, the verdict was soon overturned on appeal.

Schultz's lawyers then successfully argued that their client could never get a fair retrial in New York City.

The appeal judge agreed and moved the second trial to the small town of Malone in rural upstate New York just south of the Canadian border.

When Schultz arrives in Malone, he begins hosting parties for local officials.

A week before his trial, the Jewish mobster tries to ingratiate himself so much that he decided to convert to Catholicism.

His goal was to present himself as a man of respect.

And just as Luciano promised, Dutch Schultz is found not guilty.

Schultz stood trial twice for tax evasion, but two juries could not convict him.

Thomas Dewey and his team worked tirelessly to put together a new case against Dutch Schultz for his illegal policy racket.

A month and a half after the trial in Malone, Dewey was able to identify Schultz as the leader of the largest illegal gambling ring in New York State.

Thomas Dewey then sends officers on a citywide raid to shut down Schultz's most lucrative racket.

Dutch Schultz goes into hiding and decides there's only one way to avoid being prosecuted by Dewey and his men.

That is to kill Thomas Dewey.

Thomas Dewey has issued a second warrant for the arrest of Dutch Schultz.

And once again he is labeled as the most wanted man in America.

Schultz felt that if Dewey or his assistant David Asch were killed it could ward off his conviction.

In mid-October, 1935 Schultz went before an emergency meeting of the Commission and asked for permission to kill Thomas Dewey, which they adamantly opposed and ordered Schultz to drop his plans to murder Special Prosecutor Dewey.

Luciano argued that assassinating Dewey would cause a massive law enforcement crackdown on their families.

The Commission has a long-standing rule that police officers, federal agents, and prosecutors are not to be harmed.

The Commission voted unanimously against Schultz.

Bonanno family crime boss Joseph Bonanno thought Schultz's idea was "insane."

When Schultz heard the outcome of the vote; he was furious and accused the Commission of trying to steal his rackets and "feed him to the law."

Schultz refused to accept the Commission's ruling and told them that he was going to kill Dewey or his assistant David Asch in the next three **days.**

Schultz then turns to Murder, Inc. hitman Albert Anastasia for help in killing Dewey.

Albert Anastasia informs Luciano that Schultz had asked him to stake out Dewey's apartment building on Fifth Avenue.

After hearing the news from Anastasia, the Commission held a meeting to discuss the matter.

After hours of deliberations, the Commission orders a hit on one of his own.

The Commission called on the services of Albert Anastasia's Murder Inc. to arrange Schultz's assassination before he could kill Dewey or Asch.

Albert Anastasia assigned Jewish mobster Louis "Lepke" Buchalter to take care of the hit.

On October 23, 1935, Schultz was at The Palace Chophouse at 12 East Park Street, Newark New Jersey.

The Palace Chophouse was just two blocks from the hotel where he ran his organized crime operations.

He was at the restaurant with his bodyguard Bernard "Lulu" Rosencrantz, chief henchman Abe Landau, and his accountant Otto Berman.

Schultz was in the men's room just after 10:15 p.m. when Charles Workman and Emanuel "Mendy" Weiss, two hitmen working for Murder, Inc., entered the restaurant.

Workman managed to slip past Schultz's men and entered the bathroom to find Schultz.

Workman quickly fired two rounds at Schultz; however, only one struck him.

The bullet entered Schultz, slightly below his heart, and exited out the small of his back. Schultz collapsed onto the men's room floor, and Workman joined Weiss in the back room of the restaurant where a shootout occurred with Schultz's crew.

Schultz's accountant, Otto Berman, collapsed onto the floor immediately after being shot.

The other two men, Schultz's bodyguard Bernard "Lulu" Rosencrantz, and chief henchman Abe Landau were also shot.

Rosencrantz was struck multiple times at point-blank range with lead buckshot and Landau's carotid artery was severed when a bullet passed through his neck.

Both men rose to their feet and returned fire against Workman and Weiss, driving them out of the restaurant, despite being mortally wounded.

Weiss jumped into an awaiting getaway car and told the driver to leave and abandon Workman.

With blood pouring out of his neck wound, Landau followed Workman out of the restaurant and fired his last remaining bullets in his gun at him, but was unable to hit him.

Workman quickly fled the scene on foot and Landau collapsed onto a nearby trash can.

Not wanting to die in the bathroom, Schultz staggered out of the bathroom clutching his side, and sat down at his table; he called out for someone to get an ambulance.

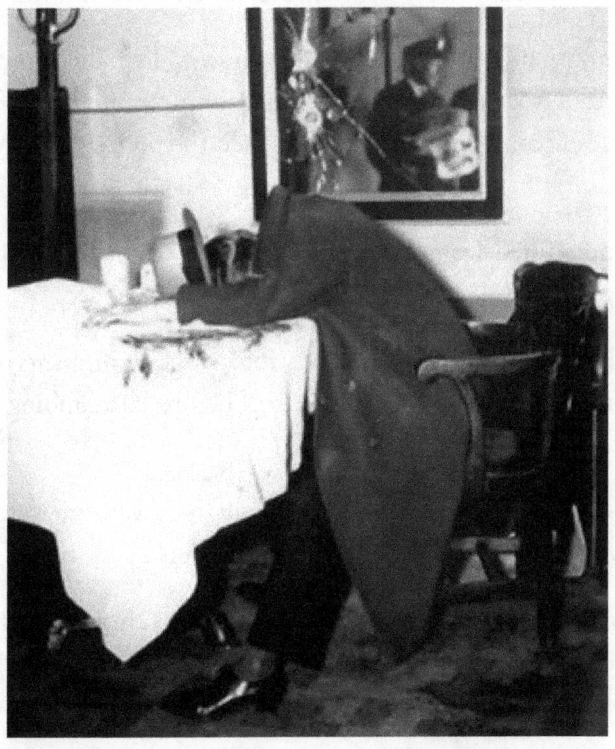

Rosencrantz placed the call for an ambulance before losing consciousness in the telephone booth.

Schultz was given brandy in an attempt to relieve his suffering because the medics lacked pain-relieving medication.

Schultz gave one of the responding medics $10,000 in cash to ensure that he received the best possible treatment available.

After surgery, when it looked as if Schultz would live, the medic was so worried that he would be indebted to the mobster for keeping the money that he shoved the money back in Schultz's hospital bed.

Schultz's accountant Otto Berman, died at 2:20 that morning.

At the hospital, Landau and Rosencrantz waited for surgery and refused to say anything to the police until Schultz arrived and permitted them; even then, they provided the police with only very minimal information.

Abe Landau died from severe loss of blood, eight hours after the shooting.

Meanwhile, Rosencrantz was taken into surgery; and survived for twenty-nine hours after the shooting before succumbing to his injuries.

The Doctors performed surgery on Schultz but were unaware of the extent of damage done to his abdominal organs by the bullet.

They were also unaware that Workman had intentionally used rust-coated bullets in an attempt to give Schultz a fatal bloodstream infection should he be lucky enough to survive the gunshot.

It was reported later that Schultz's death was slow and painful. The mobster writhed and babbled for twenty-two hours, speaking in various states of lucidity with his wife, mother, a priest, police, and hospital staff, before dying of peritonitis.

His final words were transcribed by the police.

"A boy has never wept...nor dashed a thousand kin."

"You can play jacks, and girls do that with a softball and do tricks with it."

"Oh, Oh, dog Biscuit, and when he is happy he doesn't get snappy."

Charles Workman was later convicted of Schultz's murder and sent to Sing-Sing to serve a 23-year sentence.

When he arrived at the prison, Workman requested to see Warden Lewis Lawes. Workman wanted to be housed in the same cell block as several of his old friends who were also incarcerated there; his request was not granted.

Dutch Schultz was not allowed to kill Dewey and many believe that this may have been a mistake made by Luciano.

By 1935, Lucky Luciano and his crew were pulling in today's equivalent of over $100 million a year.

Meyer Lansky is revolutionizing their gambling rackets, turning their low-rent gambling dens into high-class gambling establishments.

Meyer Lansky was the first guy to take craps, which was a street game, and put it up on green felt on a table and thereby making it appear respectable and fancy.

As Lansky is inventing the first modern casinos Vito Genovese is running a heroin racket that's pulling in millions of dollars a year.

He also begins running high-stakes poker games luring in unsuspecting wealthy businessmen and fixing the games to make sure he always wins.

In the mid-1930s gambling was the strength of the American Mafia.

Bugsy Siegel makes sure the money is collected and that the Mob's authority is understood.

And as part of Murder Inc., Siegel carries out murders sent down by the Commission.

Now that they were running these criminal organizations, very profitable ones, Lucky Luciano lived in the presidential suite at the Waldorf-Astoria with his new girlfriend, a 20-year-old Broadway dancer named Gay Orlova.

Lucky Luciano is determined to expand his criminal empire and take advantage of the oldest profession in the world, prostitution.

In the 1930s, prostitution is illegal, but Luciano knows that underground brothels are still making money and he wants a cut of their profits.

Like all of his other illegal rackets, Lucky Luciano quickly streamlines the prostitution business.

He has madams to oversee the customers and men known as bookers who deliver the prostitutes to the brothels.

Soon, Luciano has a citywide network of up to 200 brothels and 1200 prostitutes.

Lucky Luciano quickly created a prostitution empire that makes $12 million a year, the modern-day equivalent of over 200 million.

Meyer Lansky didn't like the idea of getting involved in prostitution.

He considered it a dirty business.

He also did not like the fact that the girls get sick, they get diseases, they get pregnant, and they need doctors, which will cost money.

He was also not happy being connected to hundreds of drug-addicted girls who would turn them in to the police for another hit of heroin.

Lansky has been a close trusted friend and business partner with Luciano for decades and while he's always trusted Lansky's advice this time Luciano ignores his Lansky's warning.

Within months, Luciano begins leading a double life, spending days with his girlfriend Gay Orlova and nights at his brothels with prostitutes.

Luciano then begins frequenting one of his own brothels, run by a madam named Florence Brown, her nickname was Cokey Flo.

New York Governor Herbert H. Lehman appointed Thomas E. Dewey, a special prosecutor to combat organized crime in the city.

As Dewey builds his case against Luciano in June 1935, he brings in an ambitious young prosecutor named Eunice Carter.

Eunice Carter was an assistant district attorney and the very first African-American woman to serve in that capacity in New York City.

Carter led an investigation into prostitution racketeering that connected Luciano to this prostitution network.

Carter soon discovers a break in the case that Dewey has been looking for.

More than half the prostitutes that had been arrested in the city had the same bail bondsman and the same attorney.

They also discover that the man bailing out the prostitutes is a known criminal with ties to the Mafia as a booker for Luciano's brothels.

Thomas Dewey believes he's found the weak link in Luciano's operation and brings in the booker tied to Luciano's prostitution ring.

Now they just have to get him to talk.

They bring the booker in and ask him what he knows about Lucky Luciano and his prostitution ring.

He denies knowing Luciano or anything about his prostitution ring.

Dewey lets the booker leave, but he has a plan as assistant district attorney Eunice Carter has introduced a new crime-fighting technology known as "wiretaps".

Dewey's investigators tap the booker's phone and listen to hundreds of hours of calls waiting to hear any evidence that they can use against Luciano.

It doesn't take Dewey long before he has the evidence he needs to arrest Luciano.

Carter investigated the flow of money in the New York and New Jersey prostitution network, and she began to build a case on evidence from interviews with prostitutes, and wiretaps.

On February 2, 1936, Dewey authorized Carter to raid 200 brothels in Manhattan and Brooklyn, earning him the nationwide recognition as a major "gangbuster".

Carter took measures to prevent police corruption from interfering with the raids: she assigned one hundred and sixty police officers outside of the vice squad to conduct the raids.

Still not sure that one of the officers wouldn't tip off Luciano, the officers were instructed to wait on various street corners until they received their orders, just minutes before the raids were to begin.

By doing this the officers didn't know until the very last minute that the target was Charles "Lucky" Luciano. And this did not allow any of them to tip off Luciano.

They raid brothels across the city but Luciano escapes, but for Dewey, the raid isn't a total loss.

Ten men and one hundred women were arrested. However, unlike previous vice raids where arrestees were soon released, this time the arrestees were not immediately released. They were taken to the court, where a judge set bails of $10,000, (About $185,000.00 at today's dollar value) which was far beyond their means to pay.

Carter had quickly gained the trust of a number of the arrested prostitutes and madams, some of whom reported being beaten and abused by the Mafia.

She easily convinced many of the women to testify rather than serve additional jail time.

By mid-March, several defendants had implicated Luciano. Three of these prostitutes implicated Luciano as the ringleader, who made collections. Luciano associate David Betillo was in charge of the prostitution ring in New York; any money that Luciano received was from Betillo.

Finally, in March 1936, New York State had enough evidence to charge Luciano and members of his gang with running several prostitution rackets and extortion.

In late March 1936, Luciano had received a tip from someone in the police department that he was going to be arrested.

With no luck, the police search all of the places that they expected Luciano to be in New York City.

But Luciano is in the last place Dewey would ever look, more than 1200 miles away, in Hot Springs, Arkansas.

Hot Springs is known to have one of the most corrupt police forces in the country.

It is the best hideout for gangsters on the run from the law filled with casinos, overrun with gamblers, and completely under the control of the Mafia.

Back in New York, Dewey knows if he can't find Luciano soon, all the evidence he's collected against him will mean nothing.

Dewey expands his citywide search into a nationwide manhunt after he comes to realize that Luciano may not be in New York.

On April 3, 1936, a New York City detective working an unrelated case recognizes Luciano walking down the street while passing through Hot Springs.

After months on the run, Lucky Luciano, the most powerful gangster in America has finally been arrested.

The very next day back in New York, Dewey indicted Luciano and his accomplices on sixty counts of compulsory prostitution.

Luciano's lawyers in Arkansas then began a fierce legal battle against his extradition back to New York.

Luciano believes if he can arrange for his trial to be held in Arkansas, he'll be able to bribe his way out of the charges.

On April 6th, someone offered a $50,000 (about $925,000.00 at today's dollar value) bribe to Arkansas Attorney General Carl E. Bailey to facilitate Luciano's extradition case.

However, the Attorney General refused the bribe and immediately reported it.

Luciano bribes the local sheriff and in return, he refuses Dewey's demand to return Luciano to New York to stand trial.

And back in New York, Vito Genovese is making millions the sales of heroin, Lansky is overseeing Luciano's network of casinos, and Frank Costello is continuing to use his connections to keep Luciano out of Dewey's reach.

From a jail cell in Hot Springs Arkansas, Charles Lucky Luciano is still in full control.

With Lucky Luciano protected by a corrupt Arkansas sheriff, Thomas Dewey goes to the press and names Luciano, Public Enemy Number One to personalize the corruption and Luciano's criminal conduct.

He also accused Hot Springs of being afraid to release Luciano into his custody.

To counter Dewey's attack, Luciano launches his own press campaign.

He tells the media that he may not be the most moral man in this world, but he has never supported or participated in the practice of prostitution.

The two men wage war through press conferences and national headlines for days.

With lawyers fighting Luciano's extradition and the local sheriff refusing to release him, Luciano believes it's only a matter of time before he's released.

With public pressure on state officials, the Arkansas governor is forced to send a team of heavily armed state troopers to Hot Springs to remove Luciano from the jail and return him to New York.

On April 17, 1936, Luciano was handed over to three NYPD detectives for transport by train back to New York for trial on charges of compulsory prostitution.

When the train reached St. Louis, Missouri, the detectives and Luciano changed trains. During this switchover, they were guarded by 20 local policemen to prevent a rescue attempt.

The men finally arrived back in New York on April 18, and Luciano was sent to jail and his bail was set at $350,000. (About $6,500,000.00 at today's dollar value)

This amount was a New York record for the highest bail amount given to an individual.

The prosecution of Luciano was the first time that a Mob member with that much power had been called to account for his crimes in a courtroom.

It was very dangerous for a prosecutor to take the Mafia on.

They had law enforcement and the courts on their payrolls.

So there was a very substantial personal risk for Thomas Dewey.

Thomas Dewey launched his case by calling prostitutes from around the city who worked for Luciano to take the stand.

They mostly stated that they were afraid to go to the police in fear of their lives for being a rat.

In total, Dewey calls 68 witnesses, and while the prosecutor's strategy to shock and outrage the all-male jury, Luciano sits at the defendant's table looking unfazed.

Luciano is convinced it will take more than just the testimonies of some drug-addicted prostitutes to take him down.

The main witness against Luciano was his own Madame, Florence Brown, better known as Cokey Flo.

She testified that Luciano used drugs to control her and the prostitutes that she oversaw.

She stated that Luciano wanted to run the brothels just like the grocery stores, where people come in, they pay for the merchandise, and then they leave happy.

Luciano's goal was to get as many customers in and out of the brothels as quickly as possible.

When the defense had their opportunity to make their case, against his lawyer's advice, Luciano does the unthinkable and decides to take the stand in his own defense.

Luciano denied any acquaintance at all with any of the women who've testified to his involvement in the prostitution racket and including Al Capone.

They questioned Luciano about his tax records indicate that his income was only $22,000 over the previous four years, and yet he lived in a massive suite in the Waldorf Astoria.

They asked him to explain the phone records from his suite at the Waldorf showing calls to Al Capone in Chicago.

He responded that someone else must have been using his phone.

Luciano knew that his testimony on the stand was not favorable to his defense and he knows that if he wants to sway the jury, he'll need to exercise his power outside the courtroom and try to bribe a juror.

Unfortunately, Luciano had no luck in his quest to bribe a juror and Thomas Dewey was able to successfully prosecute Luciano, on 62 counts of compulsory prostitution on July 18. Which people thought was impossible.

In the remote town of Malone New York, on the border of Canada Lucky Luciano was sentenced 30-to-50-years in a maximum-security prison.

It was learned later that even Dewey was surprised at the severity of the sentence that Luciano was given on the prostitution charges.

They sent Luciano to Dannemora prison in Saranac, New York, over 300 miles north of the Waldorf Towers.

Luciano must now figure out how to run his Mafia Empire from Dannemora prison in Saranac, New York, over 300 miles north of the Waldorf Towers.

Luciano kept his Mafia Empire running despite being in a maximum-security Dannemora prison in Saranac, New York; over 300 miles north of the Waldorf Towers.

People still took care of Luciano while he was in prison, and Luciano practically ran the prison he was in.

The prison guards were paid off, and Luciano soon enjoys the luxuries of the free world, including better clothing and even furniture from his home.

He also had phone access to New York, and Luciano could also run his business from his prison cell, and just like home, his associates can come and go as they please.

Back in New York, all major rulings are made by the Commission run by the other heads of the four remaining New York families.

The four remaining bosses still meet in New York and must run their decisions by Luciano in prison.

Luciano knows he needs representation at the Commission, and until he can find his way out of prison, he'll have to decide on an acting boss of his family.

Faced with the biggest decision of his life, Luciano turns to his closest adviser, Meyer Lansky.

Luciano knows the Jewish gangster can't be his acting boss of the Mafia's strict Sicilian code.

Instead, he'll have to pick his family's acting boss between Frank Costello and Vito Genovese.

Frank Costello was a gentleman gangster and more intelligent than Vito. He is also is one of Luciano's closest advisors, the man who gave Luciano his first real break in the Mob.

However, Genovese was almost a classic Mafioso and has been a ruthless but loyal ally to Luciano for over a decade.

Luciano's knows that his choice will ultimately determine the success of his crime family and the future of the American Mafia.

Luciano decides to name Vito Genovese as his acting boss and Frank Costello as Vito's underboss.

Luciano's still running the family from prison through his new acting boss, Vito Genovese.

Costello and Genovese carry out his orders to make sure the business runs smoothly.

Genovese finally has the power he's been waiting for with his promotion to the acting boss and lets the power go straight to his head.

The structure of Luciano's crime family begins to collapse as Genovese starts playing by his own rules.

He starts wasting money, abusing his authority, and killing off anyone who disagrees with him.

His biggest mistake is that he is doing this all without the approval of the Commission.

In November 1936, while acting boss of Luciano's crime family, Genovese became a naturalized United States citizen in New York City.

Genovese starts flaunting his power in the city's most expensive restaurants and nightclubs.

But in his quest to assert his power Genovese is getting sloppy and starts to draw unwanted attention to not only the Luciano Family but to all of the crime families.

Costello realizes he has to get his own family's boss under control before his actions take them all down.

The more Costello tries to rein in Genovese, the more out of control the boss becomes.

Luciano knows Vito Genovese has become a major liability to the family and he knows that he needs to deal with him quickly.

But before Luciano can with Genovese, he was implicated in the 1934 Ferdinand Boccia murder by fellow mobster Ernest "The Hawk" Rupolo who was facing a murder conviction.

Rupolo had decided to become a government witness against Genovese when Boccia's body was pulled from the Hudson River.

Rupolo had decided to become a government witness against Genovese and admitted to police that the order had come from Vito Genovese rather than spending the rest of his life in prison.

Later, another jailed associate of Genovese named Peter LaTempa agreed to become a government witness against Vito Genovese to shorten his prison sentence.

This information has the potential to destroy Luciano's crime family.

Thomas Dewey has already taken down Lucky Luciano and now he has a witness who is willing to testify against the new boss of the Luciano crime family.

Dewey quickly files murder charges against Vito Genovese.

It isn't long before Frank Costello, is tipped off about the warrant for Vito's arrest.

Genovese must now make a life-changing decision.

He could fight the murder charge and try to keep his power as the boss, or he can return to Italy and go on the run.

He knew that he did not stand a chance fighting the charges seeing that Luciano was convicted just a year earlier.

Now, less than a year after becoming the acting boss of Luciano's crime family, Vito Genovese is forced to flee to Italy to escape prosecution.

Genovese fled to Italy with $750,000 cash and settled in a small town named Nola, just east of Naples.

With Genovese's departure to Italy, Costello now became the acting boss of the Luciano crime family.

In 1937 Paul Castellano married Nina Manno, the sister-in-law of Carlo Gambino.

The couple had three sons Paul, Philip, and Joseph, and one daughter, Constance.

For the next several years Castellano kept a relatively low profile and was involved in bootlegging and gambling.

Luciano's legal appeals continued until October 10, 1938, when the U.S. Supreme Court refused to review his appeal case. At this point, Luciano stepped down as family boss, and Frank Costello formally replaced him.

With Costello as the newly-appointed boss of the family, business is once again running smoothly.

From his prison cell, Luciano decides it's time to expand his family outside of the U.S.

Luciano sees an opportunity to expand his family's gambling empire in Cuba.

He sends Meyer Lansky to convince the new Cuban leader, *General* Fulgencio *Batista,* who's just risen to power after a violent coup to let the Mafia build a casino in Havana.

Luciano sends Bugsy Siegel to Los Angeles to set up a stronghold for the New York Mafia by taking control of the Hollywood labor unions while Meyer Lansky works to make a deal with the Cuban leader

Once Bugsy Siegel arrived in L.A. he quickly focused on the projectionists' union.

As Costello and Luciano, focused on building their criminal empire another threat was coming from within their own ranks by a founding member of Murder, Inc named Abe Reles.

Abe Reles' girlfriend was raped by a rival gangster and Reles decides that he is going to kill him.

In the heat of the moment, Reles gets sloppy and leaves a trail of incriminating evidence that makes it easy for the police to find him

After his arrest he also agrees to cut a deal, testifying against the head of Murder Inc, Albert Anastasia, Lepke Buchalter, and his partner Bugsy Siegel.

Once word gets to Costello that Reles has been cooperating with Dewey to take down Murder, Inc., Costello orders Siegel to go into hiding.

The fate of the five families now rests in the hands of Frank Costello.

Costello knows if he doesn't take out his own hitman, Abe Reles, his testimony could destroy the American Mafia.

However, before Costello could take out Reles he has to find him.

To track down Reles, Costello turns to his political and law enforcement sources around the city.

Costello soon learns that law enforcement is hiding Reles in a heavily-guarded hotel called the Half Moon Hotel, in Coney Island.

They had almost twenty police officers guarding Reles and he was never left alone.

Costello knew that getting to Reles will be next to impossible but he soon finds a way.

But Costello knows he has to find a way.

Frank Costello had a strong influence not only into the police department but into the political system.

And with the help of the police that was on Costello's payroll, Reles died while being guarded by the police in the early morning of November 12, 1941, the very same day that he was scheduled to testify against Albert Anastasia.

It was reported worldwide that Reles fell to his death from a window with police guarding the door.

The police reports claimed that Reles was trying to lower himself out of a sixth-floor window using two bedsheets tied together and then tied to a four-foot length of wire that had been attached to a valve in his hotel room.

However, the wire knot to the valve came undone, and Reles fell to a second-floor outdoor landing.

The newspaper headlines read: "The Canary Who Could Sing, But Couldn't Fly".

Many doubted the police version of events because Reles had shown no inclination to escape from protective custody.

He was afraid of what might happen to him if he was out of the police's protection.

Many believed that he had been thrown or pushed out of the window and that the room had been arranged to look like he was trying to escape.

However, in 1951, a grand jury concluded it was an accidental death during an attempted escape.

The case against Albert Anastasia was dismissed because the evidence was based solely on Reles' testimony.

Frank Costello has now solidified his authority as the head of the Luciano crime family.

Luciano is now certain that the system he's built works.

Before Costello and his men were able to get to Reles, he also names another one of Murder Inc's top killers, Lepke Buchalter.

At the time, Buchalter has a garment industry racket worth the modern-day equivalent of over $17 million per year.

Thomas Dewey believes that if he can gather enough evidence against Buchalter he'll be able to bring down the rest of Murder, Inc.

Reles tells Dewey that on September 13, 1936, Murder Inc. killers, acting on Buchalter's orders, gunned down Joseph Rosen, a Brooklyn candy store owner.

Rosen was a former garment industry trucker whose union Buchalter took over.

Buchalter believed Rosen was cooperating with District Attorney Thomas Dewey and demanded that he leave town.

Rosen had angered Buchalter by refusing to leave town as Buchalter demanded.

At the time, no one was indicted in the Rosen murder. But now Dewey had a suspect and a cooperating witness.

With the evidence against Buchalter, Dewey orders his men to sweep the city to pick him up.

Buchalter gets word of the search and with the mob's connections and hideouts throughout New York, he simply disappears.

The FBI is also looking to arrest him on a separate narcotics charge and joins in on the international manhunt.

The federal government offered a $5,000 reward for information leading to Buchalter's capture in November 1937.

The following month Buchalter was indicted in federal court on conspiracy to smuggle heroin into the United States.

It was believed that Buchalter was hiding heroin in the trunks of young women and couples traveling by ocean liner from China to France, then to New York City.

Buchalter would then bribe the U.S. customs agents not to inspect the trunks.

Buchalter spent about two years on the run while the authorities followed leads of Buchalter's sightings all over the world.

Thomas Dewey requested that the City of New York offer a $25,000 reward for Buchalter's capture, in July 1939, citing a string of unsolved gangland murders.

Unknown to Dewey and the FBI, Buchalter was hiding out in a basement apartment in Brooklyn the entire time.

Director of the FBI, J. Edgar Hoover, knows once Buchalter is captured he could put him away for the narcotics charges.

But with the Buchalter in hiding, the FBI will need the help of Charles "Lucky" Luciano.

Luciano knows that giving up Buchalter would be a huge gamble, as Buchalter could easily turn on Luciano and cooperate with Dewey to help take down the Mafia.

But for Luciano, getting out of prison and reclaiming his place at the head of his crime family is more important to him.

Lucky Luciano and Meyer Lansky set a plan in motion to bring down Louis "Lepke" Buchalter.

Luciano knew that if he could convince Buchalter to turn himself in on the lesser drug charges that he faced with the FBI, they would hand him over to Dewey on the 1936 Rosen murder, giving Luciano the leverage he thinks he needs to get out of prison.

To carry out the plan, Lansky sends Buchalter's trusted associate Murder, Inc. co-founder, Albert Anastasia to convince him to turn himself in.

Anastasia meets with Buchalter and tells him that they can make the Rosen murder rap go away.

He tells him to turn himself in to the FBI on the heroin charges and he will do three years in prison, tops.

With the convincing of Anastasia, Buchalter decides to surrender himself to the FBI.

He didn't want the New York police to get him first and end up in the electric chair.

Because of the high-profile nature of the arrest, FBI Director J. Edgar Hoover personally wants to bring the most wanted man in America into custody.

On August 24, 1939, Buchalter surrendered to FBI chief J. Edgar Hoover.

But to his dismay, the charges that he was arrested on was not the drug charges, but the murder charge from New York

With the arrest of Buchalter, Luciano gained leverage with the FBI and just gave Thomas Dewey a huge victory.

While Lucky Luciano was working with the FBI on capturing Louis Buchalter, future Gambino Crime family boss John Gotti was born in the Bronx on October 27, 1940.

He was the fifth child of John J. Gotti, Sr. and his wife, Philomena "Fannie" Gotti (de Carlo). The family grew to 13 children – seven boys and four girls.

Two of his siblings died during childhood Due to poor medical care.

Many reports say that John Gotti's father was a hardworking immigrant from the Neapolitan section of Italy.

However official records show that John Gotti's father was born in New Jersey on March 28, 1907.

Years later, John Gotti himself would tell Salvatore "Sammy the Bull" Gravano, *"These fuckin' bums that write books, they're worse than us. My fuckin' father was born in New Jersey. He ain't never been in Italy his whole fuckin' life. My mother neither. The guy never worked a fuckin' day in his life. He was a rolling stone; he never provided for the family. He never did nothin'. He never earned nothin'. And we never had nothin'."*

On May 9, 1941, Buchalter was arraigned in New York state court on the 1936 Rosen murder along with three other murders.

Just seven months later, on December 2, 1941, Buchalter was sentenced to death along with his lieutenants Emanuel "Mendy" Weiss and Louis Capone. (No relation to Al Capone)

Future Gambino family member Roy Albert DeMeo was born on September 7, 1942, in Bath Beach Brooklyn to working-class Italian immigrants.

On March 4, 1944, Louis "Lepke" Buchalter was executed in the electric chair in Sing Sing Prison.

Louis Buchalter was the only mob boss to ever be executed for his crimes.

Dewey has taken down another high-profile gangster, and he launches a campaign to become the next governor of New York.

Luciano's certain that if Thomas Dewey wins the office of Governor; he'll sign a pardon freeing him from prison.

And while Luciano waits for word from Thomas Dewey, an attack almost 5,000 miles away on December 7th, 1941 on Pearl Harbor Hawaii is about to change everything.

The country braces for another attack on American soil and New York City could be the first target.

German submarines were prowling along American shores.

And the United States didn't have the naval force yet to counteract an attack from the sea.

Just two months after the attack on Pearl Harbor America's worst fear is realized as a massive fire breaks out on a naval troopship on the docks along the West Side of Manhattan in February 1942.

As the "SS Normandy" burns, fear spreads that war has finally reached New York City.

The government was worried about sabotage on the New York City waterfront and that the Italian-American dockworkers might secretly support Benito Mussolini in these attacks.

They know that they need the help of the mob guys who run the waterfront.

Since Probation, organized crime has asserted its power over New York's harbor and they now control more than 200 ports.

The Mafia's control over the ports, and their affiliations with the Longshoreman's Union, meant that they had a hand in everything coming into and going out of the country.

Now at war, the federal government is forced to make another unlikely alliance and reach out to the Mafia to prevent sabotage on the waterfront.

And to accomplish that they needed the help of Charles Lucky Luciano.

The government speaks to Meyer Lansky and explains that they need Luciano's help.

Lansky agrees to lock down the docks. And that nothing gets in or out of New York harbor without them knowing about it.

And in return, the navy agrees to work to reduce Luciano's fifty-year prison sentence for information and assistance in their operation dubbed "Operation Underworld" because underworld boss Charles "Lucky" Luciano operated as the eyes and ears of the American Navy.

With Luciano now calling the shots from prison, Frank Costello and Meyer Lansky orchestrate a citywide plan.

They pay armed guards to work around the clock and put a system in place to keep track of all shipments so that nothing gets in or out of New York harbor without the Mafia's approval.

By 1943, Thomas Dewey has been successful in his race for Governor of New York State.

There have been a lot of reports that Luciano helped in the invasion of Sicily in 1943, and that's actually just a myth.

Through his own public relations efforts, Luciano tried to create the myth that would help him get a pardon from Governor Dewey.

In fact, it was Frank Costello who tipped off columnist Walter Winchell, who initially reported that Luciano helped in the invasion of Sicily.

It turned out that Luciano wasn't the only high ranking Mafioso working for the United States Government in Italy at that time.

After feeling to Italy to escape a murder charge, Vito Genovese has been forced to abandon his dream of ruling his own crime family.

In the 1940s, heroin is legal in Italy. Now, Genovese is determined to exploit this new opportunity for himself in Italy.

But before he can make his fortune, he'll need to go through fascist dictator, Benito Mussolini.

Genovese donates the modern-day equivalent of $3.6 million to Mussolini's fascist party over the first few years that he is in Italy.

With Mussolini now on his side, Genovese has the freedom to set up a lucrative heroin racket.

For almost a year, Genovese exports narcotics out of the country in small packages, disguised in luggage and automobiles.

Then in July of 1943, the Allies successfully invaded Sicily.

Genovese realizes that he is on the losing side and quickly switches his allegiance.

Genovese quickly offered his services to interpret for the U.S. Army.

Completely unaware of his criminal history, Genovese was appointed to the position of interpreter/liaison officer at the U.S. Army headquarters in Naples Italy.

Genovese quickly became one of the Government's most trusted employees.

But true to form, Genovese sees a way to make money illegally by diverting illegal supplies from the American army to sell on the black market.

In August of 1944, the U.S. military police arrested Genovese during an investigation into his running of a black market ring in Italy.

Genovese had been stealing trucks, flour, and sugar from the Army. When the Criminal Investigation Division examined Genovese's background, they discovered that Genovese was a fugitive wanted for the 1934 Ferdinand Boccia murder.

The man with evidence against Genovese is Peter LaTempa, a low-level gangster who was willing to exchange his testimony against Genovese to reduce his own prison sentence.

However, the Army or the federal government had no interest in pursuing Genovese for his black-market crimes.

On January 15, 1945, while Vito Genovese sat in his jail cell in Italy awaiting extradition back to New York, the government's witnesses, Peter LaTempa, was found dead in his cell after taking medication for his gallstones.

An autopsy allegedly revealed that his medicine was tampered with and replaced with rat poison.

The coroner stated that LaTempa had ingested enough rat poison to kill eight horses.

Those responsible for arranging LaTempa's murder were never apprehended.

Back in Italy, Genovese personally offered Agent Orange C. Dickey of the Criminal Investigation Division a $250,000 bribe to release him, then threatened the young agent when he refused.

Genovese was held for almost ten months in jail before being sent back to New York to face trial.

After seven years on the run, Vito Genovese is on his way back to America facing the murder charge he tried to escape from.

On June 2, 1945, after arriving in New York by ship the day before, Vito Genovese was arraigned on murder charges for the 1934 Ferdinand Boccia murder.

The government was convinced that even with the death of LaTempa they still had a strong case against Genovese.

The Allies soon declare victory in Europe and Japan.

And now, Luciano wants to make sure the help he's given to the war effort doesn't go unrewarded.

Luciano thought that as a reward for his service, he would be released from prison and allowed to resume his power.

Luciano drafts a letter pleading his case for parole to New York's newly-elected governor, Thomas Dewey.

Almost six months pass without word from Dewey.

Luciano has now been in prison for nearly ten years.

In his quest to gain his freedom, Luciano has done favors for the FBI, the United States Navy, and even Thomas Dewey himself.

But with no response to his for freedom, it seems it's all been for nothing.

With Luciano's request for freedom in hand, Thomas Dewey must make a crucial decision because he's built his political career on the publicity of Luciano's conviction.

The pressure was put on Dewey from the United States Navy because of Luciano's war service, which was extensive.

But Luciano's work on behalf of the military is classified so if he does pardon Luciano he will not be able to say why.

The commutation of Luciano's sentence was a politically controversial issue at the time mainly because Dewey had aspirations of one day running for President of The United States.

And for a politician with presidential aspirations, releasing America's most notorious gangster could be a major liability.

Thomas Dewey comes up with a solution to appease the military, protect his political future, and deal with Luciano once and for all.

After ten years, Luciano has finally won his freedom, but it's come with a price.

Thomas Dewey issued Luciano a pardon for his "wartime services" on January 3, 1946, with the condition that he'd be deported back to Italy and not return to the United States.

Luciano accepted the deal, although he still maintained that he was a US citizen and not subject to deportation.

On February 2, 1946, two federal immigration agents transported Luciano from the prison to Ellis Island for deportation proceedings.

On the night before his departure, Luciano shared a final spaghetti dinner on his freighter with Anastasia and five other guests.

For the first time since his incarceration, Luciano's original crew is together again.

They inform him that the D.A. is going to drop the charges against Vito Genovese.

The following day, February 10, Luciano's ship sailed from Brooklyn harbor for Italy.

Now, Luciano's been forced to leave the future of the American Mafia in the hands of his crew and will have to figure out how to keep control of the American Mafia from 4,000 miles away.

After a 17-day voyage, Luciano's ship arrived in Naples On February 28.

Luciano told the local reporters that he would probably reside in Sicily.

During his exile, Luciano frequently encountered American tourists and US soldiers during his train trips in Italy in which he gladly posed for photographs and signed autographs.

With Luciano in Italy, Frank Costello is the acting boss of Luciano's family in New York and must keep the peace between the five New York crime families.

While Luciano back in Italy and Frank Costello in the position of acting boss of Luciano's family in New York, Benjamin "Bugsy" Siegel has set up a stronghold for the family in California.

Siegel has infiltrated the movie industry, using mob-run unions to gain leverage with the movie studios.

But after his years of loyalty, Siegel realizes that he still has nothing to really call his own.

Each of Siegel's childhood crew has either been the boss of the family or has had the freedom to run his own criminal operation.

Siegel sees his opportunity in a stretch of barren Nevada desert known as Las Vegas, just 300 miles east of Las Angeles.

Las Vegas was a patch of sand with no buildings taller than two stories high.

Nevada is one of the few states in the country that has legalized gambling and Siegel sees what no one else can, a gambling Mecca that will make a fortune.

Hollywood nightclub owner and one of the founders of *The Hollywood Reporter*, Billy Wilkerson started to build a hotel in Las Vegas.

By the mid-1940's it was an unfinished project and In May 1946, Wilkerson was forced into selling all stakes in the hotel under the threat of death.

Wilkerson went into hiding in Paris for a time and the hotel soon became a dream of Siegel's.

But to make his dream a reality, Siegel needs money to fund the construction of such an elaborate casino.

Siegel names his hotel after his nickname for his long-legged girlfriend, Virginia Hill, "The Flamingo".

The Flamingo Hotel and Casino project became Siegel's obsession. Siegel persuaded Meyer Lansky to help him to ask the New York and Chicago crime bosses to invest in this project.

The Five Families invest millions of dollars to help fund Siegel's Flamingo Hotel & Casino and Siegel's vision to turn Las Vegas into the gambling capital of the country.

Siegel promised the bosses that the hotel and casino would be a smart and profitable financial investment.

Frank Scalice was sent to Las Vegas to help Siegel open the Flamingo Hotel & Casino.

However, the Flamingo Hotel & Casino project immediately ran into financial problems.

Siegel made his first mistake by appointing his girlfriend Virginia Hill as the project overseer.

His contractors were stealing Siegel blind; they would sell him building materials one day, then steal them from the building site the very same night, then resell them back to Siegel the very next day.

The project was also impacted financially by the rising cost of building materials and labor costs from the post World War II building boom.

The project that projected to cost the Mafia $1.5 million to complete would eventually reach $6 million.

To make matters worse, the crime family bosses suspected Siegel and Hill of stealing money they invested in the project.

They had discovered that Virginia Hill was taking frequent trips to Zürich, Switzerland, and depositing money into a Swiss bank account.

Siegel later told the crime family bosses that he was running the California rackets by himself and that he would return the money that they invested in The Flamingo in his "own good time".

Despite his defiance to the crime family bosses, they were patient with Siegel because he had always proven to be a valuable man.

However, they soon suspected that Siegel was also skimming money and would quickly flee the country if the Flamingo failed.

Vito Genovese sat in a jail cell in the United States for over a year, with the possibility of a death sentence waiting for him if he is found guilty of the crime that he is now facing.

Genovese's case took a turn on June 10, 1946, when another prosecution witness, Jerry Esposito, was found in Norwood, New Jersey, shot to death beside a road.

Without anyone to corroborate Rupolo's testimony, the government's case collapsed and the charges against Vito Genovese were dismissed and he was set free to rejoin the Luciano family in New York.

However, neither Frank Costello nor his underboss Willie Moretti was willing to return the leadership power over to him and Genovese found himself demoted within the organization.

Genovese felt that he had been short-changed, and it was no question that he was an archrival of Costello.

While Costello is left to deal with Genovese, Meyer Lansky is still in Cuba expanding the Luciano Empire.

Luciano seizes what's left of Genovese's heroin smuggling operation in Italy and makes it his own.

The drug business was huge during the war, and Genovese made millions exporting Italy's legally manufactured heroin to the United States.

Luciano knew that the amount of money that you could make in one day with drugs would take you years to make gambling. Luciano knows with his vast criminal network in the United States, he already has a market of millions of customers.

However, after the war, heroin was made illegal in Italy.

Luciano decides to invest thousands of dollars converting Sicilian candy factories into underground heroin labs.

He needs to now find a way to smuggle the drugs into America undetected.

Luciano knows that Cuba is the missing piece to what could be a billion-dollar drug operation for selling his heroin in America.

And to do that, he would need the help of all five of the New York Crime families.

By the summer of 1946, Luciano wanted to be back in the United States.

After seven months in exile, Luciano leaves Italy in secret and heads to Cuba that's become a safe-haven for the mob and is only 90 miles away from America.

Luciano boarded a freighter from Naples that was heading to Caracas, Venezuela.

When he arrived in Caracas he quickly departed by plane to Rio de Janeiro, Brazil.

He then flew to Mexico City and doubled back to Caracas, where he took a private plane to Camaguey, Cuba, where he finally arrived on October 29th.

When Luciano arrived in Cuba he was met by Lansky's men who secretly drove him to Havana, where he moved into an estate in the Miramar section of the city.

Lansky was already established in Cuba.

In December 1946, Luciano calls for a gathering that will bring the Five Families to the island country to reaffirm his status and announce a plan to expand the Mafia's power.

Lansky knew that he could not let anyone know that Luciano was in Cuba, so he told the other mafia leaders that the meeting was going to be held at the Hotel Nacional de Cuba to see singer Frank Sinatra perform.

This meeting convened on December 20, and lasted a little more than a week, and would later become to be known as the Havana Conference.

Mafia members were present representing New York City, New Jersey, Buffalo, Chicago, New Orleans, and Florida.

Several major bosses from the Jewish crime families were at the conference to discuss joint Italian Mafia-Jewish crime family business.

They had a big party and everybody came and they brought money and gifts to Luciano.

Frank Sinatra flew to Havana with Al Capone's cousins, Charlie, Rocco, and Joseph "Joe Fish" Fischetti from Chicago.

Joseph "Joe Fish" Fischetti acted as Sinatra's chaperone and bodyguard.

Charlie and Rocco Fischetti delivered a suitcase to Luciano containing two-million dollars. This was Luciano's share of the U.S. rackets he still controlled.

They thought that Luciano would be on the next boat back to the United States.

During the meeting, Luciano discussed the position of "capo di tutti capi" or "boss of all bosses".

Luciano decided to resurrect the "capo di tutti capi" or "boss of all bosses" position and claim the title himself. He hoped the other bosses would support this decision, either by officially affirming the title or by acknowledging that Luciano was still, "First Amongst Equals".

Since Luciano's deportation back to Italy, Frank Costello had been the acting boss of the Luciano family.

As a result, tensions between the Costello and Genovese factions had started to grow and split the family.

Luciano had no intention of stepping down as the family's Boss; however, he knew that he had to do something about Genovese.

Luciano soon realized that Vito Genovese threatened his overall authority and influence within the Mafia, probably with support from some of the other crime bosses.

Luciano presented the motion to retain his position as "capo di tutti capi" the top boss in La Cosa Nostra.

Albert "The Mad Hatter" Anastasia seconded the motion because he also felt threatened by Genovese's attempts to muscle in on his waterfront rackets.

With Luciano in the position of "capo di tutti capi" the top boss in La Cosa Nostra, Genovese was forced to forget his ambitions and plan for the future.

Luciano encouraged Albert Anastasia and Vito Genovese to settle their differences and shake hands in front of the other Family bosses. This symbolic gesture was meant to prevent another bloody gang war.

During the conference, Luciano and Genovese had a private meeting in Luciano's hotel suite.

Luciano had never trusted Genovese. In the meeting, Genovese tried to convince Luciano to become just a figurative "Boss of Bosses" and let him run everything. Luciano rejected Genovese's suggestion.

For decades, Lucky Luciano and Vito Genovese have been loyal business partners.

However, Luciano realizes that from now on, Vito Genovese can't be trusted.

With Luciano in the position of "Capo di tutti Capi" and squashing Genovese's ambition, for now, Luciano brought up the discussion of the Mafia's future narcotics operations in the United States.

He explains to the other Family leaders that he wants to bring a lot more heroin into the country.

His goal is to ship it from Italy to Cuba and then to Florida and then from New York to Los Angeles.

Luciano detailed the proposed drugs network to the bosses and tells the other families to organize the transportation, storage, and distribution and they will make ten times more than they did last year and then ten times more the year after that.

Luciano explains to the other crime family leaders that the Mafia would ship the narcotics to US ports after the heroin arrives in Cuba from North Africa.

The drugs would go to ports that they controlled primarily New York City, New Orleans, and Tampa Florida.

The narcotics shipped to the New York docks would be overseen by the Luciano crime family and the Mangano crime family.

In New Orleans, the operation would be overseen by the Marcello crime family.

In Tampa, the narcotics shipments would be overseen by the Trafficante crime family led by Santo Trafficante, Jr.

The other Mafia leaders agreed to Luciano's plan to bring Heroin into the United States.

While the assembled families agree to Luciano's proposals, Genovese felt that he deserved a cut from the heroin operation because he was the one who initially set up the operation in Italy.

The Families agree to Luciano's plans of importing heroin into the United States.

And soon Luciano's converted candy factories in Italy begin producing tens of thousands of pounds of heroin.

His heroin is then smuggled across the Atlantic Ocean through the Caribbean and eventually smuggled into the United States.

Luciano is now in control of a global narcotics empire.

The next item on the agenda at the Havana Conference was what Meyer Lansky called the "Siegel Situation".

Following a discussion regarding the failure of The Flamingo Hotel and Casino, and the missing money that the Mafia members sent for the project, they voted unanimously to execute Bugsy Siegel.

The contract to kill Siegel was given to Mob hitman, John "Frankie" Carbo, a Lucchese crime family soldier.

However, at the last moment, Bugsy Siegel got a reprieve. The partly completed Flamingo Hotel and Casino was scheduled to open just that week, on December 26.

Meyer Lansky convinced the Mafia members to see how the hotel did financially in its opening.

The Family leaders agreed with Lansky and then took a break for Christmas Day.

2,000 miles from Cuba in the middle of the Nevada desert, Siegel finally opened his luxury Flamingo Hotel and Casino on December 26, 1946.

A huge storm hits Las Vegas on The Flamingo's opening night.

And with many of the hotel rooms still unfinished, only the casino, lounge, theater, and restaurant were finished and The Flamingo's big opening is a financial bust.

While gambling tables were operating, the luxury rooms that would have served as the lure for people to stay and gamble were not ready to be occupied.

In the first week, The Flamingo Hotel and Casino lost the modern-day equivalent of $3.6 million and Siegel's Las Vegas dream has turned into a nightmare.

After two weeks, the Flamingo's gaming tables were over a quarter of a million dollars in the red and the entire operation shut down in late January 1947 to resume construction.

The Crime Family leaders soon learned that the Flamingo's opening night was a financial disaster.

And his boss, Lucky Luciano wants answers for the enraged mobsters who are now demanding Siegel's murder.

Meyer Lansky manages to buy more time for Bugsy Siegel to make the Flamingo a success.

And Siegel knows that this time, he has to pull it off.

However, Lansky once again convinced them to wait. He argued that Siegel could still save The Flamingo and make money.

While Bugsy Siegel is trying to build the flamingo into a gambling empire, Vito Genovese is convinced it's time he gets a bigger cut of the profits for laying the groundwork for Luciano's Italian heroin racket.

As Genovese looks for a way to be the boss once again, the U.S. Government learned that Luciano was now in Cuba.

Luciano had been seen publicly with Frank Sinatra as well as visiting nightclubs in Havana. The United States started to immediately pressure the Cuban government to send Luciano back to Italy.

The US even threatened to block all shipment of narcotic prescription drugs to Cuba while Luciano was there.

Two days later on February 23, 1947, the Cuban government informed the United States that Luciano was in their custody and would be deported immediately to Italy.

Within 48 hours Luciano was placed on a Turkish freighter that was sailing back to Italy, destroying his dreams of returning to America, where he remained under close surveillance.

One week after Luciano boarded a freighter back to Italy, Siegel finally completes the construction of the guest rooms and The Flamingo Hotel and Casino reopened with Meyer Lansky now present, and began turning a profit.

Bugsy Siegel pays publicists to publicize the event and calls in favors from all of his celebrity friends back in Hollywood.

On a clear Las Vegas night, just months after closing its doors, The Flamingo was ready for its second grand opening on March 1, 1947.

And gamblers from all over the country showed up to spend their money.

After more than a year of delays and budget overages, Bugsy Siegel's big gamble on a forgotten desert town finally pays off.

However, by the time profits began improving for The Flamingo, The casino is packed every night and they're turning people away at the door.

However, none of the mob bosses who invested are getting their cut and the mob bosses are tired of waiting.

When Luciano arrived back in Genoa Italy in mid-April 1947, the Italian police arrested Luciano and sent him to a jail in Palermo where he remained for a month.

On May 11, 1947, a regional commission in Palermo released Luciano from jail with a warning to stay out of trouble and was not allowed to leave Naples.

Lucky Luciano's control of his empire continues to crumble after being deported once again to Italy, and he's made a dangerous new enemy out of Vito Genovese.

In New York, the other families have lost patience with Bugsy Siegel and are going forward with the plans to murder him.

On the night of June 20, 1947, as Bugsy Siegel sat with Allen Smiley, one of his closest associates, in Virginia Hill's Beverly Hills home reading the *Los Angeles Times*, an unknown assailant shot him through the window with a .30 caliber military M1 carbine.

Siegel was shot twice in the head and twice in the torso and died instantly.

No one was charged with killing Siegel, and the crime remains officially unsolved.

The next day, The *Los Angeles Herald-Express* carried a photograph on its front page from the morgue of Siegel's bare right foot with a toe tag.

The day after Siegel's murder, Meyer Lansky's men walked into the Flamingo and took over the operation of the hotel and casino.

Bugsy Siegel becomes the first of Luciano's original crew to be killed.

There has never been any official statement as to why Bugsy Siegel was killed.

Many believe it was from the money owed from the construction of The Flamingo. Others believe that he was killed because he and

Virginia Hill had a very difficult relationship, and Siegel had been physically abusive to Virginia.

And that Virginia's brother was avenging that, and it had nothing to do with the mob.

According to the Beverly Hills Police Department, it is still an open case.

And while Luciano's authority has been restored Vito Genovese begins organizing his own fight for control.

He is frustrated by his lack of power within the Mafia and wants to be boss again and begins to look outside the Luciano family for help.

He reaches out to Carlo Gambino, a 46-year-old Sicilian underboss in the Mangano family.

Genovese sees an ally in Gambino who also has ambitions of climbing the ranks of the New York Mafia.

And While Genovese and Gambino wait for their chance to make their move, Luciano was settling back down in Naples Italy.

Igea Lissoni and Lucky Luciano

After Luciano arrived back in Naples, he had a relationship with a Milanese ballerina who was twenty-years younger than him, named Igea Lissoni in the summer of 1948.

He later described Igea as the love of his life.

It was reported in 1949 that they had married, although people who knew the couple claim that wasn't the case and that they only exchanged rings.

Luciano and Lissoni lived together in Luciano's house in Naples. It was said that Luciano continued his womanizing causing many arguments between him and Igea. It was said that at times had even turned abusive towards Igea.

In May of 1950, U.S. Senator Estes Kefauver formed a committee to investigate the Mafia.

It's the largest effort to expose organized crime in U.S. history in what will come to be known as the Kefauver Hearings.

A Senate investigating committee held a series of hearings to get at organized crime and they decided to televise some of the hearings.

In front of a television audience of 30 million, the Mafia takes the stand.

The witnesses plead the Fifth, which the Constitution provides, and say they're not going to incriminate themselves.

Acting boss Frank Costello begins to see his name mentioned in the press.

When he's finally called to testify, Costello decides to take a different approach and testify to portray himself as a somewhat legitimate person.

He thought he could outwit the committee.

Costello made a mistake in thinking that he could handle a Senate investigating committee the way he handled the local politicians.

With the hearings revealing a weakness in Costello's leadership, Vito Genovese knows his opportunity has finally come to strike back at Luciano.

And with Carlo Gambino on his side, Genovese is ready to strike back at Lucky Luciano by taking down Frank Costello.

For the next ten years, Luciano continued to operate his criminal activities in Naples and had even considered sharing his life story over the years.

As Luciano was imprisoned and working with the Navy over the previous fifteen years, Vincent Mangano and his underboss Albert Anastasia built a well ran organized crime organization.

And over those fifteen years Anastasia and Mangano never entirely saw eye to eye.

Mangano wasn't pleased that his own underboss preferred the company of other mob bosses such as Luciano and Frank Costello, rather than those in his own criminal family.

Mangano also resented how the other families used Anastasia's criminal services without asking for his permission. Mangano felt that as the head of the family it was only right to ask his permission before working with anyone outside of their own criminal family.

By 1951 John Gotti's father moves the family from their four-room flat in the South Bronx to the Sheepshead Bay neighborhood of Brooklyn.

And just a year later, the family moved once again to an area of Brooklyn known as East New York.

John Gotti was soon caught up in the illegal street activity of the local mobsters. Along with his brothers Peter and Richard, John became part of a gang that ran errands for the neighborhood wiseguys.

This lifestyle made John a habitual truant, and the few times that he was in school, his teachers considered him a disturbing distraction and a class bully.

And because of this, the teachers showed little concern over his absence from school.

In February 1951, Tommy Gagliano's underboss, Thomas Lucchese, is promoted to the position of boss of what will be known for the rest of the century as the Lucchese Crime Family.

Many people believe that this promotion was based on Tommy Gagliano's death from natural causes.

However, the actual date of Gagliano's death is still uncertain.

In 1951, Lucchese stated during the Senate hearings on organized crime that Gagliano died on February 16, 1951. (This date is also inscribed on his mausoleum in Woodlawn Cemetery in the Bronx.)

However, some believe Gagliano actually died in 1953. It is believed that Gagliano only retired in 1951 and turned the family's leadership over to Lucchese

It is believed that he kept this information secret to prevent law enforcement or media scrutiny; however, there is no concrete evidence to support this theory.

According to the New York State, death Index Gagliano died on February 16. However, there is no death certificate to support this date.

On April 19, 1951, Vincent Mangano is murdered.

For the first time since the Commission was formed 20 years earlier, a mob boss has been violently removed from power.

The hit on Mangano was ordered by his underboss, Albert Anastasia, or so it is widely believed, so he could take control of the family.

It was believed that Anastasia overheard a plot by Mangano to kill him.

Shortly after this on April 19, 1951, Vincent's brother Phil Mangano was murdered near Sheepshead Bay, Brooklyn on the same day Vincent also vanished but his body was never recovered.

Anastasia never openly admitted to being involved in the Mangano murders.

He managed to convince the Commission that Mangano had been plotting his demise, a claim that was later backed up by Costello.

Anastasia was then named the new boss of the family. He soon changed the name to The Anastasia Crime Family.

While Luciano was in exile in Italy, 4,000 miles away, he is forced to watch his criminal empire turn to chaos as gangsters begin vying for power.

With no hope of returning to America, Luciano must rely on Meyer Lansky, and acting boss of the Luciano crime family, Frank Costello, to keep his criminal operation intact.

And at the same time, Vito Genovese has teamed up with Carlo Gambino to try to reclaim his position at the head of the Luciano family.

With Genovese gunning for Costello's position as boss of the Luciano crime family, Frank Costello begins to crack under the pressure.

And Costello feels that his only option is to talk to a psychiatrist about his issues.

However, going to a psychiatrist would have been perceived as a weakness. So he tries to hide this from the other family members.

But Costello isn't able to keep his visits a secret for long.

Costello knows that it would be just a matter of time before he would be killed so to keep himself safe, Costello's enlisted the protection of Willie Moretti, a ruthless mobster from New Jersey with ties to Luciano and his crime family.

Moretti and his crew of over 50 men, protect Costello around the clock guaranteeing that a hit on Costello will be next to impossible.

In 1951, Albert Anastasia was also summoned by the U.S. Senate to answer questions about organized crime at the Kefauver Hearings. Anastasia refused to answer any questions during the hearings.

By late 1951, Anastasia had Frank Costello as an ally, and Costello's main rival was Luciano's former underboss, Vito Genovese.

Vito Genovese had been scheming for over five years to remove Frank Costello from power, but he knew that he was not powerful enough to face Albert Anastasia.

Genovese and his new ally, Mangano family underboss, Carlo Gambino, meet secretly to strategize on how to get to Costello.

They know that their only hope is to eliminate his protection, Willie Moretti.

But they knew that if they were ever going to be legitimate bosses, they would have to get the Commission to give its okay.

The only problem was that Costello was on the Commission.

Carlo Gambino realizes to order a hit on Moretti; he'll have to convince Luciano himself that the mob is better off without him.

For months, Moretti has been exhibiting strange behavior and speaking too freely about mob activity to the cops, and politicians.

Many believe his brain may be deteriorating due to the effects of advanced syphilis.

When Gambino speaks to Luciano about Moretti, Luciano refuses to okay the hit.

Gambino tells Luciano that, between Moretti and Costello, the hearings and the press, his family's business is falling apart.

Luciano still refuses to approve the hit.

Now, the Genovese and Gambino must decide whether to make a dangerous move and go against Luciano's orders and eliminate Moretti, the protector of his acting boss, Frank Costello.

Moretti's murder, which happened October 4, 1951, played out in a New Jersey restaurant.

At the time of his murder, Moretti was eating lunch with four other men at Joe's Elbow Room Restaurant in Cliffside Park, New Jersey.

The waitress remembered the five men joking together before she went into the kitchen.

Just before 11:30 am, the restaurant staff heard shots fired and quickly ran back into the dining room. They found Moretti with bullet wounds to the face and head lying dead on his back on the floor. Unfortunately, the gunmen had already fled the restaurant.

Twelve years later, Joe Valachi described a conversation with Vito Genovese about the Moretti murder during the McClellan hearings:

It was supposedly a mercy killing because he was sick. Genovese told me, 'The Lord have mercy on his soul, he's losing his mind.'

After Gambino and Genovese take out Moretti, Meyer Lansky fears the future of the Luciano crime family is at stake and calls a meeting with influential Commission member, Joe Bonanno.

Because it was believed that Moretti was losing his mind to syphilis, Joe Bonanno was taking sides with Vito and Carlo.

Joe Bonanno also believed that Costello was not capable to lead the Luciano Family anymore.

With Luciano's power and influence decreasing in New York, Gambino believes the time has finally come to take on Frank Costello.

But first, he'll need to convince Genovese that this is the time to make their move.

In early 1952, Anastasia's reputation among the other Mafia family leaders suddenly changed with the murder of a 24-year-old clothing salesman named Arnold Schuster.

Many people would describe Arnold Schuster as an amateur detective.

In February 1952, Schuster recognized a wanted bank robber named Willie Sutton.

Schuster followed Sutton to a local garage and notified the police of Sutton's whereabouts.

Albert Anastasia did not like the fact that Schuster had helped the police capture Willie Sutton and considered him a "rat".

According to Joe Valachi's testimony in the 1963 McClellan hearings, claimed Albert Anastasia had ordered Schuster's death in early March 1952, after witnessing a television interview.

Schuster was shot just outside of his home, twice in the groin and once in each eye after attending a television interview.

The other New York families were outraged with Anastasia and felt that Schuster's murder was uncalled for.

Schuster's murder also violated a cardinal Mafia rule against killing outsiders and brought unnecessary public scrutiny on the Mafia.

By the mid-1950s Anastasia also alienated Meyer Lansky by expanding his empire into Cuban casinos with Santos Trafficante to compete with Lansky's.

While the other Families were dealing with Anastasia and battles within their own families, Joseph Bonanno became a powerful member of the Commission.

Bonanno was focused on building a strong relationship with fellow boss Joe Profaci. The bond between the two became even stronger when Joe Bonanno's son Salvatore Bonanno married Profaci's niece Rosalie in 1956.

This was a benefit to both Bonanno and Profaci as the Bonanno-Profaci alliance deterred the other three families from trying to move in on any of their criminal rackets.

In 1954, John Gotti was injured while participating in a robbery.

A portable cement mixer tipped over and landed on Gotti's toes crushing two of them while he and some other kids from the neighborhood were in the process of stealing it from a construction site.

He ended up losing two toes on his left foot.

He spent most of the summer of his fourteenth year in the hospital and leaving him with a gait that would last him for the rest of his life.

This injury did not deter him from the life of crime, and by the time he was sixteen, he quit school and became a member of a teenage gang with brothers Peter and Richard, named for an intersection in Brooklyn, the Fulton-Rockaway Boys.

The Fulton-Rockaway Boys differed from other "turf-minded" teen gangs in that they were into stealing automobiles, fenced stolen goods, and robbed drunks.

It was during this time in The Fulton-Rockaway Boys that John teamed up with two other young men who would become life-long friends; Angelo Ruggiero and Wilfred "Willie Boy" Johnson.

John was arrested five times, while a member of the Fulton-Rockaway Boys. Each time the charges were either dismissed or reduced to a probationary sentence.

By 1957 Meyer Lansky and Vito Genovese offered Carlo Gambino the chance to replace Anastasia.

Frank Costello's legal issues began to catch up with him. He was convicted on contempt of Senate charges in August 1952 for walking out of the Kefauver Hearings and went to jail for a year and a half.

He was released in October 1953, after serving fourteen of his eighteen-month sentence.

The IRS was investigating him, and the INS wanted to revoke his citizenship.

The following year he was charged with tax evasion and sentenced to five years in prison.

He served only eleven months of this sentence before the case was overturned on appeal.

He was once again convicted and sent to prison in 1956. However, in early 1957, he was again released when the case was overturned on appeal.

On the evening of May 2, 1957, As Costello walked into the lobby of his Central Park apartment building, The Majestic, Genovese crime family member, Vincent "The Chin" Gigante, pulled a revolver and screamed, "This is for you Frank!"

Just as Gigante fired the revolver, Costello spun around, and the bullet grazed Costello's scalp, riding around the rim of his hat.

Gigante was arrested for attempted murder even though Costello refused to cooperate with the police. Gigante was eventually acquitted at trial and thanked Costello in the courtroom after the verdict.

Although wounded and vulnerable, Costello refuses to back down.

After recovering from the assassination attempt, he reaches out to the one boss of the New York crime families that he thinks will still be loyal to him, Albert Anastasia.

Anastasia doesn't like the idea that Genovese tried to kill Costello.

While Costello and Anastasia ally to protect the Luciano crime family, Anastasia's underboss, Carlo Gambino, and Vito Genovese step up their own plan to take out Costello.

It was at this time that a sixteen-year-old John Gotti had his first brush with the law.

On May 15, 1957, Gotti is arrested and charged with disorderly conduct after a fight between street gangs.

Two months later, the case was dropped due to lack of evidence.

Vito Genovese and Carlo Gambino knew that their only option now was to kill Anastasia and that would be an easy thing to accomplish when Anastasia's underboss Frank Scalise met his demise on June 17, 1957.

The murder of Frank Scalise is believed to have been ordered by Albert Anastasia himself.

It was believed that in 1954 Scalise started selling memberships into Anastasia's crime family for $40,000 to $50,000. This was against the Mafia's long-standing tradition of only allowing men who were trustworthy and earned their way into the ranks.

Before 1954 there were no new memberships handed out since the early 1930s.

Many believe that when Anastasia heard the accusations against his underboss, he immediately ordered his murder. While others believe that the murder was ordered not out of anger, but to prevent further speculation that Anastasia was getting a cut of the membership money.

This version of the story was repeated by Joe Valachi during the McClellan hearings in 1963. He claimed that Scalise was killed because he had been selling memberships into the Anastasia crime family.

Others believe that the killing of Scalise was not ordered by Anastasia but by Vito Genovese.

Genovese was making a play to become the boss over all five Families and wanted Anastasia's family handicapped by the killing of their underboss.

On the afternoon of June 17, Frank Scalise was shot and killed inside a small fruit shop in Little Italy area of the Bronx.

As Scalice talked to the fruit shop owner inside, a black sedan pulled up and double-parked just outside the fruit shop.

Two men walked into the store and walked up to Frank, and pulled out .38 caliber revolvers, and started to shoot.

They fired five times, two of the bullets hit Scalice in the throat, and another bullet entered his right cheek.

The first shot missed its target and the last one hit Scalice in the right shoulder, spinning him around before he dropped to the floor.

The two men climbed into the black car, which pulled away and disappeared into the afternoon traffic. It was all over in a matter of seconds.

After his death, Carlo Gambino became Anastasia's underboss. This put Gambino and Genovese in a position to take out Anastasia once and for all.

Shortly afterward, Carlo's cousin and brother-in-law, Paul Castellano took over as capo of Gambino's old crew.

Just four months later, on the morning of October 25, 1957, the opportunity to kill Albert Anastasia came to pass when Anastasia walked into Grasso's barbershop in The Park Sheraton Hotel located at 870 7th Avenue and ordered a shave and haircut.

Anastasia sat back and let his barber cover his face with hot towels.

Anastasia threw caution to the wind and had gotten lax. On the day of his assassination, his bodyguard and chauffeur, Anthony Copolla, was nowhere to be found.

Copolla dropped Anastasia off at the barbershop, and parked the car in an underground garage, and then took a walk outside, leaving Anastasia unprotected. Some people believed that Copolla was aware of what was to play out on that fateful day.

Even more unthinkable, Anastasia took a barber chair with his back facing the door.

Identically dressed gunmen hidden beneath scarves wrapped around their faces walked into the hotel lobby. A wheelman and lookout in the lobby were waiting for them outside.

The gunmen entered the barbershop and quickly walked directly to Chair No. 4, aiming at Anastasia's back. One hitman stood to the left of Anastasia and shoved the barber out of the way, and started shooting.

The other stood to Anastasia's right.

Five bullets tore into Anastasia as he sat in the barber chair with hot towels around his face.

Anastasia stood to his feet and lunged at his own reflection in the mirror.

The gunmen continued firing until Anastasia finally fell dead on the floor into a heap of bloody towels.

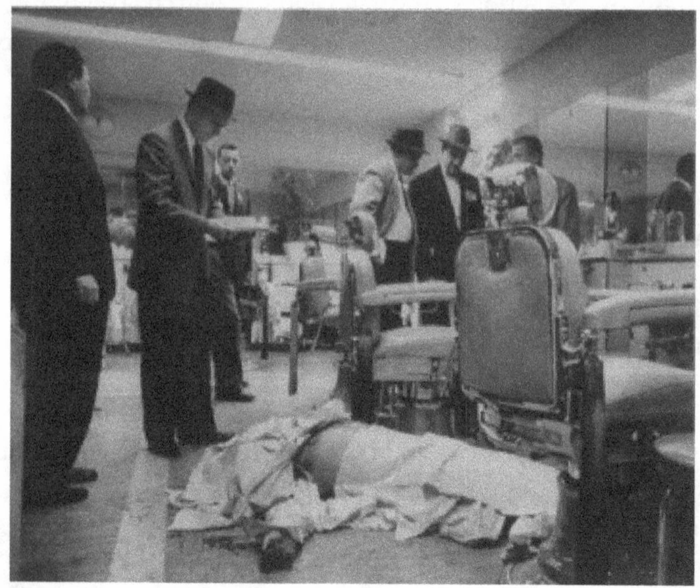

The police never apprehended the mob hitmen and to this day the murder of Albert "Lord High Executioner" Anastasia officially remains unsolved.

Initially, the NYPD concluded that Anastasia's murder had been arranged by Carlo Gambino and Vito Genovese and that it was carried out by a crew led by Crazy Joe Gallo.

Crazy Joe Gallo

At one point, Gallo boasted to an associate of his part in the hit, "You can just call the five of us the barbershop quintet."

Many believe that Gambino ordered caporegime Joseph Biondo to kill Anastasia.

And in turn, Biondo gave the contract to kill Anastasia to a group of Gambino drug dealers.

Gambino's bold plan has paid off. By taking out Anastasia, he's gone from just a mid-level gangster to the head of his own crime family.

Carlo Gambino became boss of what was now called the Gambino crime family.

Caporegime Joseph Biondo became Gambino's underboss, as a reward for killing Anastasia.

In partnership with Vito Genovese, Carlo Gambino has successfully eliminated the head of his family, Albert Anastasia.

With Anastasia's now dead, Vito Genovese was now the most powerful mobster in the country and had positioned himself to control the Mafia's Commission.

After the murder of his only ally on the Commission, Frank Costello does the unthinkable.

With Luciano's approval, Costello ends his 20-year reign as the head of the Luciano crime family.

Costello goes and visits the Commission, and retired from the Mafia as an elder statesman.

The Commission allowed Costello to retire because they trusted him. After all, he didn't give up the guy who tried to kill him.

Two decades after losing his position as acting boss, Vito Genovese now takes his seat at the head of the Luciano crime family.

Because of his deportation to Italy, Lucky Luciano was powerless to stop the transfer of leadership

Now with Luciano in Italy and Costello now removed from the position of boss, Genovese called a meeting of bosses in Apalachin, New York to approve his takeover of the Luciano crime family and to establish his power as the "Boss of Bosses".

Carlo Gambino was expected to be officially proclaimed the new boss of Albert Anastasia's family.

On November 14, 1957, Vito Genovese called the meeting to discuss various matters and to attempt to take control of the governing body of the Mafia.

Genovese knew that the recent murders of Frank Scalise and Albert Anastasia needed immediate attention since men in the Anastasia Family were still loyal to the Albert Anastasia and Frank Scalise regime.

Genovese also had the responsibility of dividing up the illegal operations controlled by the recently killed Anastasia.

At the time of the meeting, the powerful caporegimes Aniello "The Lamb" Dellacroce and Armand "Tommy" Rava were ready to go to war against Vito Genovese and his allies.

The meeting was held at the home of Joseph "Joe the Barber" Barbara in Apalachin, New York along the south shore of the Susquehanna River, near the Pennsylvania border, about 200 miles northwest of New York City. Barbara owned a beverage company in the Binghamton New York area.

Vito Genovese did not know that Barbara had been under surveillance by the New York State Police before the November meeting.

Local law officials, led by Sgt. Ed Croswell of the New York State Police, had been suspicious of Joseph Barbara Sr. who owned a beverage company in the Binghamton area.

Sgt. Croswell looked into Barbara's past and found his involvement in criminal activity, including murder in Pennsylvania, but in each instance, he was released without prosecution.

This made Croswell believe that there was more to Joseph Barbara than just a beverage company owner.

Croswell sensed something was up when he learned that Barbara's son Joseph Jr. had made multiple room reservations at some of the local hotels for November 13th and 14th.

On the evening of the 13th, Croswell and another officer drove past the Barbara residence at 625 McFall Road, noting a few expensive automobiles parked in the driveway.

Croswell believed that Barbara was preparing for something big the following day, additional troopers gathered and Treasury agents were notified.

The next day, Croswell and additional law enforcement officers returned to Barbara's home.

The Barbara home was located on a country road that came to a dead-end at the Apalachin creek.

With only one way to drive out of the area, Croswell set up a roadblock a mile away.

When Sgt. Croswell pulled up to the Barbara home, they found the driveway lined with luxury cars and many more scattered about the property.

Undetected by the high ranking Mafioso, the troopers began scribbling down license plate numbers.

Suddenly, some of Barbara's guests stepped around the corner. Stunned to see the troopers investigating around the vehicles, they panicked and ran toward the house and shouting warnings t the other guests.

The well-dressed mobsters quickly ran to their cars, attempting to flee via the road out of the area, while others ran through open fields and scaling fences heading toward the cover of the nearby woods.

As the Mafioso's cars reached the roadblock at the end of the road, cars were stopped, and each man was searched, and then transported to the New York State Troopers' substation in Vestal for questioning.

The men who fled into the woods were soon apprehended and joined the others at the State Trooper's substation.

Up to fifty men escaped, but 58 members of the Mafia were arrested.

During the interrogations as to why they were at Barbara's house that day, the reply was "to cheer up their friend Joseph Barbara who had been feeling a little under the weather."

Carlo Gambino's official appointment was postponed to a later meeting in New York City.

News of the event was splashed across the headlines of every major newspaper throughout the country by the following morning.

Twenty of those who were arrestedwere charged with "Conspiring to obstruct justice by lying about the nature of the underworld meeting".

In January 1959 they were all found guilty and were fined, up to $10,000 each, and given prison sentences ranging from three to five years.

All the convictions were overturned on appeal the following year.

For the Mafia, the Apalachin meeting was a long term disaster as it confirmed to the public the existence of the Mafia.

J. Edgar Hoover, the head of the FBI could no longer ignore the Mafia. To Hoover, this was now personal, because just six years earlier, he pronounced at a 1951 congressional hearing that "there is no Mafia. No single individual or coalition of racketeers dominates organized crime across the country."

Many say that the Apalachin Meeting was the start of the war began between the Federal government and the Mafia.

The enraged Mafioso leaders personally blamed Vito Genovese for the disaster and the focus of the FBI, opening a window of opportunity for Genovese's opponents Costello, Luciano, and Gambino to take down the leader.

Vito Genovese made the ultimate mistake of getting the Mafia noticed, and this mistake reduced Genovese's impact and influence.

For Luciano, the botched Mafia summit is just another blemish on Genovese's list of failures.

And the unpredictable mob boss is threatening to destroy everything that Luciano has built in America.

Luciano felt that Genovese had almost destroyed the mafia.

He wanted Genovese removed from power.

Luciano gets the help he needs from Genovese's closest ally, Carlo Gambino.

After the Apalachin meeting, Gambino sees an opportunity to use Genovese's failure to his advantage.

Carlo Gambino approached Luciano and told him that for the sake of the Mafia, they needed to make some changes.

Luciano watched Gambino rise through the ranks of the New York Mafia by any means necessary, the same way Luciano did decades earlier.

Luciano has every reason to get rid of Vito Genovese. But he knows if that if he does, he's effectively giving Carlo Gambino ultimate control of the American Mafia.

Luciano must quickly decide whether getting rid of Vito Genovese for good is worth giving up the power of the New York Mafia to Carlo Gambino.

However, he knows that if he doesn't, Genovese may destroy it all.

His other concern was that Gambino has been Luciano's bitter rival.

He knew that Gambino had arranged the murders of Willie Moretti and Albert Anastasia, and ordered the failed hit on Frank Costello.

Luciano respects Gambino's fearless tactics and Genovese's reign as the boss is about to come to an end.

Gambino and Luciano create a plan to get Genovese out of the way for good.

Luciano was struck with another blow when Cuban President Fulgencio Batista was overthrown by Fidel Castro.

On February 16, 1959, Castro was sworn in as Prime Minister of Cuba and the mob now had to look elsewhere for a landing and storage facility for their narcotics shipments.

On June 2, 1958, Vito Genovese testified under subpoena in the McClellan Hearings.

Genovese refused to answer any questions put to him, citing his Fifth Amendment rights under the U.S. Constitution 150 separate times during the questioning.

Vito Genovese had one goal and that was to become boss of all bosses, and he believed that Carlo Gambino would support him in this quest.

Unbeknown to Genovese, Gambino secretly joined forces with Luciano and Costello to eliminate Genovese.

Gambino, Luciano, and Costello met in a hotel in Palermo to discuss their plan to eliminate Genovese.

Soon after their meeting, Luciano allegedly paid an American drug dealer $100,000 to help them falsely implicate Genovese in a drug deal.

Gambino helped lure Genovese into a lucrative drug deal in Atlanta where a huge shipment of heroin was arriving.

However, when Genovese arrived he was met by the local police, the FBI, and the ATF.

Genovese was indicted on charges of conspiring to import and sell narcotics.The government's star witness was Nelson Cantellops, the drug dealer Lucky Luciano allegedly paid off, who claimed Genovese met with him.

In April 1959, Genovese was found guilty of selling a large quantity of heroin and sentenced to 15 years in the Atlanta Federal Penitentiary.

While in prison, Genovese used a series of acting bosses to maintain control of the family from prison.

His three acting bosses were acting boss Thomas "Tommy Ryan" Eboli, Underboss Gerardo "Jerry" Catena, and Capo Michele Miranda.

The three acting bosses were known to authorities but in 1962 Joseph Valachi stated before a US Senate subcommittee that Philip "Benny Squint" Lombardo was also one of the acting bosses.

Another FBI informant named Vincent Cafaro would later say that Philip Lombardo had been boss since 1969 and had only been using the others as decoys to insulate himself from the FBI.

With Genovese in prison, Luciano has gotten rid of his biggest rival and placed the Mafia he created into the hands of Gambino; the man he believes is most able to lead the Mafia into the future.

With Luciano's blessing, Carlo Gambino becomes the new head of the Commission ushering in a new era of the American Mafia.

Luciano remains influential in the underworld and remains in Italy with Italian dancer Igea Lissoni.

They lived together in Naples until she died in 1959 from breast cancer. The two never had any children between them.

By 1959 Joe Profaci's family was starting to unravel from the inside.

Profaci was very generous when it came to his relatives and the church.

However, he was just the opposite when it came to his criminal family.

Profaci required each of his family members to pay him a $25 a month tribute or tithe as it is known in the old Sicilian Mafia custom.

The money amounted to approximately $50,000 a month and was meant to support the families of family members that were in prison.

However, most of this money never went to the families.

Besides, if any of his family members expressed discontent with his policies they were murdered.

Profaci's bookmaker Frank Abbatemarco stopped paying tribute to Profaci and owed him $50,000.

Abbatemarco controlled a lucrative *numbers racket* that earned him over two million dollars a year with an average of $7,000 a day.

Profaci allegedly ordered his capo Joe Gallo to kill Abbatemarco. However, other versions of the story indicate that Joe Gallo played no part in Abbatemarco's murder.

It is believed that Profaci promised Gallo, who worked with Abbatemarco at the time, his criminal rackets if Gallo killed him.

This offer was very enticing to Gallo as Frank Abbatemarco's numbers racket provided a great deal of money.

On November 4, 1959, Abbatemarco walked out of a bar in Brooklyn and was shot and killed by two hitmen.

Profaci then ordered the Gallos to hand over Abbatemarco's son Anthony. They refused and Profaci refused to give them the numbers racket.

Profaci split the bookmaking business but left nothing for Gallo and his crew.

With the encouragement from Gambino crime family boss Carlo Gambino, Profaci's main rival on the Mafia Commission, the Gallo brothers and the Garfield boys (led by Carmine Persico) were aligned against Profaci and his loyalists.

This was the start of the first family war that lasted for the next three years.

Part Three

The Gambino Crime Family

The 1960s brought the Mafia into a whole new light.

With J. Edgar Hoover and the FBI in full war against the American Mafia, the leaders knew that they had to take a new approach to organized crime.

By the mid-20th century, twenty-four known crime families were operating in cities across the country, comprised of over 5,000 "made," or inducted, members, and thousands of associates.

America's capital of organized crime was New York City, which had five major Mafia families. Each family had its own leader, also known as the "Boss" or "Don".

And the most powerful of all the Bosses was, "Don" Carlo Gambino.

In the early part of the 1960s, Carlo Gambino moved against the last remaining loyalists to Anastasia.

With Joseph Biondo as his underboss, Joseph Riccobono as the Gambino family's consigliere, and with his top caporegimes Aniello Dellacroce, and brother-in-law Paul Castellano, the last remaining Anastasia loyalists could never make a move against the Gambinos.

Gambino wasted very little time expanding his rackets all over the United States and quickly built the Gambino crime family into the most powerful crime family in the United States,

Carlo Gambino built close ties to Meyer Lansky's offshore gaming houses in Cuba and the Bahamas.

Carlo Gambino and his family controlled more than 90% of all of the New York City's ports including the New York Longshoreman Union.

The family acquired behind-the-scenes control of Teamsters Local 282, which controlled access to most building materials in the New York area and could bring most construction jobs in New York City to a halt.

It was believed that they had as many as 800 soldiers spread out in 30 crews across the United States.

The Gambino Crime Family was making more than $500 million a year.

The Gallo brothers were still mad at Profaci's decision not to give them Abbatemarco's numbers racket and launch a bloody civil war within the Profaci family on February 27, 1961.

Joe, his brother Larry Gallo, and their ally Carmine Persico kidnapped Profaci's underboss Joe Magliocco, his brother Frank Profaci, and then-capo Joseph Colombo.

They tried to get Profaci, but he managed to flee his New York mansion in his pajamas and made his way to Florida and took refuge in a hospital there.

After three weeks of negotiation with Profaci's consigliere Charles "the Sidge" LoCicero, the Gallos reached an agreement with Profaci in the way profits were divided between crews and released the men.

However, Profaci had no intention of honoring this peace agreement. He was simply biding his time before taking revenge on the Gallos.

While the Gallos were negotiating with LoCicero, Profaci made a secret deal with Carmine Persico to switch sides and assist him in taking out the Gallos.

Profaci ordered the murders of Gallo members Joseph "Joe Jelly" Gioielli and Larry Gallo.

In May Profaci's gunmen allegedly killed Joseph "Joe Jelly" Gioelli, who at the time was Joe Gallo's top enforcer, after inviting him to go deep-sea fishing.

To send a message to the Gallo Brothers, they stuffed Gioelli's clothes with dead fish and dumped it in front of a diner that was frequented by the Gallo crew.

This was a common mob-style message that the deceased was now, "sleeping with the fish."

Three months later, on August 20th, Larry Gallo was lured to a meeting at the Sahara Lounge in Brooklyn.

Once inside, Profaci hitmen, including the man he believed to be his own ally; Carmine Persico, tried to strangle him.

However, Gallo avoided death when a passing policeman interrupted the assassination.

The Gallos then began calling Persico *"The Snake"*; because he had betrayed them, the war between the Gallos and Persico continued resulting in nine murders and three disappearances.

As the year progressed and the war with Persico went on, the Gallo brothers were unable to run their usual rackets and started to quickly run out of money.

Joe Gallo saw a quick money-making scheme when he tried to extort payments from a cafe owner

Unfortunately for Gallo the café owner immediately went to the police and he was soon arrested.

In November, Joe Gallo was convicted on conspiracy and extortion charges for attempting to extort money from the businessman.

On December 21, 1961, he was sentenced to seven to fourteen years in state prison.

While Joe Gallo was serving his prison sentence, Profaci's health was failing.

Carlo Gambino and Tommy Lucchese tried to convince Profaci to resign from his position as Boss to end the war with the Gallos

However, Profaci suspected that Gambino and Lucchese were secretly supporting the Gallo brothers and just wanted to take control of his family.

Profaci refused to step down as Boss and warned that any attempt to remove him would spark a larger war.

Unbeknown to Gambino and Lucchese, shortly after they meet with Joe Profaci, the position of Boss would open up in the Profaci family.

In 1962, Carlo Gambino's eldest son Thomas Gambino married the daughter of Tommy Lucchese.

It has been rumored that Gambino personally gave Lucchese $30,000 as a "welcome gift" that same day.

As repayment, Lucchese gave Gambino some of the rackets at J.F.K. International Airport where all unions, management, and security were controlled by Lucchese himself.

It was the beginning of a perfect partnership and Carlo Gambino now became the most powerful man in the Cosa Nostra.

In an odd twist of fate, 64-year-old Lucky Luciano suffered a fatal heart attack at a Naples Airport on January 26, 1962.

Luciano had been there to meet with a film and television producer to tell his life story.

Ironically, His death came just days before the Italian authorities were going to arrest him for drug trafficking. And had he been convicted, he would most likely have spent the remainder of his life in prison.

It was later said that Lucky Luciano said, "*I didn't want no son of mine to go through life as the son of Luciano, the gangster. That's one thing I still hate Dewey for, making me a gangster in the eyes of the world.*"

Hundreds of mourners line the streets of Naples to pay their respects to the man responsible for creating the American Mafia.

Two weeks later, on February 7th, nearly 16 years after being deported, Luciano finally gets his wish of returning to America one last time.

Luciano's body was brought back from Italy for burial in his family's vault in St. John's Cemetery, Middle Village, Queens.

The Pan American World Airways cargo plane that delivered his body to New York International Airport was met by his brothers, Bartolo and Joseph.

His hearse was escorted by the single mourner's car and two dozen automobiles containing the law officers, reporters, and photographers.

There was no ceremony for Luciano at the cemetery.

He was interred in a vault on consecrated ground.

Already interred in the simple vault with its Greek columns are his mother and father and an aunt and uncle.

Carlo Gambino was the only boss of the Five Families who attended the burial of Luciano.

Although he spent much of his life as Charles "Lucky" Luciano, he was laid to rest by his parents under his birth name, Salvatore Lucania.

In the late 1950s, when John Gotti was almost twenty, he met and fell in love with eighteen-year-old Victoria DiGiorgio. Victoria was two years younger than John.

John and Victoria were married on March 6, 1962, almost a full year after the birth of their first child, Angela.

The marriage proved to be a stormy one, yet despite their problems, the couple went on to have a second daughter, Victoria born on November 27, 1962.

On June 7, 1962, after a long illness, Profaci died in South Side Hospital in Bay Shore, New York of liver cancer. Profaci's underboss Joe Magliocco took over the family and continued the battle with Gallo's brothers.

Gambino and Lucchese gave their support to the Gallo brothers.

Joseph "Joe Bananas" Bonanno gave his support to Joe Magliocco and the Profacis.

With their caporegime Joseph "Crazy Joe" Gallo behind bars, the Gallo crew knew that they didn't have enough manpower to continue the war against the Profacis.

The Gallo crew gave up later that year and Magliocco and Bonanno had won the Gallo war.

And together they intended to "take care" of their "Boss of Bosses," Carlo Gambino.

In 1962, Vito Genovese supposedly accused Joseph Valachi; both were serving sentences for heroin trafficking in the Atlanta Federal Penitentiary, of being an informer.

Valachi later told the FBI that, Genovese supposedly gave Valachi the "kiss of death" because he suspected Valachi of informing.

A $100,000 bounty was put out on Valachi by Genovese. Valachi knew that his days were numbered in the prison.

On June 22, Valachi used a pipe to bludgeon an inmate to death after he had mistaken the man for a Mafia member who he believed had been sent by Genovese to kill him.

After receiving a life sentence instead of the death penalty for that murder, and the bounty now placed on his head by Genovese, Joseph Valachi decided to become a government witness.

No one knows exactly why he decided to turn on the mafia. Valachi claimed he did it because he wanted to help the public and because the mafia had ruined his life.

Others believe that Valachi may have agreed to testify to secure a life sentence and protection instead of facing execution for the murder he carried out.

In October 1963, Valachi testified before Arkansas Senator John L. McClellan's Permanent Subcommittee on Investigations of the U.S. Senate Committee on Government Operations, stating that the Italian-American Mafia existed.

Valachi described the history of the Mafia, including its structure, operations, rituals, and membership.

Valachi also described its organization structure, from soldiers to capo régimes (lieutenants) to bosses, with the so-called Commission moderating disputes between the nation's major crime families.

Valachi also revealed that Vito Genovese is the "Boss of Bosses" of the American Mafia.

Valachi spent the rest of his life in prison, fearing for the contract Genovese put out on his life.

No one was ever able to carry out the hit: He died of a heart attack at the Federal Correctional Institution, La Tuna in Texas on April 3, 1971.

Shortly after the birth of his second daughter Victoria, John Gotti spent his first time in jail, a 20-day period, in 1963 when he was arrested with Angelo Ruggiero's younger brother Salvatore. They were in an automobile that had been reported stolen from a rental car agency.

The following year his first son John A., who became known as "Junior", was born on February 14, 1964.

Throughout the mid-1960s Gotti's crimes were mostly petty crimes like larceny, unlawful entry, and possession of bookmaking records.

Around this time, John had a legitimate job as a coat factory presser and a truck driver's assistant.

It was later said that Victoria Gotti looked down on her husband's career. She disliked how it made her live.

With the Gallos now out of the way, Magliocco was able to consolidate his position and concentrate on the business of running the family's criminal affairs.

Joe Bonanno now felt threatened by the alliance between new boss Carlo Gambino and Tommy Lucchese

He was also dealing with issues within his own family.

One family issue that he was dealing with was with one of his own capo régimes named Gaspar DiGregorio.

DiGregorio had aspirations of becoming the Bonanno family's consigliere.

Instead, Joe Bonanno made his son Salvatore consigliere, leaving hard feelings with DiGregorio.

Many of his family members also complained that he spent too much time away from New York, and more time in Canada and Tucson, Arizona.

Bonanno was also becoming unpopular with some of the other Mafia bosses.

For instance, Stefano Magaddino was mad that Bonanno was moving in on some of the criminal activities in the Toronto area, which belonged to the Buffalo family.

Some even felt that Bonanno was getting too power-hungry.

Santo Trafficante, Jr. a boss from Florida, once said in anger, "He's planting flags all over the world!"

Joe Bonanno knew that if he was going to survive in the world of the Mafia, he needed to murder the heads of the other three families, and take over the Mafia Commission.

Bonanno felt that the only person that he could turn to for help with this plan was Joe Magliocco.

Bonanno met with Magliocco and as Joe predicted he decided to go along with Bonanno's plan.

The assassinations went to Profaci capo, Joseph Colombo, who quickly realized that the plot would never amount to anything.

Colombo either feared for his life or sensed an opportunity for advancement and betrayed his boss and went instead to warn Gambino and Lucchese about Bonanno and Magliocco's plan to take over the Commission.

Bonanno and Magliocco were called to face the judgment of the Commission.

Bonanno quickly went into hiding, while Magliocco faced up to his crimes.

The Commission realized that Magliocco was just following Bonanno's lead.

The Commission agreed to let him off with a $50,000 fine and forced him to retire as the head of the family.

Joseph Colombo, an ally of Gambino was appointed as the new Profaci family Boss.

The Profaci family soon became known as the Colombo crime family.

One month later, 65-year-old Magliocco died a heart attack at Good Samaritan Hospital.

Carlo Gambino had other plans for Joe Bonanno.

Even though Carlo Gambino took pity on Bonanno and gave him one last chance to retire.

When Bonanno refused to give up his position as Boss, the other Commission members felt it was an act of disrespect and knew that it was time for drastic action.

Gambino reached out to Joe Bonanno's cousin Stefano "Steve the Undertaker" Magaddino to relay the offer to retire to Bonanno.

In October 1964, Bonanno was kidnapped by Buffalo crime family members, and taken to Stefano Magaddino in upstate New York.

Stefano told Bonanno that he represented the Commission and Gambino, and told his cousin that he "took up too much space in the air," a Sicilian proverb for arrogance.

Bonanno was eventually released and the Commission and Gambino believed that Bonanno would finally retire and relinquish his power.

After several months with no response, the Commission removed Bonanno from the position of Boss and replaced him with his caporegime, Gaspar DiGregorio in early 1965.

DiGregorio made Pietro "Skinny Pete" Crociata the new underboss and Nicolino "Nick" Alfano the new family consigliere.

This resulted in the Bonanno family breaking into two separate groups and war soon erupted within the Bonanno family.

One side led by DiGregorio and his supporters, and the other side which was technically still the Bonanno crime family, was headed by Joe's brother-in-law, Frank Labruzzo, and his son, Salvatore Bonanno.

The Newspapers referred to this as, "The Banana Split."

Joe Bonanno wasn't heard from again for almost two years as Salvatore Bonanno led the family.

At one point, DiGregorio arranged a meeting to broker a peace treaty with the Bonannos at a house on Troutman Street in Brooklyn.

DiGregorio and his men arrived first; when the Bonannos arrived, DiGregorio's men opened fire on Salvatore Bonanno and his associates with rifles and automatic weapons from doorways, windows, and rooftops along Troutman Street.

Salvatore Bonanno and his associates were armed only with pistols.

More than 500 shots were fired but remarkably, no one was hurt.

The shooting became known as "The Troutman St. Ambush".

Capo Paul Sciacca and a family lieutenant, Frank Mari were suspected of masterminding the botched hit, but ultimately Gaspar DiGregorio was blamed for the bad publicity and added police scrutiny that surrounded the shooting.

The Bonanno war went on for another two more years.

In the mid 1960s Gambino family underboss Biondo started working with mobster Sam DeCavalcante of the DeCavalcante crime family.

Biondo had gained a share of revenues from a landfill in New Jersey and hid this new revenue from Carlo Gambino to avoid sharing it with the family.

However, in 1965 DeCavalcante revealed the deception to Gambino, who then removed Biondo from power and replaced him as underboss with capo Aniello Dellacroce.

Aniello "Neil" Dellacroce

By 1966 Roy DeMeo was starting to make a name for himself on the streets of New York.

After leaving high school DeMeo married and fathered three children and worked at the Mafia-connected Canarsie junkyards. At the same time, he started a loan shark business bringing in hundreds of dollars each week.

It was around this time that DeMeo met Harvey "Chris" Rosenberg who was a smalltime drug dealer in 1966.

DeMeo recruited Rosenberg to steal cars, which would then be sold off through connections DeMeo had within the Canarsie junkyards.

Rosenberg eventually opened his own car repair shop named Car Phobia Repairs, which soon became a hotspot for criminals to sell stolen vehicles.

It was also around this time that DeMeo caught the attention of the Gambino crime family and in particular Nino Gaggi, who was one of Frank Scalice's men.

It was believed that Nino Gaggi was a made man in the Gambino crime Family after killing Vincent Squillante in 1960 after he was indicted on extortion charges.

Some believe that Carlo Gambino ordered Squillante's death because Gambino was worried that Squillante could not handle the upcoming trial and probable prison sentence.

Nino Gaggi found out that it was Squillante who had killed his mentor Frank Scalice and Gambino gave Gaggi the okay to kill Squillante.

By killing Squillante, Gaggi was getting the revenge that he felt he needed for the killing of Scalice. For Gambino, it guaranteed that Squillante would not tell the authorities about the killing of Scalice to try and secure a sentencing deal.

On September 23, 1960, Squillante disappeared and his body was never found and no murder suspects were ever arrested.

This would be Gaggi's first killing and for it, he would become a made man in the Gambino Family.

In 1963, Government informant Joe Valachi claimed that Squillante was one of the hitmen in the 1957 slaying of Anastasia underboss Frank Scalice.

Gaggi quickly saw the potential in having Roy DeMeo working for him.

DeMeo and Gaggi immediately set up their own loan sharking business.

Once the loan sharking business was running, the two branched out and formed a crew for DeMeo that specialized in car theft.

His crew would be known as the DeMeo crew and the Gemini crew and included his cousin Joe Guglielmo, a local drug dealer named Chris Rosenberg, and murderer and hitman Richard "Iceman" Kuklinski.

DeMeo also developed himself as a legitimate businessman. He joined the Brooklyn Credit Union as a member of the board of directors and used his position to launder drug money for Rosenberg.

DeMeo soon had several loan sharking businesses running from the credit union and was making hundreds of thousands each year.

In 1966 John Gotti became an associate of a Mafia crew headed by Carmine Fatico and his brother Daniel who were operating out of a social club called the Bergin Hunt and Fish Club in Ozone Park, Queens.

Gotti's criminal career as a hijacker began as a member of Carmine Fatico's crew who targeted the massive John F. Kennedy International Airport.

At that time, the Fatico brothers answered to Gambino Family underboss, Aniello Dellacroce.

When Joe Bonanno returned to New York in 1966, he sent out a message to his enemies.

He boldly said that for every Bonanno family member killed, he would retaliate by killing a capo régime from the other side.

DiGregorio had the full support of the Mafia Commission members such as Gambino, Lucchese, Colombo, and Genovese at the beginning of his reign as Boss.

However, by 1966, they all had lost faith in DiGregorio's ability to lead the family and became dissatisfied with DiGregorio's efforts at ending the family war.

The Mafia Commission turned their support to Paul Sciacca and sanctioned acting him as the new boss of the Bonanno crime family.

Sciacca promoted Frank Mari to be his underboss, while another Sciacca soldier, Michael "Mike" Adamo was promoted to consigliere of the family.

Unknown to Sciacca, Mari and Adamo began to plot against him and planned to remove him from power.

But Sciacca soon learned of their plans and on the night of September 18, 1968, both men disappeared, never to be heard from again.

DiGregorio and Pietro Crociata still led their faction of soldiers in the war against Bonanno.

Joe Bonanno suffered a heart attack just as the Bonannos were sensing victory.

Bonanno decided that he and his son would retire to Arizona, leaving the now broken Bonanno crime family to Paul Sciacca. The Commission accepted Bonanno's offer, as long as Bonanno promised to never involve himself again in New York Mafia affairs.

However, they stipulated that if Bonanno broke his promise, he would be killed on the spot.

With Joe Bonanno now stepping down, Carlo Gambino now stood as the victorious and most powerful mob boss in the United States.

Gambino's showing of mercy to Bonanno made him even more respectable in front of the Commission.

By 1968, DiGregorio was in ill health and stepped down as boss and retired and lived with his family in Long Island before dying only two years later on June 11, 1970.

Natale "Joe Diamonds" Evola became the boss of the faction of the Bonanno family that DiGregorio held. The other faction was still led by Sciacca.

Evola cooperated fully with Carlo Gambino and the Commission.

Hostilities continued within the two factions of the Bonanno crime family into 1969.

With Mari and Adamo now gone, Sciacca attempted to unite both factions of the Bonanno Family by promoting the leaders of the two factions into his own.

Bonanno soldier and former Mari soldier Philip "Rusty" Rastelli, a former Bonanno loyalist, who switched allegiance to the DiGregorio-Sciacca side at the start of the war, was promoted to consigliere following the disappearance of Adamo.

Rastelli gained a great deal of influence with the younger members of the crime family and was now the leader of the "young Turks" faction.

Head of the other Faction of the Bonanno family, Natale Evola was promoted to underboss in place of Mari.

By promoting Evola to underboss and Rastelli to consigliere, Sciacca hoped to realign the Bonanno crime family.

He also intended to bring the Bonanno crime family back to the level of power and influence within the New York Mafia it once occupied before the Bonanno War.

Gaetano "Tommy" Lucchese developed a fatal brain tumor and died at his home in Lido Beach, Long Island on July 13, 1967.

Before his death, Lucchese codified his intent that all his interests in the garment industry were to go directly to his son-in-law, Thomas Gambino at the time of his passing.

Carlo Gambino organized Lucchese's funeral and hand-picked Carmine "Gribbs" Tramunti as Lucchese's successor.

By nearly all accounts, Anthony (Tony Ducks) Corralo was Lucchese's choice to succeed him.

It is believed that the Mafia Commission only appointed Tramunti as "acting" or "front" boss for the next three years until Lucchese's preferred successor, Anthony Corallo, was released from a three-year prison sentence.

Corallo became boss immediately upon his 1970 release from prison.

On August 2, 1967, Carlo Gambino was seen at the Desert Inn in Las Vegas where he met Frank Sinatra, Sammy Davis, Jr., Dean Martin, Peter Lawford, and Joey Bishop, who all are known as, "The Rat Pack".

Gambino said to Paul Castellano: "I want a picture of me and Frankie".

Sinatra of course, happily obliged and Gambino and other mobsters got a picture with Frank Sinatra.

Sinatra would later testify about this in court, but stated that he "didn't know any Carlo Gambino".

John Gotti eventually moved his family to a nicer apartment in Brooklyn. He and Victoria soon had their fourth child, a second son on October 18, 1967, whom they named Frank.

On November 27, just one month after the birth of his son, John Gotti and another crew member forged the name of a forwarding company agent and then took a rented truck to JFK's United Airlines cargo area and drove off with $30,000 worth of merchandise.

Four days later, the FBI was watching at a Northwest Airlines cargo terminal as Angelo Ruggerio and John Gotti loaded up again with women's clothing.

The two were net by John's brother Gene as soon as they left the airport. The FBI swooped in and arrested the three men. They found John hiding in the rear of the truck behind several boxes.

During the FBI's investigation, the United Airlines employees identified John Gotti as the man who had signed for the merchandise that was stolen earlier.

Three months later in February 1968, Gotti was arrested for the United Airlines hijacking. In April, while he was out on bail, Gotti was arrested a third time for stealing a load of cigarettes worth nearly $500,000 outside a restaurant on the New Jersey turnpike.

The charge was hijacking this time.

The Gotti brothers and Angelo hired defense attorney Michael Coiro to represent them at the urging of Carmine Fatico. John was advised to plead guilty to the Northwest hijacking and was sentenced to four years in Federal Prison in Pennsylvania.

In return, the prosecutors dropped the charges in the cigarette hijacking, and his lawyer was able to get the judge to let Gotti plead guilty in the United Airlines theft while allowing his current prison sentence to serve as the penalty.

When John Gotti was away serving his prison sentence, his wife was forced to apply for welfare to support her and the children.

In total, John Gotti served less than three years of his sentence at Lewisburg Federal Prison, from May 1969 to January 1972.

On February 14, 1969, seventy-one-year-old Vito Genovese died of a heart attack at the United States Medical Center for Federal Prisoners in Springfield, Missouri.

He's buried just 100 feet from Lucky Luciano.

In March 1970, Carlo Gambino was arrested by federal agents on charges of conspiracy to violate a federal statute against the interstate transportation of stolen goods.

It was believed that Gambino masterminding a plot to pull off a multimillion-dollar armored car robbery.

Gambino allegedly was already sitting on $3 million to $5 million in illicit earnings from armored car heists. Gambino was also making plans to stage a $25 million heist at the offices of the U.S. Trucking Co.

The FBI had gathered the information from a Boston armored car heist expert, named John J. Kelley.

Kelley, who was being held in protective custody in Boston, confessed after his arrest in another case and named Carlo Gambino as the kingpin in the alleged conspiracy.

In court, the special prosecutor asked for $100,000 bail. But as the prosecutor read the complaint, Gambino's face brightened, breaking into a broad grin at the mention of the $25 million conspiracy, and again when John Kelley's name was mentioned.

Gambino's lawyer described Gambino as an unfortunate man in ill health, devoted to his family to the judge.

When the judge ruled that his bail was $75,000, Gambino flew into a rage.

"I'll stay in jail," Gambino yelled.

Gambino then said: "I am innocent from this accusation. I won't put up five cents for bail."

Gambino's lawyer attempted to calm him down and told him. "You're not well enough to stay in jail."

"I stay in jail!" Gambino shouted.

Gambino's lawyer turned to the judge and asked: "Let me talk to his son, your honor."

"*Don't talk to my son. I stay in jail*," Gambino said.

Next, Carlo's son Thomas stepped to the center of the room, embraced his father, and kissed him.

The two chatted briefly, and then the judge allowed them to leave the courtroom for a half hour and talk.

When Gambino returned to the courtroom, he agreed to pay the bail.

Joe Gallo was released from prison on April 11, 1971.

After Gallo's release from prison Colombo and Joseph Yacovelli met with him and delivered a $1,000 homecoming gift.

Gallo reportedly told Colombo that he wasn't bound by the 1963 peace agreement the commission had established while he was in prison and demanded $100,000 to keep the peace.

When the commission heard Joe Gallo's response to their gift, they issued an order to kill him.

However, just two months later another gunman struck first.

However, Joe Colombo soon alienated Carlo Gambino with his establishment of the Italian-American Civil Rights League and the media attention that it was generating.

It is possible that at this time, Gambino encouraged Joe Gallo to continue his challenge to the Colombo leadership.

By early 1970, Joe Colombo, head of the Colombo crime family's name made the newspapers on a fairly regular basis.

Not only as a "Mafia boss", but also as the frequent and very vocal speaker of a new organization called, The Italian-American Civil Rights League.

The organization's overall goal was to remove the stigma of the "Mafia" and "La Cosa Nostra" associated with Italian-Americans.

The Italian-American Civil Rights League accused the FBI of hiring informants to give false testimony and manufacturing conspiracies against Italian-Americans.

It was estimated that 100,000 people attended the group's first "Unity Day" festival was held in New York's iconic Columbus Circle in the summer of 1970.

The group's second Unity Day festival was held once again in New York's Columbus Circle in the summer of 1971.

On Monday, June 28, 1971, the 48-year-old crime family boss greeted guests who arrived for the big Unity Day festival at Columbus Circle.

A colored guy brandishing both press credentials and a revolver approached Joe Colombo and fired three shots into Colombo's head at point-blank range.

Within seconds, police officers descended upon the gunman, but with the chaos of the crowd and confusion, another series of shots rang out.

An unknown shooter shot and killed the suspected shooter of Joe Colombo and was never apprehended.

Investigators recovered several handguns from the scene, and identified the assailant, who was pronounced dead on arrival as Jerome A. Johnson, a 25-year-old resident of New Jersey and described as a "gun buff" and "an admirer of Adolf Hitler."

Colombo was rushed to Roosevelt Hospital in critical condition.

Surgeons quickly began the task of removing a slug from the mid-brain and one from his neck.

The operation took five hours and left Colombo with a "less than 50-50" chance of survival.

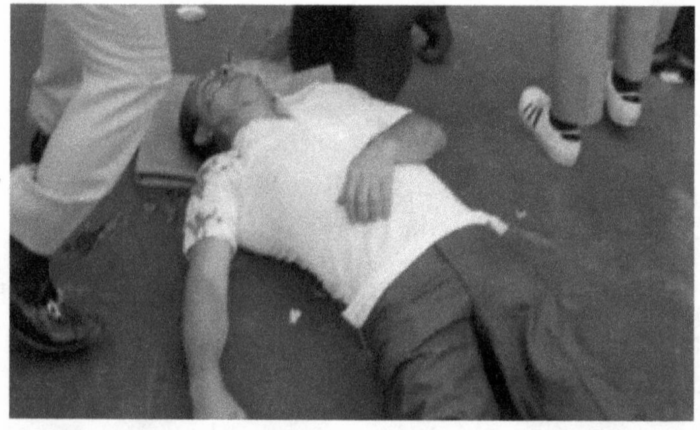

Colombo's condition had slightly improved by the next morning.

The crime boss was still in a coma but was able to breathe on his own and move his left arm.

After the shooting, Joseph Yacovelli became the acting boss for one year before Carmine Persico took over the leadership position.

Joe Colombo lived out most of the next seven years at his Brooklyn home, still comatose and paralyzed.

The official police investigation concluded that Jerome Johnson acted alone and that he had no direct ties to organized crime.

The mafia Commission received information that while in prison, Joe Gallo had recruited several African American men into his crew.

Jerome Johnson was thought to be one of Gallo's men.

Apparently, the style of the killing didn't sit well with the Commission, who did not like the fact that Gallo allegedly hired a black associate to kill Colombo in the presence of his family.

Because of this, the Commission increased its intensity to have Gallo killed.

Some believed that Carlo Gambino was the person who ordered the hit and Joe Colombo for bringing too much attention to the Mafia. However, this theory has not been proven as Carlo Gambino had nothing to gain from Colombo's death.

Colombo's increasing media attention was not liked by the other members of the Commission.

The Lucchese crime family withdrew support was evidenced by Capo Paul Vario rescinding his membership from the Italian-American Civil Rights League.

Others believed that Joe Gallo organized the attack himself using black gang relationships he developed while in prison.

However, the police accepted the Gallo theory as did the Colombo family, but as time went on the theory that Carlo Gambino masterminded the hit became more believable.

No matter who shot Joe Colombo on that day in June 1971, the following April it would be Joe Gallo who would be shot and killed.

By1971 Neil Dellacroce still managed to stay out of law enforcement's radar.

However, Dellacroce refused to answer any questions about the mafia after being summoned to appear before a grand jury. He was cited for contempt and received a one-year prison sentence.

On April 7, 1972, Joe Gallo celebrated his 43rd birthday with his family.

The night began at the Manhattan restaurant the Copacabana to see comedian Don Rickles and singer Peter Lemongello perform.

After leaving the Copacabana, Gallo's sister Carmella, wife Sina Essary, her daughter Lisa, his bodyguard Peter "Pete the Greek" Diapoulas, and Diapoulas's female companion moved to Umberto's Clam House in Little Italy.

At 4:30 a.m. a large lone gunman entered Umberto's and open fired at Joe Gallo.

According to witnesses Gallo pulled a revolver, flipped over a table, and quickly returned fire.

Gallo was hit in the back, elbow, and buttock, and Gallo's bodyguard Peter "Pete the Greek" Diapoulas was shot once in the buttocks as he dove for cover.

After the gunman fled Gallo staggered through the front door of the restaurant and collapsed just outside on Mulberry Street.

Some say he was trying to draw the gunfire away from his family and friends. Others say he was trying to flee.

When police arrived, the badly wounded Gallo was placed in a squad car and rushed to the nearest hospital where he died.

He was taken in a police car to Beekman-Downtown Hospital, just about ten minutes south of the restaurant where he died in the emergency department.

The police released to the press that three Italian men stormed the restaurant with guns blazing and killed Gallo.

The NYPD knew that was not the truth and that it was a large lone gunman who killed Gallo and he certainly wasn't Italian.

They did this to prevent people from coming forward with false information on the case.

Years later, lead Gallo case detective Joe Coffey confirmed that the NYPD would hang up on phone callers who would try to sell the police information on the "three killers" who claimed to have killed Gallo as an integrity test.

A differing account of the murder was offered by hitman and union activist Frank Sheeran, who claimed that he was the lone triggerman in the Gallo hit.

Also, an eyewitness from the night of the shooting has confirmed that Frank Sheeran was the man who killed Gallo.

In the book, *I Heard You Paint Houses,* Frank Sheeran said that killing a man in front of his own family was against the mafia's rules, but that it was no more than what Gallo had reportedly ordered done to Joe Colombo a year earlier: "Right there in front of his family; they turned the man into a vegetable. So that's the way it was going to be for Crazy Joey."

Gallo's funeral was held on April 11th, his sister Carmella declared over his open coffin that "the streets are going to run red with blood, Joey!"

Joe Gallo's murder brought a lot of heat to the Colombo family from the FBI and the family's consigliere, Joseph Yacovelli decided to go into hiding.

The Colombo family, led by the imprisoned Persico, was plunged into a second civil war which lasted for several years until a 1974 agreement allowed Albert Gallo and his remaining crew to join the Genovese crime family.

It was rumored that Joe Gallo was spotted by Colombo associate Joseph Luparelli who promptly left the restaurant for a Colombo hangout a few blocks away from where he recruited Colombo associates Philip Gambino, Carmine DiBiase, and two other men to kill Gallo.

Shortly after Gallo's murder, Luparelli fled to California, where he contacted the FBI and reached a deal to become a government witness.

Many believe that he did this because he was falsely accused of being associated with Gallo's murder and knew that the FBI would be able to protect him from any of Joe Gallo's loyalists.

It was reported that Luparelli then implicated the four gunmen in the Gallo murder.

However, the police could not bring charges against them; as there was no corroborating evidence to support this story.

After the FBI spoke to the NYPD Luparelli was deemed an unreliable witness. No one was ever charged in the murder of Joe Gallo.

By 1972 Roy DeMeo's crew member Chris Rosenberg had most of his friends stealing cars for him. Two of these friends were Joseph Testa and Anthony Senter who would come to be known as, "the Gemini twins".

Rosenberg would introduce the twins to DeMeo and become members of Roy DeMeo's crew.

Testa and Senter, who were both full-blooded Italians, had known Rosenberg since their teenage years.

After John Gotti's release from prison in 1972, he was put on the payroll of Victoria's stepfather's construction company.

Shortly after his release Victoria was pregnant with the couple's last child, another son whom they named Peter.

Even though he had a job at his father-in-laws' company, Gotti still returned to the Bergin club which by now only consisted mainly of associates.

The Mafia's made members had grown old and a Mafia edict in 1957 had prevented the making of any new ones.

By late April 1972, Carmine Fatico used Gotti to oversee the day-to-day activities when he was indicted for loansharking and stopped frequenting the Bergin club.

At the age of 31, John Gotti became the acting capo of Carmine Fatico's Bergin crew, with the blessing of Neil Dellacroce.

Several members had already become confidential informants for the FBI by the time Gotti gained control of the Bergin crew.

They included Gotti's friends, Willie Boy Johnson who was identified by the FBI as "Source Wahoo" and William Battista.

On May 2, 1972, Aniello Dellacroce was indicted on federal tax evasion charges for failing to pay federal income tax on 22,500 stock shares worth $112,500.

The Yankee Plastics Company of New York gave Dellacroce the stocks in return for labor peace.

In May 1972 Carlo Gambino's nephew, Giuseppe "Joseph" Gambino's son Manny Gambino was kidnapped and his wife, Diane, received a letter demanding $350,000 for the return of her husband.

Only $31,500 of the $350,000 ransom was paid.

The initial attempt by the Gambino family to deliver the ransom failed when went to the wrong restaurant in New Jersey to make the ransom drop.

A few days later, an attorney for the Gambinos called and asked the FBI to get involved in finding Manny.

After receiving the new ransom orders from the kidnappers, Manny's brother Tommy Gambino was told where to drive to pick up the next set of instructions.

An FBI agent and a business partner of Tommy Gambino went with Gambino.

They were told to cross over the George Washington Bridge into New Jersey and to park next to a set of payphones at a gas station on the Palisades Parkway in Fort Lee, New Jersey.

The kidnappers called the payphone with instructions for the money to be thrown over a railing about a mile down the road on the Palisades Interstate Parkway.

After making the ransom drop, the group went back to the Gambino home only to be disappointed when Manny was not returned as promised.

Over the next few months, the FBI continued investigating Manny Gambino's disappearance.

During their investigation, they had learned that Manny had fallen in love with a young woman named Nancy Masone.

He wanted to leave his family because the girl refused to have anything more to do with him unless he left his wife.

The FBI wasn't sure as to what degree this affair played on Manny's disappearance.

The FBI also discovered that Manny had financial problems, most likely due to trying to maintain two households; one with his wife, the other with his girlfriend.

It was common practice for the local police to go around at night and write down the license numbers of all the vehicles that were parked in the area where the ransom money was dropped off.

And they come up with a license plate that was on a rental van that was rented to 37-year old, Henry Robert Sentner.

The van was driven by John Kilcullen, a 42-year-old bartender who had been sent to Fort Lee, N.J., to pick up the ransom money that was paid by the Gambino family.

The FBI soon discovered that Henry Sentner owed Manny a large sum of money.

They would bring him into the city and start talking to him in hopes that he would provide any information as to what had happened to Manny.

Unfortunately, Henry Sentner was not willing to talk.

All changed once Manny's car was located parked at the Newark Airport parking lot on June 2, 1972.

Unfortunately, Manny was still nowhere to be found.

All the glass is taken off Gambino's vehicle and sent to the FBI's Washington crime lab to be fingerprinted.

On the driver's side window, the F.B.I found Henry Sentner's thumbprint inside the window quite a distance from the edge.

When questioned by the FBI, Sentner claimed that the kidnapping began as a hoax. Manny worked out the scenario with Sentner, a friend of Sentner's, and two others.

The FBI charged him and his accomplice, John E. Kilcullen, on December 4, 1972, with kidnapping Gambino and demanding a ransom from his family. Without a body, the FBI would not be able to bring murder charges against the two men.

The FBI started to put pressure on Gambino by parking a van marked "Organized Crime Control Bureau" outside Gambino's home at 2230 Ocean Parkway in Brooklyn, in December 1972.

The FBI monitored events inside the house using lip-readers, audio-surveillance equipment, cameras, and including microphones and wire-taps that were planted in Gambino's home.

The FBI was hoping to connect Carlo Gambino to organized crime.

Even with the FBI sitting just outside of his home, Gambino continued to conduct business using a combination of silent gestures and coded language.

According to FBI officials they once recorded a meeting between Gambino, Aniello Dellacroce, and Joseph Biondo, where Biondo said only, "Frog legs," and Gambino simply responded with a nod.

In late January 1973, seven months after Manny Gambino's car is discovered, Henry Sentner finally admits to killing Gambino.

He tells the FBI that Manny had threatened him because he owed Gambino a $76,000 in gambling debts.

He still maintained the story that the kidnapping was a hoax.

However, midway through the plot, Sentner and his men began to have their doubts. They could see that if things went sour Manny would give them up to the law.

He told the FBI that there was an argument between Manny and Sentner and his men inside Manny's Cadillac and Sentner said that he took out a 22 caliber gun, which he had in his pocket, placed it behind Manny's left ear, and shot and killed him.

At this point, the FBI had a confession but still did not have a body.

And to the FBI agent's amazement, Sentner takes them to Colts Neck, N. J., to where he buried Manny's body just days after killing him.

The FBI exhumed the partly decomposed body of Emanuel Manny Gambino, near the Earle Naval Ammunition Depot in Colts Neck.

Manny's body was found on January 26, 1973, wrapped in a blanket in a four-foot-deep grave.

During the trial, Kilcullen pleads guilty to extortion in the kidnapping of Gambino.

Henry Sentner admitted on the stand that he shot and killed Gambino after a quarrel about gambling debts. However, he now claimed that it was an accidental shooting.

On June 1, 1973, Henry Sentner pleaded guilty to manslaughter and was sentenced to fifteen years in prison.

Even though Carlo Gambino had managed to rise to the top of the American Mafia by keeping a low profile and managing his businesses quietly, he was under watch by the FBI.

He had dealt with family members being kidnappings and death and was growing increasingly upset by the actions of his own underboss Neil Dellacroce who was convicted of the tax evasion charges from his May 1972 indictment and sentenced to five years in prison and fined $15,000 In March 1973.

Thomas "Tommy Ryan" Eboli continued as the "front boss" of the Genovese family for two years before he wanted to be the real head of the Genovese family.

To further his advancement in the Genovese family, Eboli borrowed $4 million from the Carlo Gambino to fund a new drug trafficking operation.

Unfortunately for Eboli, law enforcement soon shut down his drug racket and arrested most of his crew.

Carlo Gambino and his underboss Paul Castellano allegedly came to Eboli to get their $4 million back, but he did not have it.

Gambino then allegedly ordered Eboli's murder due to a lack of payment. However, it is believed that Gambino wanted to replace Eboli with Gambino ally Frank "Funzi" Tieri and that Gambino used the drug trafficking operation to set up Eboli.

Around 1:00 A.M on July 16, 1972, Eboli left his girlfriend's apartment in Crown Heights, Brooklyn, and walked to his chauffeured Cadillac.

An unidentified gunman in a passing truck shot him five times As Eboli sat in the parked car.

Eboli was hit in the head and neck and died instantly.

Frank "Funzi" Tieri would replace Eboli as front boss shortly after his murder.

However, it is widely believed that Tieri was merely a front for the Genovese's' actual boss Philip "Benny Squint" Lombardo.

The police never discovered who killed him.

With Carmine Fatico now keeping a low profile and Neil Dellacroce in prison, John Gotti, who was running the Bergin crew but still in the status of an associate, began making regular visits to Carlo Gambino.

On the outside it seemed as though Gotti was happy with his position in the Gambino family, however, years later, he would be overheard on an FBI bug calling Carlo Gambino a "rat mother fucker" and a "back door mother fucker" for never promoting him.

Carlo Gambino was now facing increased pressure and began to reorganize the Gambino crime family.

His first order of business was to restructure the top positions within the family and put in place a second underboss below him.

Neil Dellacroce, his longtime underboss and next in line for the title of "Boss" was already established having several men working under him and knew how to handle the up-and-coming Mafioso and the dirty side of the business.

However, Gambino promoted his brother-in-law Paul Castellano as the family's second underboss.

Castellano was put in charge of all the white-collar crimes through Brooklyn due to his businessman attitude.

Gambino's decision to create a second underboss effectively split the family down the middle, one side being led by Neil Dellacroce and the other by Paul Castellano.

This restructuring also created confusion in the FBI in the mid-1970s as to who the official underboss in the Gambino Crime Family was.

Frank Costello lived out his retirement in peace, remaining an influential figure in the New York Mafia.

Many say that Costello "had one foot in the underworld, one foot in the legitimate world".

And as a result, he becomes known as the "Prime Minister of the Underworld."

In early February 1973, Frank Costello suffered a heart attack at his Manhattan home.

He was rushed to Doctors Hospital in Manhattan, where he died on February 18.

Costello's memorial service at a Manhattan funeral home was attended by a few dozen relatives, friends, and law enforcement agents.

Galante allegedly ordered the bombing of the doors to Costello's mausoleum in St. Michael's Cemetery in East Elmhurst, Queens in 1974, after he was released from prison.

Carlo Gambino wanted revenge for his nephew's killing, and the family assembled a list of likely suspects, one of them was James McBratney, who had a history of kidnapping wiseguys for profit.

However, as it turns out McBratney had nothing to do with the kidnapping or death of Gambino.

On the advice of his underboss, Aniello Dellacroce, Carlo Gambino hired John Gotti who was loyal to Dellacroce and was becoming a known figure in the underworld of the Gambino family and longtime Gambino family associate Angelo Ruggiero, to deal with McBratney.

Gotti met with Carlo Gambino, Aniello Dellacroce, consigliere Joseph Armone and Gambino's top capo régime, Paul Castellano.

Castellano also wanted Gambino family soldier Ralph "Ralphie Wigs" Galione to assist Gotti and Ruggiero in carrying out the murder.

McBratney was shot three times at close range by Galione, after he had overpowered Ruggiero and Gotti, on the night of May 22, 1973, at Snoope's Bar & Grill in Staten Island.

In July, Angelo Ruggiero and Ralph Galione were identified from police photos by a barmaid and a customer from the bar, and the men were quickly apprehended.

However, Gotti had not been identified.

John Gotti was overheard by Willie Boy Johnson a month later bragging about the killing.

Johnson passed the information along to his FBI handlers. The FBI reported their information to the New York Police Department, which quickly showed Gotti's mug shot to the witnesses.

John Gotti was positively identified by the witnesses and on October 17, was indicted by a grand jury for murder.

Gotti immediately went into hiding.

In July 1973, at the age of 30, Roy DeMeo committed his first murder when he killed Paul Rothenberg.

DeMeo and Gaggi had forced themselves into the business as silent partners in a porn business with Rothenberg.

Rothenberg was arrested and DeMeo believed he would fold under pressure and tell the police how DeMeo and Gaggi had forcefully taken over his porn business.

Once Rothenberg was released on bail awaiting trial, DeMeo summoned him to a meeting at a local diner on Long Island on July 29th, and then beat him and shot and killed him in a nearby alley.

Law enforcement in Sullivan County said that Michael Zaffarano, a Brooklyn restaurant operator who was said to have been a bodyguard to Joseph Bonanno, was being sought for questioning in the Rothenberg killing.

John Gotti managed to evade capture for a year and was arrested on June 3, 1974.

The information as to Gotti's whereabouts had been supplied by Willie Boy Johnson, who was paid $600 by the FBI for his betrayal.

Victoria Gotti's parents provided the collateral for their son-in-law's release on a $150,000 bail.

As soon as Gotti was released, he returned to the Bergin to attend to the overseeing of his crew.

On December 21, 1973, before and Galione and Ruggiero could be tried for the McBratney killing, Ralph "Ralphie Wigs" Galione was murdered in Brooklyn.

When the state brought its case against Angelo Ruggiero the defense produced witnesses who testified that he was in New Jersey the night of the murder. The trial ended in a hung jury.

With Ralph "Ralphie Wigs" Galione now dead, Gotti and Ruggiero were to be tried together in a second trial.

Carlo Gambino now had his sights set on Henry Sentner who was sitting in the Federal House of Detention.

By 1974, Chris Rosenberg began selling drugs, again backed by Roy DeMeo.

Rosenberg acquired Quaaludes through a pharmacist connection, as well as cocaine, which at the time could be prescribed for medical purposes.

It was through this pharmacist, Rosenberg and the rest of the DeMeo crew met 22-year-old Romanian immigrant and body shop owner Andrei Katz.

When Andrei was arrested due to a stolen vehicle he blamed Rosenberg for his predicament because he purchased the stolen vehicle from Rosenberg.

When word got back to Rosenberg that Katz was placing the blame on him, Katz was pulled from his vehicle and severely beaten by two men and put in the hospital.

Andrei claimed the two men who attacked him were Testa and Senter.

While still in the hospital recovering from his injuries, Andrei swore that he would get revenge on Rosenberg and the others.

The revenge finally came on November 13, 1974, when Rosenberg opened his garage door and was shot three times.

Rosenberg survived the shooting, one bullet hitting him in the lower jaw, another hit his right arm and a third that was aimed for his chest merely glanced off. Rosenberg survived what should have been a fatal shooting.

Rosenberg's jaw was left disfigured from the bullet wound and had to wear a beard to mask the scars that resulted from this attack.

Rosenberg's would-be assassin was never identified, but it was assumed by Rosenberg and the rest of the DeMeo Crew to be Katz.

While Rosenberg was still in the hospital recovering from his wounds, DeMeo met with his crew and it was decided that Andrei Katz had to be murdered and started to put a plan together.

Katz knew that his life was now in danger and knew that his only option to save his life was to turn to the Brooklyn District Attorney's Office.

On November 22, 1974, while John Gotti and Angelo Ruggiero awaited trial, Henry Sentner, was given cocoa laced with strychnine in a cell he shared with seven other men in the Federal House of Detention on West Street.

He was rushed to St. Vincent's Hospital emergency room, where they pumped his stomach and saved his life.

Attorney Roy M. Cohn was hired by Carlo Gambino to represent John Gotti and Angelo Ruggiero. Cohn was a well-known attorney; Cohn handled many high-profile clients in New York, including Neil Dellacroce.

Although both defendants had been indicted on murder charges and identified by witnesses, knowing that the earlier trial ended in a hung jury, Cohn figured that the prosecution might be willing to make a deal.

Cohn negotiated a remarkable deal with the Staten Island district attorney's office.

On August 8, 1975, Gotti and Ruggiero plead guilty to a reduced charge of attempted manslaughter.

The plea bargain gets Gotti four years in prison (he would only serve two) and sent to the Green Haven Correctional Facility located 80 miles north of Queens.

While in the Green Haven Correctional Facility, Gotti bribed the guards to take him from the prison in upstate New York for visits to his new home in Howard Beach, Queens.

They also took him to restaurants in New York City, where he met with friends.

Also in the Green Haven Correctional Facility with Gotti was Willie Boy Johnson, who, despite his FBI informant status, had been convicted on an armed robbery charge and was serving a ten-year sentence.

In his final years, Carlo Gambino kept a low profile both from the public and law enforcement.

In late 1975, after Carlo Gambino became ill, Gambino had to choose who he would appoint as his successor after his departure. He chose to give control of the family not to the obvious choice, longtime underboss Aniello "Mr. Neil" Dellacroce, but to his cousin, brother-in-law, and underboss, Paul Castellano after he dies or steps down from the position of the family leader.

Dellacroce, at the time, was still in prison for tax evasion and was unable to contest Castellano's succession.

Some believe that another decisive factor in Carlo's choice was that Castellano was of Sicilian descent (Dellacroce was not).

Allies of Neil Dellacroce were unhappy about Gambino's decision, but Dellacroce himself kept his men in line, and in a gesture of goodwill, Castellano allowed Neil Dellacroce to remain as the Gambino family's underboss.

While Dellacroce was serving his prison sentence, James "Jimmy Brown" Failla was put into the position of acting Underboss until Dellacroce was released from prison in 1975.

As the acting boss, Castellano took over several of the family's non-legitimate businesses and converted them into legal enterprises.

Castellano started a company named Dial Meat Purveyors Inc. formerly known as Blue Ribbon Meats, that supplied over 300 butchers in New York, Dial Meat Purveyors, Inc. helped poultry magnate Frank Perdue distribute his chickens in supermarket chains.

He also had a successful butcher shop franchise that he owned with his sons Phillip and Joseph, called "Meat Palace".

Castellano not only involved his sons in the meat business. In the early 70s, he hired his daughter Constance's husband Frank Amato as a butcher at Meat Palace.

Frank Amato was a butcher and a fellow criminal associate of Danny Grillo, who was part of Roy DeMeo's crew that robbed transport trucks coming in and out of J.F.K. Airport.

Soon after Amato married Constance, Castellano set him up in a legitimate Italian ice distribution business.

Castellano soon discovered that Amato did not share the same keen business sense as Castellano and the Italian ice distribution business soon failed. Paul decided that being a butcher would be more in line with Amato's talents.

Castellano's sons, Phillip and Joseph, managed the meat butchering businesses. There is no evidence that Castellano promoted or wanted to induct his son-in-law as a "made man" into the Gambino crime family.

Although he was married to Paul's daughter, Frank had been witnessed making sexual advances and having had brief sexual encounters with the female employees who worked with him at the Meat Palace.

Castellano had the female employee fired and Amato transferred to Dial Meat Purveyors to work for his brother-in-law, Paul Castellano Jr.

After a few months of working at Dial Poultry, Amato was caught again having an affair with a co-worker.

Paul Castellano became enraged when he learned of Amato's affair and ordered Amato to move out of Castellano's mansion and fired him from Dial Poultry.

After being fired, Amato went to work with the help of cousins-in-law Thomas and Joseph Gambino, the sons of Carlo Gambino, at a clothing store in Queens.

When Constance learned of Amato's numerous affairs she filed for divorce.

In 1973 Constance was granted the divorce from Frank Amato on grounds of spousal abuse and infidelity.

After the divorce, Constance moved to Florida and lived in her father's condominium to deal with her emotional distress.

Constance would eventually start dating a Gambino associate named Vito Borelli.

In the early 1970s, Castellano also started to make a lot of money from the concrete business around New York City. His son Philip was the president of Scara-Mix Concrete.

Scara-Mix Concrete supplied Staten Island with construction concrete. Castellano also formed the Concrete Club, a group of mob families that divided revenue from New York developers.

No one could pour concrete for a project worth more than $2 million without the approval from the Concrete Club.

Finally, Castellano supervised Gambino control of Teamsters Union Local Chapter 282, which provided workers to pour concrete at all major building projects in New York and Long Island.

At the time New York City was the most expensive place to build a building.

Castellano's focus was business, by turning the family away from the illegitimate business such as drug trafficking, towards the comparatively safer practices of money laundering and extortion.

In January 1975, the man who organized the shooting of Chris Rosenberg, Andrei Katz, went to the Brooklyn District Attorney's Office and voluntarily provided them information that DeMeo's crew was involved in auto theft after an altercation with DeMeo.

DeMeo learned about the meeting in January immediately after it happened from an Auto Crimes detective that DeMeo had on his payroll.

DeMeo immediately ordered his associate Henry Borelli, Also known as "Dirty Harry", to contact one of his female acquaintances about being used as bait to lure Katz to his death.

In May, Katz testified before a Brooklyn grand jury and told them what he knew about the DeMeo crew's auto theft activities.

Due to the back and forth violence that had already occurred between Katz and Rosenberg, Henry Borelli, who had become involved with the crew shortly after Rosenberg was shot, suggested that he use a woman friend of his to lure Katz to a location where he could be dealt with discreetly.

On Friday, June 13, 1975, the female friend of Borelli's successfully lures Katz to her apartment complex for what he thought was a date.

When they arrived at the woman's apartment complex Katz was abducted by Chris, Henry Borelli, Joseph Testa, and Anthony Senter. He was then taken to the meat department of a supermarket, where Roy DeMeo was waiting.

When the group arrived at the supermarket, Katz was stabbed multiple times in the heart with a butcher knife, presumably by Rosenberg in revenge for the shooting the previous year.

After Katz was dead, he was then stabbed over a dozen more times in the back, presumably done by Rosenberg.

Katz's head was then crushed in a compactor used for cardboard after being decapitated, also presumably done by Rosenberg.

The body parts were then thrown into the supermarket's dumpster, where they were discovered two days later by a homeless man looking for food in the dumpster.

The police reported to the press that a grisly, brutal killing had occurred, but that was the extent of the information given.

Because of the damage done to the remains, dental records had to be used to positively identify the victim. It took the police two days to identify the victim as Andrei Katz.

A short time later, the woman who was used in luring Katz to his death confessed to the police about her role in the killing.

She told the police that Joseph Testa and Henry Borelli were responsible for the killing and she was unable to identify Rosenberg.

Joseph Testa and Henry Borelli were soon arrested and spent months in jail while waiting for trial.

The two men stood trial in January 1976 and were acquitted.

The nephew of Anthony Gaggi, Dominick Montiglio, later testified that he learned of the Katz murder from Rosenberg shortly after it happened.

He also testified that Rosenberg claimed Katz's murder had driven DeMeo and his crew to decide that any future murders would be dealt with in a similar manner of dismemberment to make the victim disappear.

After the murder of Andrei Katz, DeMeo and his crew began committing sanctioned hits for the mafia.

They would lure their targets to the Gemini Club where they would be lured into the back of the club at which point someone, usually DeMeo, would shoot them and quickly wrap a towel around their head to prevent blood from spreading across the floor.

Then they would stab the person in the heart to lessen the flow of blood from the gunshot wound in the victim's head.

They would then hang the victim from a shower rod in the bathtub and bleed them dry, and then cut their body into pieces and dispose of it in several different locations around the city.

In the 1990's it was learned the DeMeo crew was responsible for over two hundred murders; more than Anastasia's Murder Inc.

In 1975, Castellano allegedly ordered the murder of Vito Borelli, his daughter Constance's boyfriend.

Castellano met twice with businessman Frank Perdue, the owner and commercial spokesman for the poultry company Perdue Farms.

Perdue wanted Castellano's help in thwarting a unionization drive at a Perdue facility in Virginia. However, according to Perdue, the two men talked but never agreed to anything.

Castellano heard that Borelli had compared him to Frank Perdue.

Because of Perdue's balding, elderly appearance, and his comically awkward mannerisms Castellano considered this an insult.

Borelli was murdered the following year in 1976, and his body was dismembered and his remains have never been recovered.

After John Gotti died in 2002, he was identified as the killer of Vito Borelli by Joseph "Big Joey" Massino who served as the boss of the Bonanno crime family from 1991 to 2004.

In 2011, Massino became the first boss to turn state's evidence.

Many people place the murder of Borelli in 1980.

However, the date of 1976 is supported by the filling of court documents in the case against Salvatore Vitale.

Case 1:02-cr-00307-NGG

UNITED STATES DISTRICT COURT EASTERN DISTRICT OF NEW YORK

UNITED STATES OF AMERICA

- against -

SALVATORE VITALE

Case 1:02-cr-00307-NGG Document 989 Filed 10/26/10 Page 25 of 128

Murder of Vito Borelli (1976)

Salvatore Vitale provided information regarding the murder of Vito Borelli in this court case.

He told the court that individuals associated with both the Bonanno and Gambino family killed Borelli in the mid-1970s, based on an order from Castellano.

At the time a Bonanno associate provided a van for Joseph Massino before Borelli's murder. Vitale also was involved in the subsequent disposal of Borelli's body.

He also stated that Joseph Massino, John Gotti, Angelo Ruggerio, Frank DeCiccio, Dominick Napolitano, and Anthony Rabito were involved in Vito Borelli's murder.

Vitale was likely the first cooperating witness to provide information relating to the Borelli murder.

In July 1975, Castellano was indicted for loan sharking and tax evasion.

However, the state's case against him fell apart when their main witness refused to testify, allegedly under pressure from the defense.

After leading the Gambino crime family for 20 years and The Commission for more than 15, 74-year-old Carlo Gambino died of a heart attack in the early morning hours of Friday, October 15, 1976, while watching television at his home.

Paul Castellano was now completely in charge of the Gambino crime family.

His funeral was said to have been attended by over 2,000 people, including police officers, judges, and politicians.

His funeral mass was held on Monday, October 18, at the Church of Our Lady of Grace in Brooklyn.

The funeral mass at the church was attended by only 350 people, including many neighbors and friends who had remained after the end of the earlier funeral service.

The funeral cortege contained 13 limousines, a dozen or so private cars, and a single flower car with the usual array of roses, carnations, and chrysanthemums.

Carlo Gambino was entombed within his family's private room in the Cloister building of Saint John Cemetery in Queens.

He is interred beside his wife Catherine, who had died in 1971, and was survived by three sons Thomas, Joseph, and Carlo and one daughter Phyllis Sinatra.

On Thanksgiving Day in 1976, Neil Dellacroce was released from prison.

In December, the upper echelon of the Gambino Mafia Family met at the home of capo Anthony "Nino" Gaggi to officially name a new boss.

Paul Castellano's succession to the role of the Gambino Family Boss was then confirmed, with Neil Dellacroce present.

Joseph N. Gallo continued as consigliere of the Gambino Crime Family.

Joseph N. Gallo was not related to Joe Gallo of the Colombo crime family.

Gallo served as consigliere of the Gambino crime family under three different bosses; Carlo Gambino, Paul Castellano, and John Gotti.

While Neil Dellacroce accepted Castellano's succession to the position of Boss, the move split the Gambino family into two rival factions.

Neil Dellacroce, true to his promise to Carlo Gambino announced to all of his allies that Paul Castellano was now the boss of the family and that they should stand behind him as one.

Neil remained as underboss of the family and was given several crews to oversee, including the Bergin crew of Carmine Fatico.

Castellano would continue to run all of the white-collar businesses while Dellacroce continues to handle all of the traditional Mafia activities.

Gaggi was elevated to the position of capo régime, taking over the crew previously headed by Castellano.

Gaggi's promotion was beneficial for Roy DeMeo, whose mentor was now even closer to the Gambino family leadership.

Another advantage was that with Gambino deceased, new associates would be eligible for membership in the family.

However, Paul did not immediately "open the books" for new memberships, opting instead to only promote existing members.

Castellano opposed the idea of Roy DeMeo becoming a made man in the family.

Many believe that this was because Castellano involved himself in white-collar crime and looked down on street-level members such as DeMeo.

Others believe that Castellano felt DeMeo was uncontrollable.

However, no matter how he felt about DeMeo, Castellano did retain a degree of muscle to keep Dellacroce's allies in check, including the crew run by Gaggi and DeMeo.

While Castellano was still in charge, most of the family affairs were run and controlled unofficially by a four-man ruling panel which included Thomas "Tommy" Gambino, bodyguard and later Underboss Thomas "Tommy" Bilotti, and Daniel "Danny" Marino and James "Jimmy Brown" Failla

These men were all rivals of John Gotti.

In May of 1977, the bridge between The Gambinos and the Irish Mob the Westies started to be built with the murder of a loan shark named Michael "Mickey" Spillane.

Though the Italian Mafia dominated organized crime in New York City, the Irish Mob had long operated in an area bordered by 34th Street to the south, 59th Street to the north, Eighth Avenue to the east, and the Hudson River to the west known as Hell's Kitchen.

The Italians allowed Mickey Spillane to operate on the West Side as long as they got their cut from his loan shark business.

Spillane wasn't happy with the fact that he had to pay a cut of his money to the mafia and in return, he would kidnap members of the Italian Mafia and hold them for ransom.

And just like Castellano, he was against the sale of drugs in his neighborhood and wouldn't allow it.

In 1966 a young criminal named Jimmy Coonan attempted to take the neighborhood from Spillane.

Coonan swore to restore his father's honor and seek revenge against Spillane after he had kidnapped and pistol-whipped Coonan's father who was an accountant not involved in any illegal criminal activity.

Coonan purchased a machine gun and fired at Spillane and his associates from the top of a Hell's Kitchen tenement building. Coonan failed to murder Spillane and his followers.

Ultimately, Coonan was sent to prison in 1967. Coonan was released from prison in late 1971 and continued with his war with Mickey Spillane.

Unfortunately for Spillane, his problems didn't end with Jimmy Coonan.

Spillane soon had an issue with the Genovese crime family, as Tony Salerno sought control over the soon to be built Jacob K. Javits Convention Center.

The Convention Center was located on West 34th Street in Hell's Kitchen.

Mickey Spillane stood his ground against the takeover by the Italians.

And in return the Genovese crime family headed by Salerno responded by assassinating three of Spillane's chief lieutenants; Tom Devaney, "the Butcher" Edward Cummiskey, and "the Greek" Tom Kapatos.

Cummiskey had recently switched sides to the Coonan camp, but Salerno was not aware of the switch. Devaney and Cummiskey were murdered in late 1976, and Kapatos was killed in January 1977.

By the mid-1977 Spillane had to move his family out of Hell's Kitchen to Woodside, Queens, for their safety.

Anthony Salerno reached an agreement with Jimmy Coonan. If Coonan became boss, Salerno would run the construction site and give Coonan a portion of the proceeds.

With Spillane now out of Hell's Kitchen, his control of the rackets in Hell's Kitchen began to deteriorate; Coonan became the neighborhood's new boss, although some still viewed Spillane as boss.

Coonan felt that Mickey Spillane still had to die.

As Spillane's issues were growing with Coonan, Coonan was having issues himself with yet another loan shark named Charles "Ruby" Stein.

Stein was known as the "loan shark to the stars".

He was a close associate of Genovese family boss "Fat Tony" Anthony Salerno and Nicholas "Jiggs" Forlano, a Colombo crime family capo.

Stein was allegedly one of the biggest loan sharks in New York City during the 1960s and '70s and had around a million dollars out on the streets earning him and his partner's exorbitant interest rates.

He also ran gambling clubs on the Upper West Side of Manhattan.

After Coonan's release from prison in 1971, Stein hired him as his bodyguard, loaning him money to run his own loan shark business and using him on collections.

Many of the members of The Westies owed large amounts of money to Stein and Coonan. They owed Stein as much as $50,000 and were looking to escape these obligations which they couldn't pay.

On May 5, 1977, Stein was lured to the 596 Club in Manhattan, which was owned by a member of the Westies.

In November 1987, Westies gang member, William "Billy" Beattie stated in court that after Stein entered the bar the door was locked and the curtains were quickly closed.

Danny Grillo, who was a member of Roy DeMeo's crew who was also associated with Coonan, then came out from the kitchen and shot Ruby in the chest.

Grillo had met Coonan while in prison during the early 1970s. After their release, both men stayed in contact.

Danny Grillo was recruited by DeMeo into his crew when he was released from prison just two years earlier.

Grillo had known DeMeo through work in the Mafia-connected Canarsie junkyards. Grillo soon became involved in the hijacking of truck cargoes with DeMeo to and from J.F.K Airport in Brooklyn.

After the shooting Coonan embraced Grillo and ordered the others to shoot into Stein's corpse.

Coonan tore off the dead man's shoes and socks and $1,000 fell out. The killers then split the money on the bar.

Stein's body was placed on plastic sheets and dragged to the rear of the bar, where it was cut up.

Stein's body parts were bagged and then dumped in the Hudson River.

However, Coonan had forgotten to puncture the lungs and Stein's torso washed ashore and was found several weeks later on Jamaica Bay.

Stein's murder caused an investigation from the Mafia, especially Tony Salerno, and in particular, they wanted to know what happened to Stein's black book, which had all of the names and numbers of who owed money.

Some believe that Stein was killed so Coonan and his gang could take Stein's black book and collect the debts themselves.

The details of Stein's murder were later revealed when Westies member Mickey Featherstone also turned informant and stood trial for the murder and was found not guilty.

Word soon got around that Coonan was now collecting on Steins' loans. Paul Castellano considered killing Coonan and Featherstone for the offense, but DeMeo who was ever the businessman saw a golden opportunity to make a move in his favor.

Instead of killing Coonan and Featherstone, DeMeo insisted that a deal could be made.

Roy DeMeo used a move to gain Coonans' trust which made the whole deal possible.

Danny Grillo helped DeMeo form an alliance with Coonan who wanted to oust The Westies' current leader Michael 'Mickey' Spillane but needed money to fund a rebellion.

After Grillo told DeMeo about Coonan's predicament, DeMeo decided to help Coonan.

Roy DeMeo's crew and the Coonan faction were soon committing crimes together and splitting the profits.

DeMeo also loaned Coonan large sums of money to build a loan shark racket.

On May 13, just eight days after Stein's murder in Manhattan, Mickey Spillane was killed outside his apartment in Woodside, Queens.

Over the years many authors have written that the murder of Stein happened after the murder of Spillane.

Unfortunately, there is no rock-solid proof that Stein was killed after Spillane. And because Stein's body was discovered weeks after the actual killing, we can only base our information on court records from the testimony that was made years later.

For DeMeo, it was a smart and political move that served another purpose. By killing Spillane, nobody was standing between the Italian Mafia and the profits from the big construction job of the Jacob Javits Convention Center. Roy had killed two birds with one stone.

DeMeo then persuaded Gaggi to consider a partnership with the Westies.

Gaggi went to Castellano with this information and they started to work out a plan to meet with Coonan to create a partnership between the two criminal organizations.

In the summer of 1977 Castellano reluctantly agreed to "open the books" and officially make DeMeo a "made" member of the Gambino crime family.

Gaggi supported this move after DeMeo arbitrated an agreement with the Westies gang who was feuding with the Gambinos to sit down and meet with the Gambino leadership.

Angelo Ruggiero (paroled earlier than John) and John's brother Gene Gotti (who acted as crew boss in his brother's absence), were also both officially made in the Gambino crime family.

According to an informant, the Gambino Family planned another induction ceremony for later that year upon John Gotti's release from the Green Haven Correctional Facility.

Castellano put DeMeo in charge of handling all family business with the Westies. He was also ordered to get permission before committing any murders and to avoid drug dealing.

DeMeo's crew, however, continued to sell large amounts of cocaine, marijuana, and pills.

DeMeo and his crew also continued to commit unsanctioned killings.

One such killing was the 1977 double homicide of Johnathan Quinn, a car thief suspected of cooperating with law enforcement, and Cherie Golden, Quinn's 19-year-old girlfriend at the time.

When DeMeo found out that Quinn, who was a friend of Nino Gaggi, became a government informant he called him in for a sit-down at their hangout in Brooklyn.

Quinn came with his girlfriend. Cherie stayed in the car while Quinn went to meet with DeMeo.

Quinn was shot in the back of the head and killed as soon as he entered the club.

Soon after Quinn was killed, two of DeMeo's men went out and shot and killed Cherie and left her body in the car.

DeMeo's crew dumped the bodies in locations where they would be found to serve as a warning to anyone who may be considering cooperating with the authorities.

Quinn was found in a deserted area of Staten Island, dressed in pajamas

His hands and feet were tied together, a bullet hole in the back of his head.

Cherie's body was found four days later wedged between the floor and dashboard of a car in the Gerritsen Beach section of south Brooklyn.

When the murder of Cherie showed up in the newspapers, Castellano asked Gaggi about the murder.

Gaggi knew that the killing of Cherie would not go over well with Castellano because she was an innocent victim,

So Gaggi chose to lie to Castellano to save DeMeo's life, telling the boss that she was a potential witness too.

Many believe that Gaggi told Paul this lie was Gaggi needed DeMeo to bring him cash and Castellano needed both of them for the same reasons.

John Gotti was released from prison on July 28, 1977, having served less than two years for the murder of McBratney.

He had to have a legitimate job according to the terms of his parole.

So in the summer of 1977, he became a salesman for Arc Plumbing & Heating Corporation.

Years later, when the president of Arc Plumbing & Heating Corporation was asked at a hearing what function Gotti performed for the company, he replied, "What John does is point out locations."

Gotti quickly set his sights on Carmine Fatico's position as head of the Bergin crew. The only problem was that Gotti was still considered an associate and could not officially become the "acting capo" of the crew until he became a made member of the Gambino Family.

By this time Fatico had beaten two loansharking cases, but he and his brother Daniel, along with crewmembers Charles and John Carneglia, had been convicted of hijacking.

Gotti was hoping that Carmine Fatico would receive a lengthy prison sentence, enabling him to move ahead.

However, instead of a lengthy prison sentence, Carmine Fatico received five years probation

This would mean that his reign as capo of the Bergin crew was over because the terms of his probation required that he not associate with known criminals.

Gotti was soon promoted to a Made man in the Gambino ranks. In this second rite, Gotti and eight other men took the Mafia oath of Omerta.

Soon after becoming a Made member of the family, Neil Dellacroce promoted Gotti to the captain of the Bergin crew.

Gotti would go on to become one of Neil Dellacroce's most powerful supporters.

To celebrate Gotti's return from prison, the Bergin crew purchased him a brand new Lincoln Mark IV.

Since Gotti was still on probation at this time, he ordered the Bergin crewmembers to stop loitering in front of the Bergin and to park their cars elsewhere.

He soon found out that, while he was away, there had been a change in the leadership of the Gambino Family and that Paul Castellano was now the Boss.

Occasionally Gotti was to seek Carmine Fatico's advice, but they would never meet at the Bergin.

During the late 1970s and early 1980s, the FBI's informants reported that Gotti lost heavily at gambling and crewmembers were growing concerned because they were unable to make money.

Castellano soon became worried about the ambitions of John Gotti.

Castellano repeatedly made it clear that he would kill anyone who was dealing in narcotics.

Many people believe that he made this ruling knowing that Gotti was doing just that because Paul turned his attention away from the

DeMeo crew and the Cherry Hill Gambinos who were making a very significant amount of money in the drug trade.

The Cherry Hill Gambino's was located in Delran, N.J. and was headed by Carlo Gambino's cousins John and Rosario Gambino.

So, if Paul was against drugs; and hated everyone who was associated with dope. Why allow some of the family crews to deal and others not to?

Many people wonder if it was because they were related to him or because they brought in a lot of money for the Gambino crime family.

And was it because Paul was close with Nino Gaggi as to why he allowed the DeMeo crew to continue in the drug dealing business?

One thing that worried Paul was that if someone was caught dealing drugs and faced decades in prison they may try to make a deal and become informants to avoid prison.

And because of that, maybe Paul allowed only people they trusted and not the low-level soldiers who are more vulnerable and can easily become informants to participate in the drug trade.

Many people feel that it's a hypocrisy situation and he hated the Dellacroce faction and used the rule on drug dealing to eventually try and do away with them.

In February 1978, Castellano invited the Westies leader Coonan and his top lieutenant, Michael Featherstone, to a meeting at the Vets & Friends Social Club next door to Tommasso's restaurant a Brooklyn mob-owned restaurant.

Present at the meeting was Castellano, underboss Aniello Dellacroce, capo Carmine Lombardozzi and capo Nino Gaggi.

Castellano wanted hitmen that law enforcement could not tie directly to the Gambino family. The Westies wanted Gambino protection from the other Cosa Nostra families.

Castellano gave them the following directive:

"You guys got to stop acting like cowboys - acting wild. You're going to be with us now. If anyone is going to get killed, you have to clear it with us."

They agreed to become a *de facto* arm of the Gambino family and share ten percent of Coonan's profits.

In exchange, the Westies would be privy to several lucrative union deals and take on murder contracts for the Gambinos.

With this deal, the Gambinos got a hitman with no direct ties to the Gambino family and the Westies were protected by the Gambinos.

What Castellano didn't know, was that the Westies had several of their own heavily armed men in an apartment close by.

Years later when Michael Featherstone and Coonan's niece Alberta Ann Sachs told a federal jury their version of that meeting they said that, If they didn't hear from them in two hours the heavily armed gang members were supposed to rush to a Gambino club next to the restaurant and kill everybody in the place.

However, the meeting lasted more than the two hours and they began to get worried that any minute the rest of the Westies gang were about to show up and shoot the place up.

Coonan and Featherstone made their way outside to make sure the gang would see them; however, there was no sign of the gang.

Some reports say that the gang members had gotten spooked and decided not to carry out the orders.

While others say that Coonan rushed to the apartment where his Westies gang was waiting and found them drinking whiskey.

When Coonan asked where they had been, he was told that his men had decided to wait a few more minutes and have another whiskey just in case.

No matter what version of the story is factual. The fact is that Paul Castellano came very close to being killed that evening by the Westies gang.

Another prosecution witness testified to the federal jury that he was among those waiting at the apartment and, "if we got the call, we were going to charge out to Brooklyn and shoot up everybody out there."

He also said that a Gambino member warned them not to admit "anything about Ruby's murder or his black book."

In early May 1978, with his health deteriorating rapidly, Colombo was taken to St. Luke's Hospital in Newburgh, suffering from "intra-cerebral problems."

54-year-old Colombo passed away two weeks later on May 22, 1978.

Cardiac arrest was the official cause of death, brought on by his injury seven years earlier.

Also in 1978, Castellano allegedly ordered the murder of Gambino associate Nicholas Scibetta after he insulted a female cousin of Paul Castellano's protégées Frank DeCicco.

DeCicco's crew was one of the most powerful in the Gambino family and was heavily involved in labor racketeering with the International Brotherhood of Teamsters Union Local 282 who delivered concrete and building materials to construction sites in New York City and Long Island.

Since Scibetta was Sammy Gravano's brother-in-law, Castellano asked DeCicco to first notify Gravano that Scibetta was going to be killed.

Gravano was furious when he learned of the plan to kill Scibetta said that he would kill Castellano first.

However, DeCicco managed to calm Gravano down and accept Scibetta's death sentence as the punishment earned by his behavior.

However, Gravano's decision seven years later along with John Gotti to murder Castellano and take over the Gambino family may have been an easy decision to make as he still held bad feelings for Castellano.

Many believe that there was another motive behind the killing of Scibetta. It is believed that part of the motive for the murder was that Scibetta was suspected of being gay.

In 2003, supporters of John Gotti told some of the New York City newspapers that Sammy Gravano was involved in homosexual relationships with several young men.

They said that at least one of which was alleged to have been Nicholas Scibetta.

These accusations are unsubstantiated and have never been proven to the public.

Sammy Gravano later said, *"I was hoping that it would be like he just disappeared. It would be better for his mother and father. They knew he was a crazy kid. Maybe he had met somebody, some group of people, and run off. The bottom line is that I let it happen. That makes me just as guilty. I didn't know the body would be chopped up afterwards. That's not me."*

After Scibetta was killed, his body was dismembered and was never found other than an arm.

Gravano's relationship with Castellano was further strained after an incident at a club Gravano owned.

Gravano arranged to sell the club to a local drug dealer named Frank Fiala, who promised to pay him in gold bullion.

However, before the deal was even closed, Fiala began knocking out the wall of Gravano's office to begin remodeling the club.

When Gravano confronted Fiala, he threatened Gravano with a submachine gun.

Gravano then retreated outside the club and waited for Fiala to leave.

When Fiala walked out of the back door of the building, one of Gravano's men shot him in the head and killed him.

Gravano claims that he then urinated into Fiala's open mouth.

Castellano was upset by this unsanctioned killing, and Gravano was now at risk of being killed himself.

Gravano met with Castellano and managed to talk his way out of it.

Gravano wasn't 100% sure that he made amends with Castellano, so he still called a meeting with his crew to make sure that if it ever became necessary, they would help him kill Castellano.

By 1978, Danny Grillo was suffering from gambling and cocaine addictions and was heavily in debt to Roy DeMeo.

Grillo was constantly borrowing from other loan sharks to avoid missing his payments to DeMeo.

The drugs and financial stress were making Grillo act erratically and both DeMeo and Naggi felt Grillo would soon feel that he had no choice but to run to law enforcement for protection.

They also believed that Grillo would fold under police pressure if he were to be arrested.

In the fall of 1978, Dominick Montiglio, the nephew of Gaggi, risked his own life trying to help Grillo.

Montiglio ripped up $50,000 worth of debt markers that Danny had acquired during a night of gambling at one of the Gambino's illegal card games.

DeMeo confronted Montiglio about the way that Grillo was acting and made statements that made Montiglio believe that Grillo did not have much time left.

On November 14, Grillo received a call at home from Roy DeMeo requesting that he come to a meeting at the Gemini Lounge in Brooklyn.

Before leaving, Grillo told his wife and children goodbye. After he was gone, his wife discovered that he had left his wallet and other personal possessions behind.

Grillo voluntarily went to a meeting that he knew would be his last.

The following day Dominick Montiglio went to the Gemini Lounge in Brooklyn. Seeing crew members outside the entrance, Montiglio asked if they had seen Grillo.

One of the men allegedly smiled and replied, "No one will see Danny no more."

Roy DeMeo confirmed the man's statement, saying that "...if anybody wants to talk to Danny they'll have to talk to him at the Fountain Avenue dump."

DeMeo also told Montiglio that they had parked Grillo's car in the middle of the Manhattan Bridge and left the driver side door open to make it look like a suicide.

DeMeo later learned that Grillo had tried to use Coonan as a front to borrow even more money from DeMeo. According to Mickey Featherstone, DeMeo allegedly remarked, "I wish you would've told me earlier, I would've cut him into littler pieces."

Danny Grillo was the first known occurrence of Roy DeMeo's internal crew discipline.

But he wouldn't be the last.

By 1979, Chris Rosenberg continued his involvement in the drug trade and was Roy DeMeo's second-in-command.

His involvement in the drug trade included importing marijuana from Colombia and dealing in large quantities of cocaine.

In 1979 he visited Florida to set up a cocaine deal with a loan shark customer of Roy DeMeo's named Charles Padnick

It was reported that Padnick had entered the drug business in an attempt to pay off his debts to DeMeo.

Padnick was acquainted with a Cuban man named William Serrano who had connections with a Colombian drug cartel

Padnick told Serrano that a group of Italians in New York were interested in purchasing a large quantity of cocaine.

On March 17, Charles Padnick and William Serrano as well as the cousin and girlfriend of Serrano's Colombian drug connection, flew to New York to complete the drug deal.

Within hours of the group landing, Serrano as well as the cousin and girlfriend of Serrano's Colombian drug connection were shot to death, dismembered, and disposed of by Rosenberg and other members of the DeMeo crew.

Unbeknownst to Rosenberg and DeMeo, Serrano had told one of his Colombian Cartel acquaintances that he would call to let him know that the drug deal had been completed.

When he did not receive the phone call from Serrano, his cousin, or girlfriend that night to ensure that the sale had been completed, he contacted Charles Padnick's son Jamie.

The only information that they had was the location of New York City and the name "Chris DeMeo".

Fortunately, the Colombians had contacts in New York and eventually, the clues led them to Roy DeMeo and the Gambino family.

Jamie immediately flew to New York arriving on March 19.

Shortly after he arrived in New York he was also murdered, dismembered, and disposed of by Rosenberg and his fellow crew members.

When the Columbians learned of the murders they were looking to get revenge on the DeMeo crew and the Gambinos.

When Anthony Gaggi's nephew, Dominick Montiglio, became a government witness in 1983 he told the authorities of how DeMeo's crew handled the hostile situation with the Columbians.

Montiglio claimed that he was the man in charge of communicating between the Colombian's contact in New York and Roy DeMeo's crew and the Gambinos.

The Colombians told DeMeo that they demanded revenge for the killings of Serrano as well as the cousin and girlfriend of Serrano's Colombian drug connection.

They made a deal that if Chris Rosenberg were murdered; there would be no further issues between them.

The Gambino's agreed to this arrangement and relayed the message back to the Columbians that Rosenberg would be dealt with quickly.

The Columbians had one more demand, to make sure that Rosenberg was killed, the murder would have to be in the newspapers; otherwise, they would not believe it had happened.

Gaggi ordered DeMeo to handle the killing of Rosenberg.

DeMeo knew that Rosenberg had to be killed, however, due to the close relationship he and Chris had he stalled for a few weeks.

When the Columbians discovered that Rosenberg wasn't killed quickly by the Gambinos, they sent a group of men to New York and threatened violence if Rosenberg was not murdered soon.

Roy DeMeo knew that cartel hitmen were in New York and that they were not happy. And he felt that there was a slight possibility that he may also be on the Columbian cartel's hit list.

On April 19, DeMeo saw a young man parked in front of his house.

He immediately assumed that the man was a Colombian Cartel hitman sent to kill him.

DeMeo pursued the young man in a car chase that ended with the young man who was identified as 19-year-old Dominick Ragucci, being shot and killed after his car became too damaged to continue fleeing from DeMeo.

After the killing, DeMeo drove his family out of New York and left them at a hotel for a short time for their own protection.

After the murder, DeMeo learned that the young man was not a Cartel hitman but was an innocent man who was paying his way through college by selling vacuum cleaners door to door.

According to DeMeo's son Albert, Roy DeMeo started crying when he discovered he had murdered an innocent boy.

After Ragucci's murder, Gaggi met with DeMeo and ordered him to stop delaying and kill Rosenberg before there were any more innocent victims.

Gaggi made sure that Rosenberg was never informed about the Colombian situation so that he would have no indication that his life was in danger.

On May 11, three weeks after Ragucci's murder, Rosenberg went to a meeting at the Gemini clubhouse with DeMeo and his crew.

While at the meeting, DeMeo pulled a pistol and fired a single bullet into the unsuspecting Rosenberg's head, wounding but not killing him.

DeMeo hesitated when the still-living Rosenberg managed to rise off the floor.

Anthony Senter shot him four more times in the head when Rosenberg got up off the floor and stumbled onto one knee.

DeMeo knew that Rosenberg's murder had to be in the newspapers so Rosenberg's body was placed in his car, and left it parked on the side of Cross Bay Boulevard near the Gateway National Recreation Area in New York City.

Henry Borelli sprayed the car with machine-gun fire, to ensure the murder was seen as an assassination and would be mentioned in the local newspaper.

The following day the murder of Rosenberg was printed in the newspaper and this gave the Colombians proof of the killing and defused the situation.

Immediately the DeMeo crew was suspects in Rosenberg's murder.

After an in-depth investigation by the police, there was not enough evidence to charge any of them.

Fifteen years later, however, the murder would be among many others charges in a 1984 indictment against the surviving members of the DeMeo crew.

At the trial in 1988, cooperating witnesses Dominick Montiglio and Vito Arena provided a great deal of information on the crew's activities.

Their testimony linked the remnants of the DeMeo crew with Rosenberg's murder.

In 1989 Joseph Testa and Anthony Senter, the only core DeMeo Crew members who had not been murdered or already imprisoned, were sentenced to life in prison.

In the summer of 1979, Philip "Rusty" Rastelli imprisoned boss of the Bonanno crime family, fears a takeover, and goes to the Commission to get permission to murder Carmine Galante.

In 1976 Rastelli was sentenced to 10 years in prison on a charge of extortion. He was also serving prison time for a four-year sentence for conspiracy, criminal contempt of court, and usury.

On February 23, 1974, Rastelli was named as Boss of the Bonanno crime family by the Commission after Natale "Joe Diamond" Evola died of cancer On August 28, 1973.

Although Rastelli was officially endorsed by the Commission in 1974, the real power in the Bonanno crime family was with Rastelli's rival Carmine "the Cigar" Galante, who was released from prison at the same time.

In Rastelli's absence, Carmine "The Cigar" Galante seized control of the Bonanno crime family as the family's unofficial acting boss.

Galante was nicknamed "the Cigar" or "Lilo," which is Sicilian slang for a cigar because he was rarely seen without one in his mouth.

Carmine Galante started working for the Bonanno crime family after being released from prison in 1939.

Both Galante and then family Boss, Joseph "Bananas" Bonanno hailed from the same town in Sicily, Castellammare del Golfo.

By 1953, Galante rose to become the Bonanno Crime Family's underboss.

Galante ran the family's drug business, particularly heroin. Galante spoke various Italian dialects and was fluent in both Spanish and French.

He oversaw the family's drug business in Montreal as it smuggled so-called "French Connection" heroin from France into the United States.

Galante's power move did not go well with some of the other family Bosses.

One such boss was Genovese crime family boss Frank Tieri.

Tieri began having Joseph Massino contacting the other Family Bosses to build a consensus for Carmine Galante's murder.

Tieri even obtained approval from the retired Joseph Bonanno to kill Galante.

Finally, in the summer of 1979, Rastelli and Joseph Massino sought the Commission's approval to kill Carmine Galante; the request was officially approved.

On Thursday, July 12, 1979, Carmine Galante, 69, showed up for lunch at Joe & Mary's Restaurant at 205 Knickerbocker Avenue in Bushwick, Brooklyn with his two bodyguards Baldo Amato and Cesare Bonventre as well as a drug dealer, Leonardo Coppola, and the restaurant owner and Galante's cousin Giuseppe Turano.

However, instead of eating inside the restaurant, he chose to eat his lunch of fish, salad, and wine at a table in the quiet patio garden in the back.

At about 2:45, as the men ate their lunch; three men in ski masks ran into the restaurant and barged into the patio and opened fire on the unsuspecting Galante.

When the shooting ended, Carmine Galante, Leonardo Coppola, and Galante's cousin Giuseppe Turano were all killed.

As for the two bodyguards Baldo Amato and Cesare Bonventre, they did nothing during the attack or afterward. They simply left the restaurant unharmed – they were suspected to have assisted in the assassination.

And suspicion grew that his own crime family was in on the hit against him.

Galante died with his cigar still clenched in his teeth, and the newspaper photographs that captured the crime scene were soon an indelible part of mafia lore.

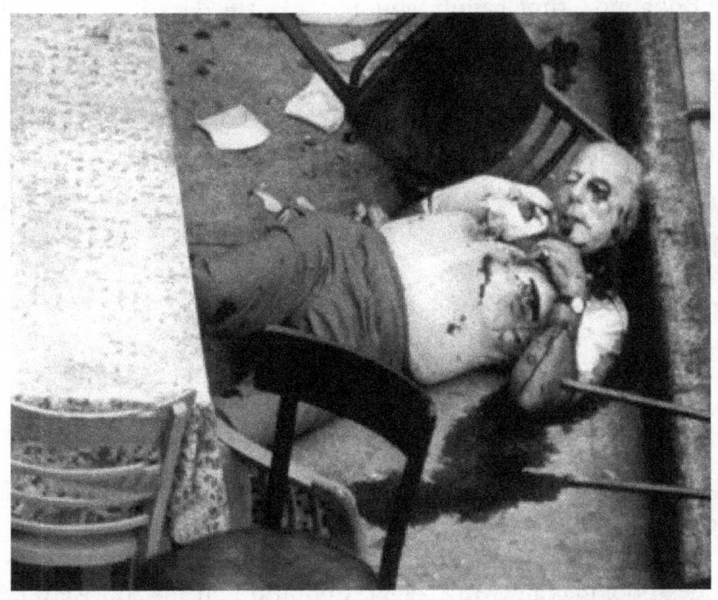

After Galante's killing, Salvatore "Sally Fruits" Ferrugia was appointed by the commission to replace Carmine Galante.

Philip "Rusty" Rastelli was now once again the undisputed boss of the Bonanno crime family, controlling things from behind bars through the use of acting boss Salvatore "Sally Fruits" Ferrugia.

Ferrugia ran the Bonanno Crime family until Rastelli was released from prison On April 21, 1983.

Rastelli returned to prison in 1986 and the Family was run by Anthony "Old Man" Spero until 1991 when Joseph "Big Joe" Massino took over.

Joseph "Big Joe" Massino was imprisoned in January 2003, and in a move that surprised everyone in the Mafia underworld, he became a government informant in October 2004.

The Bonanno Crime Family would later be ruled by, Vincent "Vinny Gorgeous" Basciano and then followed by Michael "The Nose" Mancuso.

In the summer 1979, Castellano allegedly ordered the murders of Gambino capo James "Jimmy the Clam" Eppolito and his son, James Eppolito, Jr.

Eppolito Sr. was a caporegime in the Gambino Crime Family.

Eppolito Sr. joined the Gambino Crime Family in the 1950s and was one of Carlo Gambino's caporegimes in the 1960s and 70s.

Eppolito Sr. was primarily involved in bookmaking with Anthony Gaggi.

Besides bookmaking with Gaggi, Eppolito and his son were both involved in a children's charity scam that had been supported by First Lady Rosalynn Carter and Senator Edward Kennedy.

The charity was set up by James Eppolito and from all aspects appeared to be legitimate.

The money that was donated to the charity was supposed to go to a worthy cause but was ultimately pocketed by Eppolito Sr.

In 1979 Eppolito's scam was discovered and was broadcasted on the national television show 60 Minutes.

During that episode, a photograph was displayed that showed Jimmy Jr. and Rosalynn Carter, posing together.

When Castellano learned of this negative media attention he became concerned that Eppolito had brought unwanted negative attention to the Gambino's, and that President Carter's embarrassment might cause him to seek retaliation.

Soon after the photo was discovered by Castellano, Eppolito Sr. complained to Castellano that Gaggi was infringing on his territory and that DeMeo had cheated Eppolito's son, a Gambino soldier, in a cocaine drug deal that cost him $7000 out of pocket after the deal.

Knowing Paul's stand on drug dealing within the family, Eppolito informed him that Gaggi and DeMeo were also involved in drug trafficking and accused Gaggi of being a police informant. Both of which carried the penalty of death.

Eppolito then asked Castellano for permission to murder Gaggi and DeMeo. Eppolito believed that Castellano would side with him in the dispute, however, Castellano broke his own rules and sided against Eppolito Sr. and gave Gaggi and DeMeo permission to murder both Eppolito and his son.

Gaggi and DeMeo started to put a plan together to eliminate the Eppolitos because they knew that they needed to be killed and fast before they could cause any real problems for them.

Gaggi and DeMeo reached out to one of Eppolito's oldest and closest friends, Peter Piacenti, to encourage Eppolito and his son to have a sit down with Gaggi and DeMeo to resolve their dispute.

Piacente even agreed to accompany the Eppolitos to the Gemini Lounge so they would feel at ease.

What Piacente did not know was that Gaggi's plan was that, once the Eppolitos were in the lounge, they would be killed and dismembered.

On October 1st, 1979, as the five men made their way to the Gemini Lounge, Gaggi sat in front with Jimmy, Jr. Piacenti sat between DeMeo and Eppolito Sr. in back.

Sometime during the journey, the elder Eppolito knew that he was going to be killed when they arrived at the Gemini Lounge and decided he had to get out of the car.

He told his son to stop the car so he could get out and use a bathroom.

The younger Eppolito pulled the car over on the Shore Parkway near Brighton Sixth Street in Coney Island. As the car came to a stop, Gaggi shot Eppolito Jr. several times in the head. DeMeo reached across Piacenti and fired into the head of Eppolito, Sr. killing each man instantly

Up to this point, the actions of the four men are only conjectured as none of the men ever came forward and told authorities about what happened that night before the Eppolito's killings.

What we do know for certain is that the car pulled over in Coney Island, Brooklyn and they were both shot and killed in their car.

A witness named Patrick Penny was driving by right as the shots were fired managed to alert a nearby off-duty policeman, who found Gaggi walking away from the crime scene.

The two had a brief shootout, and the policeman wounded Gaggi in the neck and arrested him.

DeMeo fled the scene in a different direction as Gaggi as they left the scene, and he was not arrested or identified by Penny.

Gaggi was charged with the Eppolitos' murders and the attempted murder of the police officer.

Part Four
The 1980s
The Beginning
Of The End

Nino Gaggi's trial was finishing up in March 1980.

At his trial, the eyewitness, Patrick Penny testified against Gaggi.

Gaggi knew that he could have Penny killed at any time during the trial, but feared that if he did, he may face a stiffer penalty if convicted of Eppolitos' murders and the attempted murder of the police officer.

When the trial was finished, Gaggi was found guilty of assault and sentenced to 5-to-15 years in federal prison. Roy DeMeo would take over as acting captain.

After the trial, the authorities warned Penny that his life was in danger and he should consider leaving town.

Unfortunately, Penny didn't act quickly enough on the advice of the authorities, and shortly after the trial; Gaggi gave DeMeo the orders to kill Penny.

Roy DeMeo's crew tracked down Penny and on May 12, DeMeo shot him dead in the street.

On the following day, the front page of the New York Times read "Mob Witness Rubbed Out".

By 1980 John Gotti was quickly rising through the family ranks.

After being released just three years earlier, Gotti and his crew made the Gambino Crime family a large amount of money and his dedication to Neil Dellacroce was stronger than ever.

Life at home in Howard Beach, Queens was going well for Gotti. In 1980 his wife Victoria DiGiorgio, and he had five children; Peter J., Frankie, John Jr., Victoria, and Angel.

John and Victoria celebrated their eighteenth wedding anniversary on March 6th. For John, life couldn't be better. He was on his way to the top in The Gambino crime family and his family at home was doing great.

However, on Tuesday, March 18, 1980, the Gotti family members' lives would be changed forever.

On that afternoon, after school, 12-year-old Frankie Gotti met up with some neighborhood friends and went out to play on his friend Kevin McMahon's, minibike.

Frankie Gotti

While riding in a construction site on 157th Ave., Frankie darted out from behind a garbage dumpster near the side of the road and into the path of an oncoming car driven by fifty-one-year-old John Favara.

Mr. Favara was driving home in the Howard Beach neighborhood of Queens, New York, from his job as a service manager at a Castro Convertibles furniture plant.

John Favara and his wife, Janet, lived on 86th St. in Howard Beach, and were back-fence neighbors of the Gotti's who lived at 160-11 85th Street.

The Favara's had two adopted kids and their son, Scott, was friends with John and Victoria's oldest son, John Jr.

Favara told the police he was momentarily blinded by the sun and did not see Frankie suddenly shoot out from behind the garbage dumpster until it was too late.

The crash was ruled an accident by the police and concluded that the driver had done nothing wrong, but Victoria wasn't going to accept that.

Years later, Victoria Gotti, Frankie's sister, claims that Favara was drunk and speeding at the time of the accident. (The police never officially determined either of these claims) She even went on to say that he had dragged Frankie's near-lifeless body 200 feet before bystanders stopped the car, pounced on his hood, and stopped him from crossing the avenue.

She said that Favara then cursed him when he finally did stop.

Victoria said that Frankie's blood seemed to leave a trail down the entire block, leading up to Favara's car.

She said that her mother ran to Frankie, knelt, and was cradling his head and screaming his name over and over.

Frankie's sudden death crushed John Gotti and drove his wife, Victoria, into a deep depression.

For days following the accident, the Gotti family was distraught.

Frankie's funeral was heavily attended by family and friends.

John Gotti sr. kept his composure during the funeral and greeted each of the mourners as they paid their respects at the casket.

FBI agents, who normally held surveillance at wakes and funerals, stayed away out of respect for the death of John Gotti's child.

John Jr. said later that he heard his father go into his den after the funeral, close the door, and cry.

Frankie's death sent Victoria, whose life was her five children, into a downward spiral of rage for John Favara.

Victoria Gotti dressed only in black for weeks after the funeral.

Frankie's picture was hung over a backdrop of candles and flowers In the Gotti's living room.

Victoria Gotti was furious that Favara continued to drive the car that had killed her son. And some have said that she was furious that he had never even had the dented right fender and badly damaged quarter panel from the tragic accident repaired.

Not long after the accident John Favara started to receive written death threats in his mailbox.

It was even reported that just two days after Frankie's death, a woman called the local police and said, "The driver of the car that killed Frank Gotti will be eliminated".

John Gotti's daughter Victoria said Favara also taunted her mother with "smug" grins over the fence that divided their properties.

She said that a few nights after Frankie's funeral, they heard loud music and even louder laughter coming from the Favara's back yard.

Victoria said that her mother made her way outside and was standing against the fence, her eyes filled with hate, disbelief, and grief.

When Favara noticed her standing by the fence, Instead of getting up and going inside, he shot her a smug smile and grinned.

John Gotti soon came out to the backyard and brought his wife back inside. Luckily John Gotti never saw the smug smile or the grin that Favara gave Victoria.

John didn't say a word; he just guided his wife back inside the house.

When Victoria was sure that John was sound asleep beside her, she crawled out of bed, grabbed a baseball bat, and made her way around the corner to Favara's house.

When she arrived at the Favara's house, in the driveway was their late-model, brown Oldsmobile, with a dented right fender and badly damaged quarter panel with Frankie's blood now dried and caked on the car.

Victoria started hitting the car with the bat, and within minutes, Favara came out of the house.

She was just inches from Favara. He was pointing a finger at her and screaming at young Victoria to "Get this crazy woman off my property!"

He also yelled, "What the hell was her son doing in the fuckin' street?"

Victoria swung the bat at Favara multiple times. Each time, she only narrowly missed him.

"She's fuckin' crazy!" Favara yelled.

While young Victoria walked her mother home Favara continued to complain about his car and who was going to pay for the damages.

Two weeks later, on April 13, the Favara's car, which still had not been repaired, was reported stolen.

The car was found two weeks later abandoned on a street less than a mile away from his home.

On another occasion Favara found a funeral card and a photograph of Frankie in his mailbox and in late May, the word "murderer" was spray-painted on his car.

On May 28, in the midst of all of these threats, John Favara decided to visit the Gotti's to apologize and to offer his condolences.

When he arrived at the Gotti's residence he was confronted by Victoria Gotti who picked up a baseball bat and struck Favara over the head with it.

After being treated for his injuries at a nearby hospital, Favara sought advice from a friend Anthony Zappi, whose father was Ettore Zappi, a mob captain. Favara thought perhaps Zappi could act as a mediator and resolve this problem.

But instead of resolving the issue for Favara, Zappi urged him to get rid of his car and to move out of Howard Beach.

By mid-July Victoria was getting worse by the day, and John Gotti believed that a few weeks away would do her some good.

On July 25, John Gotti, his wife Victoria, and their youngest son Peter went on a much-needed vacation to Fort Lauderdale, Florida.

By this time Favara and his wife, Janet put their house up for sale and planned to move as far away from the Gottis as possible.

It did not take long before the Favaras had a buyer for their home and a closing date on the home's sale was scheduled for the last day of July.

Three days later, on July 28, while John and Victoria were on vacation in Fort Lauderdale, John Favara vanished.

In 2001, information from present and former law enforcement people who were connected with the Favara case was put together and eight crew members –Anthony Rampino, Willie Boy Johnson, Angelo Ruggiero, Gene Gotti, John, and Charles Carneglia, Richard Gomes, and Iggy Alogna were named as having played a role in Favara's abduction and slaying.

Just two days before the Favaras were to complete the sale of their home; John Favara left the Castro Convertibles furniture factory and walked towards his car, which was parked beside a diner two blocks away.

As Favara approached his station wagon he spotted the men and quickly turned to run.

John Carneglia shot Favara twice in the legs with a .22 caliber, silencer-equipped pistol.

Eyewitnesses at the diner said that Favara gasped, "No. No. Please, my wife," as he struggled to get up off the ground.

Richard Gomes then stuck Favara over the head with a two-by-four knocking him unconscious, picked him up and threw him into the back of a blue van, and drove off.

The van was followed by a car that had been parked in front of the diner with the van.

Another crewmember took Favara's keys and followed the other vehicles away from the crime scene.

Favara's car was driven to a salvage yard in East New York operated by John and Charles Carneglia.

As for Favara, in January 2009, Brooklyn federal court papers filed by prosecutors contained allegations that Gambino family hitman Charles Carneglia told a Gambino family associate, who is a government witness, that John Favara's body was taken to a New Jersey warehouse where he was killed and stuffed into a barrel that was then filled with acid.

Another account of Favara's death was that while he was still alive, he was dismembered with a chainsaw and stuffed into a barrel filled with concrete.

The barrel was then dumped off a Sheepshead Bay pier into the ocean or buried somewhere on the salvage yard property.

How exactly John Favara died we may never know for certain. But what we do know is that after that day, neither John Favara nor his car was ever seen again.

One week later on August 5, an FBI informant told the FBI that Favara's body would never be found.

When John and Victoria were questioned about Favara's disappearance, John Gotti said: "I'm not sorry the guy's missing. I wouldn't be sorry if the guy turned up dead."

His wife Victoria said: "I don't know what happened to him, but I'm not disappointed he's missing. He killed my boy."

After the killing, Favara's wife sold their home and moved out of Howard Beach; John was declared legally dead in 1983. His widow, Janet, died in 2000.

Every year on the anniversary of Frankie's death, Victoria religiously places Memoriam notices in the New York Daily News. As his siblings grew and had their own families, so did the notices.

In honor of Frankie, each one of the Gotti children has named one of their children after him.

Just like John Gotti in 1980, Paul Castellano's challenges not only came from the U.S. government but from his very own family members.

In the summer of 1980, Castellano learns that during their marriage, Frank Amato physically abused his daughter Constance causing her to have a miscarriage.

After learning this he orders the murder of his ex-son-in-law Frank Amato.

Castellano turned to Roy DeMeo's crew to make Amato disappear.

It is believed that DeMeo's crew killed Frank Amato on September 20, cut up his body, and disposed of the remains.

Members of Roy DeMeo's crew were later charged with Amato's disappearance and suspected murder, but none of the men were ever convicted.

Frank Amato was pronounced legally dead in 1985.

The murder and disposal of Frank Amato earned DeMeo and his crew great respect from Paul Castellano.

However, behind the scenes, Roy DeMeo's crew was slowly falling apart.

By the early 1980s, a couple of DeMeo's associates, Dominick Montiglio who was the nephew of Anthony Gaggi, and Vito Arena, had vanished. This was very bad news for Gaggi and DeMeo.

Vito knew about the international stolen car operation and Montiglio knew about several unsolved murders done by DeMeo's crew.

Unknown to Gaggi and DeMeo, the FBI began an investigation into the DeMeo Crew's activities.

Vito Arena had been calling in anonymous tips; regarding the DeMeo crew's stolen car racket.

Federal prosecutors eventually charged the Boss of The Genovese family, Frank "Funzi" Tieri with being the head of a crime family that was involved in racketeering, extortion, and illegal gambling.

On January 23, 1981, Tieri was convicted of violating the RICO act.

Tieri arrived in court using a wheelchair and an oxygen tank.

Tieri's lawyers argued for leniency, saying that he was dying. Prosecutors told the judge it was all just an act, and the judge sentenced Frank "Funzi" Tieri to ten years in prison.

On March 29, 1981, just over two months after he was convicted, Frank "Funzi" Tieri died of natural causes at Mount Sinai Hospital in New York.

He is buried in Saint John's Cemetery, Queens, New York where fellow mafia members Charlie "Lucky" Luciano and Carlo Gambino are also laid to rest.

Philip "Benny Squint" Lombardo stepped down as boss due to poor health following Tieri's death, naming Vincent Gigante as his successor and the acting Boss of The Genovese family.

At the same time, Lombardo made Anthony "Fat Tony" Salerno the new front boss to disguise Gigante's transition into the new acting Boss of The Genovese family.

In February 1981, John Gotti opened a gambling den for "family" men only, on the second floor of the Bergin club.

In early March, he decided to move the gambling den to a location on Mott Street around the corner from Dellacroce's Ravenite Social Club in Little Italy, at 247 Mulberry Street in Manhattan.

Soon after moving to the Mulberry Street location, a Queens' detective squad watched as Willie Boy Johnson handed a package to a drug dealer in exchange for a paper bag that he quickly threw into the trunk of his car.

Detectives followed Johnson as he drove to his home in Brooklyn. When he arrived home and opened the trunk to get the bag, the detectives approached him and asked what the bag contained.

He admitted to the police that the bag contained $50,000, which Johnson quickly claimed came from John Gotti's gambling operation.

Johnson was scared because he was still on probation after having served less than four years of his ten-year sentence

He told the officers to just take the money because if his parole officer found out about it he would violate the conditions of his parole and go back to prison to finish his sentence.

Johnson, who was at the time, working as a confidential informant for the FBI, now agreed to work with the New York City Police Department.

In May 1981 Henry Borelli and Freddy DiNome were arrested in connection with the DeMeo Crew's stolen car operation.

The FBI agents began working hard to get Freddy to provide them with more evidence against DeMeo and his crew.

The FBI knew that DiNome was not a hardened killer like the rest of DeMeo's crew, and had years of info from being close to DeMeo.

Freddy was scared for his life and the life of his brother, crew member, and car thief Richard DiNome and refused to talk.

The FBI then focused on getting Henry Borelli to talk.

But just like DiNome, Borelli was not about to make any deals. He was a hardened criminal who was ready to do his time for the sake of the DeMeo crew.

Borelli was also suspected of participating in dozens of murders.

Borelli would never be a free man again. The case would drag on for years; and he would eventually be convicted and sentenced to 150 years in prison.

In mid-1981, Vito Arena was arrested for a minor crime and quickly began cooperating with the FBI on several unsolved murders.

DeMeo tried to contact Vito while he was still in jail.

The prosecutor on the case informed DeMeo that Vito was now playing for the other team.

In June 1981, approximately thirty men were arrested after Willie Boy Johnson ratted out the Mott Street gambling den.

The men were represented by attorney Michael Coiro and pled guilty to misdemeanor gambling charges, and were fined $500 each and released.

The following night, John Gotti moved his operation right across the street from the raided location. However, due to the higher than normal risk of being arrested, the game never regained its former popularity.

It was around this time that the FBI overheard a conversation from the bug planted in Ruggiero's house of Gene Gotti discussing a hit on Roy DeMeo that Castellano had tried to assign to his brother John.

John Gotti was wary of accepting this job. He knew very well of Roy and decided to let Paul deal with DeMeo.

Using the information that they received from Vito, detectives were able to locate the body of a man named Joseph Scorney who was a close childhood friend of Vito.

Scorney worked for DeMeo, it was strictly "freelance" stating to DiNome that he would never work for "the Mafia guys."

In September 1978 Scorney was murdered, although the motives never became clear to the participants in the murder, Arena and DiNome Cut Scorney's body in half, and stuffed it into a 50-gallon oil barrel.

They then filled it with cement and rolled it off a pier in Center Moriches, New York.

In 1985 Vito was sentenced to eighteen years for the murder.

After cooperating with the FBI Vito disappeared upon release from jail'

By this time DeMeo was getting nervous and ordered Borelli and DiNome to plead guilty.

DeMeo's thinking was that maybe the FBI would be happy with just the convictions of DiNome and Borelli.

DeMeo believed that it worked out as they were only sentenced to 5 years at the time.

When a new prosecutor took over the car case, the pieces started coming together.

Slowly, the case that first seemed like just a local car theft ring turned into a racketeering and murder case.

The case soon led from the DeMeo crew, all the way up to Paul Castellano.

The prosecution had a witness named who was able to make the connection between DeMeo's crew and Castellano, and he included Dominick Montiglio as a co-conspirator.

Montiglio had recently vanished after a serious falling out with Gaggi over his drug habit.

The prosecutor had another cooperating witness who was the cousin of John Quinn, who was killed with Cherie Golden.

He was willing to testify against DeMeo and crew regarding that case.

The prosecutor then tried to find Vito Arena and Dominick Montiglio.

He knew that they were the only ones who could provide firsthand accounts to authorities about DeMeo and his crew.

DeMeo and the remaining member of his crew went on the run.

The FBI was now serving subpoenas to DeMeo and everyone else associated with the crew, including their wives.

Some people within the Gambino family ranks believed that if DeMeo was ever arrested, he might be willing to cooperate.

With as much knowledge that DeMeo had on the Gambinos, Castellano knew that he had to deal with DeMeo before that could happen.

The job to kill DeMeo was given to Gaggi and the Gemini twins; Joey Testa, and Anthony Senter.

For the Gemini twins, DeMeo was nothing out of the ordinary because they'd already killed several of their own friends and crew members before.

Castellano knew that it was only right that this job went to them.

The trio of killers started to put a plan together on how to kill their crew's leader.

Also in mid-1980, Castellano started the building of a lavish 10,436 sq ft, mansion.

The lavish home was located at 177 Benedict Rd, Staten Island, NY on the highest part of Staten Island, exclusive Todt Hill.

The mansion had seventeen rooms and twelve bathrooms, with an Olympic-size pool, waiting rooms, and an apartment for the Castellano's housekeeper

The home was completed in 1981 and cost $3.5 million.

With its grand portico, Castellano's men started calling the mansion the White House.

The home also had a spectacular view of the Verrazano Narrows Bridge arching over the entrance to New York's Upper Bay.

Shortly after moving into the new home on Benedict Rd. with his wife Nina Mano Castellano, then Sixty-five-year-old Castellano started a love affair with his thirty-year-old live-in maid, Gloria Olarte.

In late August 1991, while living in her hometown of Medellin Columbia, Gloria Olarte spoke to a reporter about her time with Paul Castellano.

She said the main problem between her and the Castellanos was the language difference.

Nina would talk to her at times in Italian and other times in English. Each time Gloria didn't understand what was said to her.

She said that she would call her sister and ask what certain words meant.

Paul eventually brought home a minicomputer that was capable of translating seven languages.

In the beginning, the messages were simple phrases like, "Bring me fruits." "Make the coffee." "Set the table."

However, over time the messages started to get more personal and Gloria began to find other messages like: "You have pretty eyes." "I like you."

She went on to say that one day, Castellano entered the kitchen and put his hand on her hip, and told her to put her head on his chest.

She put it there, and then Paul said, 'You could be my daughter.'

Gloria looked at him, and he kissed her on the cheek.

It wasn't long before Gloria had a wardrobe of the finest designer dresses.

One day Gloria smiled at him, in front of all the people. And after they left, Paul told her, 'From now on, you're going to keep smiling for me.'

That was the beginning of the end for not only Paul's marriage but his very existence.

The extravagance of Castellano's lifestyle caused resentment and envy with many of the Gambino family members.

Castellano didn't make many friends with the men in the streets under him. He considered himself a businessman and above the Capos, soldiers, and associates in the family.

And it was that way of thinking that created tension within the family.

And Castellano was all about making money, he didn't share money.

He was very greedy; typically, Gambino capos would give ten percent of their earnings as a tribute to the boss.

However, soon after moving into his Todt Hill mansion, Castellano began to demand fifteen percent or more in some cases from his men who were struggling to make money in the traditional family rackets.

And that caused resentment within the ranks of the street level guys.

To make things even worse for some of the Gambino capos, John Gotti in particular, Castellano repeatedly made it clear that he would kill anyone who was dealing with narcotics.

Even though Castellano banned Gambino Crime family members from running drug rackets, he still was accepting large drug payoffs from the Cherry Hill Gambinos in New Jersey and the DeMeo crew.

This caused further dissatisfaction with Castellano as the family's leader among the Dellacroce supporters.

John Gotti, who was a prominent Dellacroce supporter at the time, defied Castellano by secretly distributing drugs.

Gotti knew that Paul had stated that drug dealing within the family would be a death sentence; however, as long as Neil Dellacroce was alive, Gotti would defy Castellano's orders.

By the early 1980s, the government was beginning to investigate New York's five organized crime families.

On November 9, 1981, with information supplied to the FBI by Willie Boy Johnson, the FBI proceeded to "launch an electronic assault" against the mobster known as "Quack Quack".

Angelo Ruggiero was known as "Quack-Quack," because of his incessant talking. It was even said that if you dialed any random number in New York chances are Ruggiero would answer.

On their surveillance, the FBI overheard Angelo talking to Gene Gotti. During their conversation, the word "babania" (a street name for heroin), was heard and the next day the Gambino Squad approached a judge for a warrant for further electronic surveillance.

Ruggiero had moved from Howard Beach to Cedarhurst, Long Island as the FBI was listening in on Angelo's conversations during the early part of 1982.

Once again the Gambino Squad approached a judge for a warrant for further electronic surveillance of Ruggiero's new home.

Willy Boy Johnson told the FBI where the best locations would be to listen in on Angelo's conversations.

Agents disguised as construction workers planted listening devices in Ruggiero's kitchen, dining room, and basement den.

They also tapped the phone in his daughter's bedroom that Angelo used regularly.

Angelo Ruggiero's house in Cedarhurst was bugged during April, May, and June of 1982 hoping to gain evidence into some of the illegal rackets that he, John Gotti, and Gene Gotti operated.

Then on May 6, 1982, a tragic plane accident that would claim the life of Gotti's closest crew member Angelo Ruggiero's brother Sal, would drop Gotti and his crew right in the middle of an internal war with Castellano.

Salvatore Ruggiero and his wife, Stephanie, were killed when their private Gates Learjet 23 N100TA crashed in the Atlantic Ocean 12 miles southeast of Savannah, Georgia.

They were flying from Teterboro, New Jersey, to Orlando, Florida where the couple was interested in purchasing a McDonald's franchise chain restaurant in Magic Kingdom, Disney World.

The plane was piloted by George Morton and a stand-in pilot, Sherri Day.

Pilot George Morton flew the aircraft for the first hour of the flight before turning the controls over to pilot Sherri Day.

The day was clear and perfect for flying. Then at noon, from over the Atlantic Ocean, Day radioed the air traffic control center in Jacksonville, Florida requesting landing status for their arrival in Orlando.

An air traffic controller instructed her to lower the plane's altitude.

Then 90 seconds later, Day made another brief transmission, which was unintelligible. It was at this time that the Learjet plunged into the Atlantic.

A fishing boat crew spotted a huge water geyser on the surface of the water and sped to the scene.

When the fishing boat arrived they found debris of the Learjet's outer skin and interior, scattered across the surface of the ocean.

The crew searched but did not find any survivors. The National Transportation Safety Board was notified ninety minutes after the crash. A team of three investigators was dispatched from Washington, D.C. that same day.

On May 13, one week after the plane entered the Atlantic Ocean, a search team, using sonar equipment, began an underwater scan of the crash site.

The next afternoon, fifty-five feet below the surface, the main wreckage was found, scattered over seventy-five feet of the ocean floor.

George Morton's body and those of Salvatore and Stephanie were recovered from the wreckage. All had suffered multiple traumatic injuries. Sherri Day's body was never recovered from the crash site.

After examining the debris, the NTSB was unable to determine the cause of the crash. An explosion and an onboard fire were both eliminated as a possible cause of the crash.

The National Transportation Safety Board later concluded that the probable cause of the accident was an "uncontrolled descent from cruise altitude for undetermined reasons from which recovery was not, or could not be, affected"

Until his body was identified, Ruggiero had been listed as a fugitive from justice and a large scale heroin trafficker.

In the mid-70s, Salvatore was one of the largest and wealthiest dealers in New York City.

Salvatore and Stephanie went on the run after they were charged with tax evasion in 1977; they assumed new identities and fled. Salvatore changed his name to Steve while his wife never changed her first name. The couple changed their last name from Ruggiero to Teri.

Even though they changed their identities, Ruggiero continued selling heroin.

He had been running a profitable heroin business that even leaders of the Gambino family were unaware of.

After Sal's brother Angelo was notified of his brother's death, he, along with John Gotti's brother Gene Gotti and John Carneglia, went to Sal's hideout in Franklin Lakes, New Jersey, searching for a yet-to-be-sold shipment of heroin and cash.

Two days after the plane crash, Attorney Michael Coiro, who had represented Angelo and the Gottis in the past, arrived from Florida to help Angelo resolve legal issues involving his brother's estate.

Gambino Family capo Frank DeCicco arrived at Angelo's home to offer his condolences while the two men were meeting.

As the FBI agents listened in, they heard Coiro tell DeCicco, "Gene found the heroin."

A memorial service was held in Howard Beach at Mary Dellacroce's house. Mary Dellacroce was the sister of the Gambino crime family underboss Aniello Dellacroce.

After the crash, the Gambino's had to take action to protect their interests.

What they didn't know was that they got into things just as the FBI was starting to closely watch high-level members of the Gambino family.

Michael Coiro was still around helping Angelo several weeks after the memorial service.

During a conversation at Angelo's home, the FBI overheard Angelo, Michael Coiro, and Gene Gotti talk about unloading the heroin:

Ruggiero: If I get some money, will you hold it?

Coiro: Yeah.

Gene: Nobody is to know but us. You're not our lawyer; you're one of us as far as I'm concerned.

Coiro: I know it, Gene, I feel that way too.

Ruggiero's conversations revealed that in the aftermath of Salvatore's death, his former associates set out to avoid being indicted for having harbored Salvatore and his wife while being on the run as a fugitive and to locate and liquidate Salvatore's assets.

In its initial request to wiretap Ruggiero's telephone, the F.B.I listed John's brothers, Peter and Richard Gotti as loan shark collectors.

They also stated that Angelo Ruggiero was a "known murderer who would, without question, seek physical retribution and possibly murder a shylock victim who is unable to pay his debts."

Ruggiero's constant talking on the phone and around his house with other criminals provided the FBI with a wealth of intelligence on the Gambino crime family.

The FBI recorded Angelo's attorney offering condolences to Angelo on the death of his brother, and then saying, "Gene found the heroin."

The investigation into Ruggiero suddenly held promise in leading to indictments of Gambino family leaders.

Angelo provided the FBI a running commentary on everything going on in his life.

To the benefit of the agents listening in, everyone who visited Ruggiero had to endure endless gossip, complaints, and general indiscretions within the Gambino Crime family.

Ruggiero was often overheard on the wiretaps speaking of his brother to his two drug trafficking partners.

The FBI later revealed that Ruggiero allegedly sold 46 kilos of heroin in six months of 1982.

The FBI also overheard that Ruggiero and Gotti were concerned about whether they should give some of their street-level dealers, heroin on consignment, or demand the money for it on delivery.

The wiretaps throughout Ruggiero's home also overheard him saying how difficult it was for him to accept his brother's death, "because the body was in "fucking pieces." He added: "If he would have been shot in the head and they found him in the streets- that's part of our life, I could accept that."

As the FBI gathered the information from the hidden bugs in Ruggiero's house, they had enough to launch an investigation into drug trafficking that involved Gene Gotti and Ruggiero.

Years later during John Gotti's trial, it was learned that the FBI tapes recorded Ruggiero saying that Paul Castellano considered putting John Gotti in a leadership position in case the family's hierarchy was imprisoned.

In the tapes, Ruggiero tells of 'a little rumor' he heard that Castellano was looking for candidates who could replace him if he was imprisoned.

Ruggiero said Paul Castellano and Neil Dellacroce, told him 'every family has groomed (someone), or has put somebody on the side in case something happens to them ... and Johnny's name came up three times.'

Ruggiero then said that he was told to 'tell Johnny to be cool.'

Also recorded at Ruggiero's house was Robert DiBernardo, who offered the following advice: 'Live to be an administrative position.'

Although John Gotti was not directly implicated on any of the tapes, he would be on the spot as far as Paul Castellano was concerned if the tapes were ever released.

If Castellano ever heard the tapes he would assume that Gotti was either involved and thus had violated his ban on drug trafficking, or he had failed to control his crew.

For the next eighteen months, Angelo Ruggiero's conversations were recorded by the F.B.I.

And just like Ruggiero, Roy DeMeo didn't know that he was gaining the attention of someone who wanted to have him taken out. However, unlike Ruggiero, it wasn't the FBI focusing on him, but his own crime family.

On January 10, 1983, Gaggi and the Gemini twins made their move on killing DeMeo.

The plan was the same that they used to kill Harvey "Chris" Rosenberg.

In his last days, Roy's son claimed that DeMeo was paranoid and anticipated his time was up and DeMeo even considered faking his own death and leaving the country.

DeMeo was summoned to a meeting at the body shop of Patty Testa, brother of Joey.

When DeMeo left his home that day, he left behind his watch, wallet, and ring in his study. He also left behind a religious pamphlet indicating that he had gone to church and attended confession.

When he got to the body shop, Gaggi began firing bullets immediately.

Many people feel that DeMeo must have seen the attack coming because he had his hands up. But the bullets just tore through his arms into his head and upper body.

DeMeo's bullet-riddled body was then stuffed into the trunk of his own car.

On January 15, Meyer Lansky dies in Miami Beach, with only $37,000 to his name.

The FBI believes that Lansky stashed away more than 300 million in secret bank accounts.

Three days later, on January 18, DeMeo's car was located at a boat club in Sheepshead Bay, with his frozen body partially covered by a chandelier in the trunk.

Paul was happy to have DeMeo out of the way. However, it turned out to be a bad thing for Paul because DeMeo served as a layer of protection for him.

After the DeMeo hit, Dominick Montiglio reappeared and joined Vito Arena and Freddy DiNome as cooperating witnesses for the F.B.I.

Over the few months, Henry Borelli, Joseph Testa, and Anthony Senter were imprisoned for life after two trials where they were convicted of twenty murders in all, in addition to extortion, car theft, and drug trafficking.

Gaggi was not charged with DeMeo's murder. He died of a heart attack during a trial in 1988 at age 62.

In March 1984, The FBI would indict Paul Castellano for ordering the murder of DeMeo, as well as other crimes.

When the murder of DeMeo was brought up to Richard Kuklinski, he said it "couldn't have happened to a nicer guy".

Years later Richard Kuklinski became famous with a 2012 biographical film on his life titled, "The Iceman"

Kuklinski, not surprisingly, claims to have killed DeMeo.

With Roy DeMeo now eliminated, Paul would have some sort of comfort knowing that the knowledge that DeMeo had on the Gambino family was now silenced.

Back in Castellano's Todt Hill mansion, tensions were growing thick between Paul and his wife Nina because of the attention that Paul was showing to their housekeeper.

In 1983 Nina finally left the mansion and separated from Paul for having an affair with Gloria Olarte, their live-in Colombian housekeeper, and maid.

Paul's daughter Constance also left her father and moved with her mother into a nearby where she remained at her mother's side constantly.

After the separation from Nina, Castellano became a recluse, rarely venturing outside of his hilltop mansion.

Castellano's Capos visited Castellano on a regular basis at the mansion to provide information and receive orders.

Over time this would ultimately prove to be his undoing.

Castellano was abandoning his presence in the family's social clubs; he began to lose touch with the men on the streets.

This decision to stay away led to a widening division between the Paul Castellano and Neil Dellacroce factions in the family.

In March 1983, the FBI obtained a warrant to install secret listening devices in Castellano's house just as they did with Angelo Ruggiero.

The FBI used the information that they had gathered on the Ruggiero recording to obtain the warrant to plant listening devices in Castellano's home.

How they managed to get the devices into the mansion has been speculation for many years.

One story that was put into a book by two of the F.B.I.'s agents goes that the FBI waited until Castellano went on vacation to Florida; agents disabled his security system, drugged his watchdogs, and then planted devices in the dining and living rooms.

It was said that they placed the listening device inside a lamp that was located in the perfect area to pick up all of Castellano's conversations.

Many disregard this theory as the FBI wouldn't want it known how they installed "bugs" inside a private residence. And the fact that two agents were so willing to share this information makes it doubtful.

The official and more believable version of how the listening devices were planted is that they knocked out Castellano's cable television and an undercover agent went into the house dressed like a repairman.

Once inside of the mansion, he installed the listening device directly under the nose of Castellano's bodyguard, Thomas "Tommy" Bilotti.

These listening devices provided law enforcement with a wealth of incriminating information to lead to the eventual arrest of the bosses of all of New York's major crime families; they also recorded embarrassing personal information about Castellano.

The devices picked up conversations between Castellano and his maid, discussing his recent penile implant.

The FBI now had two locations bugged and both were providing a wealth of information.

Just over a year after planting the listening device in Ruggiero's home, the FBI moved in to make their arrests on August 8, 1983.

The FBI's "Gambino Squad" arrested Angelo, Gene Gotti, John Carneglia, Michael Coiro, Peter "Little Pete" Tambone, and Mark Reiter.

In addition to the heroin discussions caught on tape, the bugs and phone taps picked up Ruggiero making disparaging remarks about Paul Castellano.

The following month, in September 1983, Angelo Ruggiero, Gene Gotti, and the others were indicted on charges of drug racketeering and obstructing justice.

On February 4, 1984, Gambino associate and former DeMeo Crew member Richard DiNome is shot to death in his living room with two other individuals with no known organized crime ties who happened to be at his residence at the time.

Authorities suspect members of the DeMeo Crew murdered DiNome to prevent him from becoming a cooperating witness for the government, but no evidence links them to the crime and the case remains unsolved to this day.

Then, less than two months later, on March 30, Castellano was indicted on federal racketeering charges in the Gambino case, including the Eppolito and DeMeo murders.

Other charges that Castellano was indicted on were extortion, narcotics trafficking, theft, and prostitution.

Paul Castellano was released on a $2 million bail.

On April 17, Angelo Ruggiero met with one of his associates, Jack Conroy, who had a source who worked at the telephone company, which is notified when phones are being legally tapped.

He told Ruggiero that he could find out who authorized the taps that were in his house for $800- $1,000 for his telephone company source and $200 each for his partner and him.

In a few days, Conroy told Ruggiero that the taps were legal because of the federal court order in the Southern District of New York.

Ruggiero told Conroy that he would get other telephone numbers for him to check also.

What Ruggiero did not know was that Jack Conroy was really an undercover FBI agent who was posing as a telephone repairman.

By 1985 Angelo Ruggiero spent $40,000 on remodeling his home and was overheard saying, "the bugs in this house were a bunch of bullshit, and nothing is coming."

Unfortunately what he didn't see was what was coming for Neil Dellacroce, John Gotti, and him in May.

On February 25, Castellano and many other Mafia bosses were arrested on charges of racketeering; he was released on $3 million bail.

In the final week of March, Dellacroce faced his most serious charge. He was one of ten Gambino Family members charged with federal RICO conspiracy and related counts.

The federal Racketeer Influenced and Corrupt Organizations Act, commonly known as the RICO statute was created in 1970.

Under the 1970 law, anyone found guilty of two felonies listed in a RICO indictment was considered to be engaged in a pattern of criminal activity and thus open to a conviction for violating the RICO law itself.

Federal prosecutors began using the RICO statute against organized crime figures in the 1980s with considerable success.

They were accused of conducting an 18-year-long racket enterprise operating two crews from Manhattan and Brooklyn that encompassed truck hijacking, gambling, shylocking, extortion, and murder.

Dellacroce was accused of overseeing and directing the crew.

The indictments were the culmination of several years of work by assistant United States attorney Diane Giacalone, who represented the Eastern District of New York.

His co-defendants included his son Armond, John and Gene Gotti, John Carneglia, Willie Boy Johnson, William Battista, Anthony "Tony Roach" Rampino, Leonard DiMaria, Nicholas Corozzo, and Nicholas Corozzo.

At Gotti's arraignment on March 28, 1985, Judge Nickerson ordered him released on a $1,000,000 personal recognizance bond secured by real property.

During the investigation, Giacalone discovered that Willie Boy Johnson was a confidential informant for the FBI.

She approached Johnson and asked him to become a government witness and to testify against John Gotti and the Bergin crew.

Johnson told the prosecutor that he was in fear of not only his own life but also the lives of his family if he testified.

Johnson was held in protective custody without bail for over a year before the case came to trial.

Fellow FBI informant William Battista learned that Giacalone was also looking to bring him into the case.

Battista quickly fled New York and has not been seen since.

In an attempt to convince him to plea bargain and testify against Gotti, Giacalone publicly revealed that Johnson was working as an informant for the FBI. This move by Giacalone led to a breakdown in already strained relations between the FBI and Giacalone.

The FBI tried to convince Johnson to enter the Witness Protection Program for his own safety, but for an unknown reason, he refused.

Giacalone's actions led to the FBI to cease involvement in the John Gotti case.

Then on May 11, using evidence obtained by the F.B.I., eleven organized crime figures, including the heads of New York's "Five Families," were indicted by United States Attorney Rudolph Giuliani under the Racketeer Influenced and Corrupt Organizations Act (RICO) on charges including extortion, labor racketeering, and murder.

By the time that the case went to trial, the indictments and arrests included defendants:

Paul "Big Paul" Castellano, boss of the Gambino crime family and his underboss Neil Dellacroce

Anthony "Tony Ducks" Corallo, boss of the Lucchese crime family and his underboss Salvatore "Tom Mix" Santoro along with Christopher "Christy Tick" Furnari, Lucchese family consigliere

Carmine "Junior" Persico, boss of the Colombo crime family and Gennaro "Gerry Lang" Langella, Colombo family acting boss/ underboss and Ralph "Little Ralphie" Scopo, Colombo family soldier

Anthony "Fat Tony" Salerno, boss of the Genovese crime family

Philip "Rusty" Rastelli, boss of the Bonanno crime family and Stefano Canone, Bonanno family consigliere and Anthony "Bruno" Indelicato, Bonanno family capo

This case would come to be known as, The Mafia Commission Trial (in full, United States v. Anthony Salerno, et al).

In the early 1980s, the Bonanno family was kicked off the Commission due to FBI undercover agent Joseph Pistone using the alias "Donnie Brasco" being able to infiltrate them.

And although Philip "Rusty" Rastelli, boss of the Bonanno crime family was one of the men initially indicted, this removal from the Commission actually allowed Rastelli to be removed from the Commission Trial.

After Paul was arrested for racketeering and other crimes, he learned for the first time that his home had been bugged by the FBI and that the information from the tapped Ruggiero telephone lines, recorded by FBI phone taps, provided the government with enough probable cause to enter and bug his Todt Hill mansion.

Castellano immediately went to his underboss Dellacroce and demanded he give over the transcripts of the tapes.

Castellano told Neil that he needed the incriminating surveillance transcripts to prepare his own defense in the upcoming Commission trial. Castellano said that his lawyers were trying to suppress the introduction of his own tapes in the upcoming Mafia Commission Trial.

Neil tried to placate Castellano, saying that there were personal embarrassing moments on the tapes that Ruggiero did not want anyone to hear.

This only escalated the conflict between Castellano and Gotti's faction, under the leadership of Neil Dellacroce.

Dellacroce informed Ruggiero and Gotti that Castellano wanted the transcripts of the tapes, and Ruggiero remained adamant about not giving up the tapes.

He accused Dellacroce of betrayal for even entertaining the thought of turning over the tapes to Castellano.

It was later revealed that Ruggiero even told his lawyers that he would kill them if they gave up the tapes.

Ruggiero had a good reason for not allowing the tapes to be given to Castellano. If he got hold of the tapes he would hear Ruggiero complaining about Castellano's high-handed manner.

He also stated that Castellano was a "milk drinker" and a "pansy".

Ruggiero was even heard putting down Castellano's two sons, who were running his Dial Poultry Company, as "the chicken men", and called business advisers that Castellano had around him as "the Jew club."

He also referred to Thomas Gambino, the son of Carlo Gambino and nephew of Paul Castellano, who oversaw the family's interests in the garment center as a "sissy dressmaker".

He also made comments about Castellano and Bilotti spending evenings together at Castellano's Todt Hill mansion, "whacking off."

Another reason as to why Ruggiero did not want the tapes released was because he had been lying to Castellano and Dellacroce.

He told them that he had not been dealing in drugs, but was merely cleaning up loose ends of his deceased brother Salvatore's narcotics operation.

John Gotti knew that they couldn't delay Castellano from hearing the tapes for too long.

All those tapes of Ruggiero would one day be played in court. And when they were, Castellano would know that John Gotti's crew was in the drug business.

It was believed that Castellano would've killed Gotti, along with Angelo and Gene, if the transcripts weren't handed over.

Castellano, at the very least, was reportedly planning to demote John Gotti and split up his crew, which likely would've been a fate worse than death for Gotti.

In June, Castellano again demanded that Dellacroce get Ruggiero to give him the tapes.

Some say that this time both Dellacroce and Gotti tried to convince Ruggiero to comply but Ruggiero refused, fearing he would endanger the men in his heroin racket.

Years later, Sammy Gravano said that Castellano had the Ruggiero tapes all along and was just testing his underboss to see if he would hand over the incriminating tapes against Gotti and his crew.

Castellano's legal issues were mounting over the next couple of months.

In July, he was indicted on loansharking charges and with tax evasion and pleaded not guilty.

On September 11, 1984, 35-year-old refrigerator repairman Romual Piecyk found his car blocked by a double-parked automobile outside the Cozy Corner Bar in the Maspeth section of Queens.

Piecyk laid on his horn until the owner of the double-parked automobile Frank Colletta, a Gambino Family associate, appeared.

Frank Colletta hit Piecyk in the face and took $325 from his shirt pocket.

Piecyk quickly jumped out of the car and began fighting with Colletta.

At that time, John Gotti exited the bar and also slapping Piecyk across the face.

Gotti then made a motion as if he was going to withdraw something from his waistband, and as he did, he warned Piecyk, "You better get the fuck out of here."

Gotti and Colletta returned to the bar while Piecyk went to notify the police.

Piecyk complained to New York City Police Sergeant Thomas Donohue and his partner, Police Officer Raymond Doyle, of being recently beaten and robbed by two men in a white car.

Piecyk led the officers back to the Cozy Corner Bar, near where he recognized the car. Entering the bar, Piecyk pointed out Gotti and Colletta as the men who had assaulted him

The police officers arrested John Gotti and Frank Colletta after Piecyk identified the men.

According to Officer Doyle, Gotti first said "Do you know who I am?" Looking past the officers towards Piecyk, Gotti then said "let me talk to this guy."

Several days later, Piecyk again identified Gotti as the man who had beaten him when he testified before a state grand jury.

Gotti and Colletta were indicted and charged with felony assault and theft.

In mid-September, Sammy "The Bull" Gravano was approached by Robert DiBernardo with a message from John Gotti.

DiBernardo informed him that Gotti and Ruggiero wanted to meet with him in Queens.

Gravano agreed and when he arrived only Ruggiero was present. Ruggiero informed Gravano that he and Gotti were planning to murder Castellano and asked for Gravano's support.

Gravano was initially noncommittal and told Ruggiero that he wanted to discuss this first with Frank DeCicco.

It was believed that in the event he was convicted and sent to prison, Castellano would designate his nephew, Thomas Gambino, acting boss, and his driver, Thomas Bilotti as the family's underboss.

Gravano and DeCicco ultimately decided to support Gotti's decision to carry out the hit on Paul Castellano.

John Gotti now had to recruit a respected old-timer in the Gambino family to offer more credibility to the new regime and placate Castellano's supporters.

Gotti turned to Joseph Armone for support in the plan to take out Castellano.

Luckily for Gotti, Armone had a dim view of Castellano as a true Mafioso gangster and saw Gotti's plan to take out the boss as a chance to rise to a leadership role in the Gambino family.

In the second week of October, opening statements commence in the Federal trial United States of America v. Paul Castellano, et al.

Castellano and nine others were accused of operating an international auto-theft ring that shipped stolen cars to Kuwait and Puerto Rico.

The defendants were also accused of committing five murders to protect the interests of the operation.

In November, in testimony from car thief Vito Arena, Castellano was named the head of the stolen-car ring that he worked for and gave testimony regarding the five murder charges.

For the first time in his life, Castellano found himself getting serious media attention.

The media waited at the courthouse for him daily and The New York Times published regular reports regarding Castellano's trial.

As Castellano was working on his defense John Gotti and his crew were working on his murder.

By mid-1985, Neil Dellacroce's health had begun to fail.

In mid-November 71-year-old Dellacroce used the name "Timothy O'Neill" to check into Mary Immaculate Hospital in the borough of Queens where he died two weeks later on December 2, of lung cancer.

About 100 people attended the mass in St. Patrick's Old Cathedral in Manhattan's Little Italy for Dellacroce.

In the eulogy, the priest said, "All of us are sinners and all of us need God's mercy and compassion. Very few of us will be ready to meet God and have the ecstasy of possessing God."

Outside St. Patrick's Old Cathedral before the mass a photographer was physically escorted from the church.

Nearly the entire Gambino family and many others showed up for his funeral to pay their respects to the family's underboss. One person in particular that did not show was Gambino boss Paul Castellano who claimed that he wanted to avoid government surveillance.

To John Gotti, Castellano not showing up for Dellacroce's funeral was a sign of disrespect not only to Dellacroce and his family but also to the Gambino crime family.

This was also viewed as highly disrespectful by the Dellacroce/Gotti loyalists.

He was buried in St. John's Cemetery in Queens with other high ranking members of the Mafia; Charles "Lucky" Luciano, Carlo Gambino, Joseph "Joe" Colombo, Salvatore D'Aquila, Carmine Galante, and Vito Genovese.

Castellano then named his bodyguard and driver, Thomas Bilotti, as the new underboss to replace Dellacroce.

Many people felt that this was also a show of disrespect to the Gambino Crime Family as Bilotti was only a loanshark with little of the diplomatic skill required to hold such a high ranking position within the family. Many members of Dellacroce's crew were more appropriate successors than Bilotti.

Castellano announced that he was planning to close down Dellacroce's Ravenite social club and reassign the old Fatico Bergin members to other crews.

It was also believed that with Dellacroce out of the way, Ruggiero could no longer keep the incriminating transcripts away from Paul.

Gotti also believed that if Paul heard the tapes, Castellano would go forward on breaking up John Gotti's crew.

With Dellacroce unable to stand in between Castellano and Gotti, Gotti decided to make a move against both men.

Shortly after Neil's death, Time magazine reported that he had been an FBI informer.

At a meeting after Dellacroce's death in December 1985, Paul Castellano told Gotti, "You know, there was a rumor that Neil was a rat."

It was said that Dellacroce was receiving $1000.00 a month from the FBI to be an informant.

If Dellacroce was an informant he would have brought down more than half the Gambino Crime Family, including Carlo.

And while he served as Underboss under Castellano, he could have taken down the entire Family.

To Gotti, this was the ultimate insult against Neil, especially coming from the man who had not even attended the underboss's funeral.

Those who knew Neil would never believe this because Dellacroce was probably taking in $100,000 a month as underboss, so why would he accept $1000 a month as an informant.

I personally doubt that Neil was an FBI informant simply because informants don't do numerous stretches in prison, as Neil did.

And most important of all, Dellacroce was an old school gangster and arguably the most loyal Mafioso left in the Family. If they threatened Dellacroce with the death penalty he would have taken it like a true man.

With the tensions in the Gambino Family against Castellano, John Gotti and Angelo Ruggiero recruited capo Frank DeCicco and soldiers Salvatore "Sammy the Bull" Gravano and Robert "DiB" DiBernardo into their plot to kill Castellano.

Gotti knew that he had to get the support of family old-timers, so he also recruited longtime capo Joseph "Joe Piney" Armone into the plot.

Their initial plan was to kill Castellano outside of his house on Todt Hill.

They knew that they risked the possibility of encountering federal agents outside of Castellano's house so Gravano suggested killing them while they were eating breakfast at a local diner.

DeCicco soon informed Gotti that he would be having a meeting with Castellano and some other Gambino Family members at Spark's Steak House on December 16.

Gotti and the other conspirators decided that this would be the best time to kill them both.

"Sammy Bull" Gravano testified seven years later in 1992 that in the weeks before the murder of Castellano, he was afraid to sleep in his own house for fear that Castellano might discover the plot and kill him first.

Gravano testified that he began carrying a gun and sleeping at the home of another family associate, who was not told of the plan to kill Castellano.

Many people over the years claimed that Gotti never received permission to kill Paul from the Commission. And that it was an unsanctioned hit.

Under cross-examination, Gravano said he began discussing killing Castellano with his accomplices nearly a year before the actual killing.

Gravano said that they sought permission from the bosses of the Bonanno, Colombo, and Lucchese crime families before carrying out the hit.

At the time that Gotti approached the Commission to kill Paul, each one of the Bosses of the other families was currently under indictment due to the bug planted in Castellano's house. And because of this, it is highly doubtful that he had many allies on the Commission.

Even if Gotti never approached Vincent "The Chin" Gigante with Paul getting killed, the following Bosses most likely had no issues with it.

Anthony (Tony Ducks) Corallo the Boss of The Lucchese family

Carmine (Junior) Persico Boss of the Colombo family,

Gennaro (Gerry Lang) Langella the acting boss and underboss of the Colombo family

I will also note that in the early 1980s, the Bonanno family was kicked off the Commission due to FBI undercover agent Joseph Pistone using the alias "Donnie Brasco" being able to infiltrate them.

And Gravano testified that they approached the Boss of the Bonanno family to get their consent. Maybe this was done in place of the Genovese Family we are not sure. But we do know by Gravano's testimony that the Bonanno family's permission was sought and the Genovese family was not.

So the only boss that they did not consult before Castellano's hit was Genovese family boss Vincent "The Chin" Gigante.

They knew that Gigante and Castellano were close and Gigante would most likely not approve of the hit.

On Monday, December 16, 1985, after finishing an appointment in Manhattan with his lawyer, 70-year-old Paul Castellano decided to do a little Christmas shopping with his bodyguard, chauffeur, and newly appointed underboss, 47-year-old Thomas Bilotti, before they went to their 5 p.m. meeting with Frank DeCicco, at Sparks Steakhouse at 210 East Forty-Fifth Street in Midtown Manhattan.

Sammy Gravano later testified in trial that he and John Gotti were sitting at the scene looking down at Sparks Steak House in a Lincoln sedan with tinted windows on the northwest corner of Third Avenue and 46th Street.

Just past the entrance to the restaurant was a team of armed hitmen with walkie-talkies, ready to take action.

He said that as they sat in the Gotti's Lincoln, Castellano pulled up alongside them and stopped for a red light, in another Lincoln driven by Thomas Bilotti at approximately 5:30 p.m.

He then turned and told Gotti that they were right next to them.

He said that Gotti used a walkie-talkie to notify the gunmen up ahead that they were stopped at the light, the first car, and they were coming through.

When the light turned green, Bilotti drove across Third Avenue and parked in front of Sparks Steak House, next to a no parking sign.

Waiting for the two men were four gunmen wearing black Russian hats and white trench coats.

When the car came to a full stop, the gunmen ran up to the car as both men were getting out, and shot them several times.

It is believed that John Carneglia was the gunman who shot Castellano a total of six times in the head, chest, and abdomen.

Castellano slumped to the grounded next to the open door on the passenger side of the car; his head face-up on the floorboard.

Thomas Bilotti was unarmed and after Paul had been shot, it is believed that Tony "Roach" Rampino shot him a total of six times also in the head and chest.

Bilotti fell to the street a few feet from the driver's door. A set of keys lay next to his body.

The two bodies were removed more than an hour later.

Witnesses at the scene told the police that after the killings were completed the hitmen disappeared into the rush-hour crowd and drove off in a rented luxury car that was parked close by.

That evening the New York Police issued an all-points bulletin for the rented luxury car, with New Jersey license plate ABM 43Z.

Gotti and Gravano, who observed the hit take place, drove by to take a closer look at the two bodies before they left the scene.

Gravano said that they drove slowly up to the murder scene and he looked down at Tommy Bilotti as he lay dead in the street and said to Gotti that he was gone.

Gravano and Gotti then drove back to Gravano's office in Brooklyn.

He said that later, Castellano's nephew, Thomas Gambino, entered Sparks Steak House moments later and encountered Frank DeCicco, who had been scheduled to meet with Castellano.

Frank DeCicco told him that his uncle just got shot, just go back to his car and leave.

Thomas Sheer, deputy assistant director of the FBI`s New York office, first speculated that the slayings were either ordered by Mafia "young Turks" who wanted to replace an aging leadership or by associates who feared Castellano would cooperate with prosecutors for a lighter sentence in his trial.

Some even speculated that the hit was punishment for a major security breach—the planting of a microphone in his house by the FBI that led to the arrests of the Bosses of the other Mafia families.

Paul Castellano's funeral was held on the night of Wednesday the 18th, at The Cusimano and Russo Funeral Home in Brooklyn where his body was laid out in an open casket.

The Cusimano and Russo Funeral Home is the same funeral home where Carlo Gambino's funeral was held.

Several hundred people attended Paul Castellano's wake, which one of his two sons said was, "just for the family."

Cardinal John O'Connor from the Catholic Archdiocese of New York refused to allow a public funeral mass for Castellano.

Cardinal John O'Connor made his decision 'out of deference to hundreds of thousands of people who could assume the church condones or is apathetic to organized crime' if such a mass was held.

A chief spokesman for the archdiocese said permission was given for a priest to say prayers at Castellano's wake and at the grave.

In addition to being denied a Mass of Christian burial, he was also refused burial in St. John's Cemetery, the family's first choice.

Instead, he was buried the very next morning around 9 a.m., Thursday the 19th, at the Moravian Cemetery on Staten Island in a secret and hasty burial just one and a half miles from his Todt Hill mansion.

A private Mass also was approved and held at Blessed Sacrament R.C. Church in West Brighton, but only after his burial.

To this day, the location of his crypt, on the cemetery grounds, remains unmarked and private.

Castellano was not the first mafia figure to be denied a public funeral mass.

In 1979, Carmine Galante was also denied a funeral Mass by Cardinal Terence Cooke after he was gunned down in a Brooklyn restaurant.

However, a priest had agreed to recite prayers at the funeral home service as what he called "an act of charity."

The Funeral Home had said that Castellano would be buried Friday, an apparent ruse to prevent press coverage of the funeral.

Even the FBI was not aware that Paul was being buried on Thursday.

A few days after Castellano's funeral, his mistress and housekeeper, Gloria Olarte returned to Colombia.

When she left New York she had $18,000 in cash and a porcelain clown, a gift from Castellano.

She now lives Medellin Columbia with her mother and is a secretary at a local travel agency.

Thomas Bilotti is also buried in the Moravian Cemetery.

At the time of his death, Bilotti left behind ten children, including a baby daughter who was only six-weeks-old.

The Murder of Paul Castellano enraged Vincent Gigante, boss of the Genovese crime family.

Gigante considered it an unsanctioned hit because Gotti never received permission from him which meant that he never received permission from all members of the Commission.

Gigante solicited the help of Lucchese crime family boss Anthony Corallo to kill Gotti.

Shortly after the killings, during a court hearing to decide whether Angelo's Ruggiero's bail should be revoked, an FBI agent testified that an informant said that Gotti and Angelo Ruggiero helped choreograph the murders of Thomas Bilotti and Paul Castellano.

Angelo blurted out in the courtroom, "This is like Russia."

Later, when the judge revoked his bail and ordered him to jail, Angelo lost his temper and appeared to threaten a prosecutor.

He pointed his finger and said, "Go home and celebrate with your family! Go ahead and laugh!"

Part Five
There's a New Boss In Town

Two weeks after Thomas Bilotti and Paul Castellano's murder, all captains of the Gambino family meet and Frank DeCicco nominates John Gotti for the new boss of The Gambino Crime Family.

John Gotti and his brother Peter

Forty-five-year-old John Gotti is elected unanimously and declares Frank DeCicco his underboss while Joe Gallo remains consigliere.

Frank DeCicco took control of all of the "white collar" rackets that once belonged to the Castellano faction.

Years later Sammy Gravano said in his book that he had told Frank DeCicco that he, DeCicco, not Gotti, should become the new boss, with John Gotti as his underboss.

By March 1986, John Gotti was busy preparing for two trials. The first was for the September 11, 1984 felony assault of Romual Piecyk.

By that time that the Romual Piecyk felony assault and theft trial started, Gotti's face had been seen all over the newspapers and television in the wake of the Castellano and Bilotti murders.

In February 1986, just one week before the trial was to start; Sergeant Anthony Falco of the Queens County District Attorney's Detective Squad went to Piecyk's home to arrange for Piecyk's testimony in the case.

According to Falco, Piecyk told him that he would not testify, saying that "because of Gotti's people" he was in fear of his life and his wife's safety.

He had received anonymous threats over the phone late at night and said that Gotti's people had cut the brake lines of the work van he used.

The police offered to provide Piecyk with protection and investigate the brake tampering incident, but Piecyk flatly refused.

The threats against Piecyk prompted Queens District Attorney John J. Santucci to request an anonymous jury for Gotti's upcoming trial.

The trial, scheduled to begin on March 2, was delayed for five days while Justice Ann B. Dufficy considered, and then denied, the prosecution's request for an anonymous jury.

On March 5, Piecyk spoke to a New York Daily News reporter and denied receiving any threatening phone calls or having his vehicle tampered with.

He then told the reporter that he would appear as a witness for John Gotti.

He said, "I am not going to go against Mister Gotti, I'm going in his behalf. I don't want to hurt Mister Gotti."

Piecyk also sent a letter earlier that year to the Queen's district attorney's office saying, "I saw the name of the man who assaulted me appearing in the Daily News and the media printed that he was next in line for godfather. Naturally, my idea for pursuing the matter dropped."

The trial began on March 19 with Piecyk scheduled to take the stand the following day.

The next day Piecyk didn't come to court because he was too scared to testify against John Gotti.

The Assistant District Attorney told the judge that the prosecution was unable to proceed with the trial, due to the absence of the People's witness.

Piecyk was located at Mercy Hospital in Rockville, Long Island Later that evening. He had gone there to have elective surgery performed on his right shoulder, thinking that he could avoid having to testify in the trial.

The next day The Assistant District Attorney told Justice Dufficy that Piecyk would appear in court on Monday to testify.

Gotti's attorney, Michael Coiro, Jr. told the court, "I think it's obvious the complaining witness is reluctant to testify."

To make sure that Piecyk would testify, Detectives from the Queens district attorney's office took Piecyk into protective custody as a material witness when he checked out of the hospital on Saturday morning,

He began to cry after he was brought to the station because he was still afraid of "Gotti's people."

On the afternoon of Monday, March 24, 1986, with his right arm in a sling and sporting dark glasses, Piecyk took the witness stand to begin two hours of direct examination by the prosecutor.

Piecyk was asked if he saw the men in the courtroom who had assaulted him.

To the shock of the spectators, he replied, "I do not."

When asked to describe the two men who had assaulted and robbed him, Piecyk stated, "To be perfectly honest, it was so long ago I don't remember."

Piecyk also said that "Eighteen months have elapsed; I can't identify the arresting officer, so how can they expect me to identify Gotti and Colletta? "

He did say that his pocket had been ripped and his cigarettes and money were taken, but he could not recall what had happened beyond that.

Justice Dufficy declared Piecyk to be a "hostile witness" and the trial was recessed until the following day.

The New York Daily News printed its famous headline, "I FORGOTTI" on its front page.

The following day the prosecutor tried to resurrect the case by asking to introduce Piecyk's grand jury testimony as evidence in the trial and to recall the arresting officers so they could testify about what Piecyk told them.

Justice Dufficy denied the prosecutor's request and dismissed the assault and robbery charges against John Gotti and Frank Colletta.

The Queens district attorney's office considered filing perjury charges against Piecyk but ultimately declined.

With the Piecyk assault trial over. The jury selection for Gotti's second trial, Giacalone's RICO trial, was scheduled to begin two weeks later on April 7, 1986.

On March 20, "front boss" of the Genovese crime family Anthony "Fat Tony" Salerno, along with 14 other Genovese family members, are indicted on charges including conspiracy, racketeering, and extortion.

Former Salerno soldier Vincent Cafaro would turn informant and tell testify that after Salerno suffered a stroke in 1981, he was delegated to functioning as a figurehead boss to keep the pressure off the official boss Vincent Gigante.

Cafaro would go on to testify at the trials of Gambino boss John Gotti.

Neil Dellacroce's son, Armond Dellacroce, who pleaded guilty in December 1985 to a racketeering conspiracy charge, failed to appear in Federal court for sentencing on March 31, 1986.

He left the New York City area and went to The Pocono's Mountain area of Pennsylvania to start life over on the run.

Another defendant in the trial in which Mr. Dellacroce pleaded guilty, Charles Carneglia, also fled before the trial began.

On April 13, 1986, a car bomb exploded in Dyker Heights, Brooklyn, outside the Veterans & Friends Social Club.

The only casualty was Gambino crime family underboss Frank DeCicco following a visit to Paul Castellano loyalist James Failla.

According to the authorities, an "explosive device" attached under the front end of a 1985 Buick Electra went off, causing the vehicle to burst into flames.

The two men were standing on the sidewalk by the car when the explosion occurred at 1:45 P.M. when DeCicco opened the passenger side door.

DeCicco took the brunt of the blast.

A police officer, who saw the explosion, said a black, mushroom-shaped cloud rose from the vehicle and flames burst from the car's windows. The bomb blasted a hole two feet wide in the street shattering windows in buildings near the corner of Bay 8th and 86th Streets and shook buildings for several blocks.

The blast also seriously injured a man who had been standing with DeCicco at the time of the blast. He was identified as sixty-nine-year-old, Lucchese soldier Frank "Frankie Hearts" Bellino who is said to bear a startling resemblance to John Gotti.

The two men were taken to Victory Memorial Hospital, where DeCicco was pronounced dead and Bellino was described as in very serious condition and lost several toes, but survived.

A woman who was passing by also received minor injuries.

A confidential informant said that John Gotti was very angry about DeCicco's murder.

Gotti also said that when he was out on bail, or when the trial was over, there was going to be a war and that he would take his revenge.

Gotti instructed all the Gambino made men and associates to attend DeCicco's wake, which was held over for two days at a funeral home near the bombing site.

And like many Mafiosos before him, the Roman Catholic Diocese of Brooklyn denied DeCicco a Mass before his burial at the Moravian Cemetery in Staten Island.

He is buried just 500 feet from Thomas Bilotti and less than 200 feet from Paul Castellano.

Years later, after he began cooperating with federal authorities, ex-Lucchese underboss Anthony "Gas Pipe" Casso, provided the FBI with the facts behind the DeCicco murder plot.

He said that Vincent Gigante who was the boss of the Genovese crime family had outsourced the job to Lucchese bosses Anthony "Gas Pipe" Casso and New Jersey-based Genovese capo Vittorio Amuso to plot the assassinations of DeCicco and Gotti.

Casso and Amuso recruited drug dealer and Genovese family associate Herbert "Blue Eyes" Pate to kill Gotti and DeCicco.

Pate was chosen because he had no links to the Gambino family and because of that, he would not be recognized while staking out DeCicco and Gotti.

Casso told the FBI that Pate drove up to the Veterans & Friends Social Club where Gotti and DeCicco were supposed to be attending a meeting with James Failla.

Casso and the Amuso brothers watched from a parked car as Pate walked toward DeCicco's car carrying two grocery bags. When he got close to the car he dropped one of the bags. As he squatted down to pick up the groceries, he placed a bag containing the explosives fashioned out of C-4 plastic explosive under DeCicco's car.

Casso said they decided to use an unconventional method of execution - a bomb - to divert suspicion toward Sicilian hoods that often used explosives.

Casso's effort to divert suspicion away from the real killers worked, according to a conversation later that day between Gotti and then-capo Sammy "The Bull" Gravano.

Gotti was heard saying, "The bomb was fuckin' something, the car was bombed like they put gasoline on it. You gotta see the car. You wouldn't believe the car."

"I saw it John," said Gravano, "I pulled Frankie out."

"I heard, Sammy. I heard it was too late."

"Who the fuck did it?" asked Gravano.

"I don't know...Who the fuck knows?" replied Gotti.

"Chin?" asked Gravano.

Gotti replied, "Nah, he wouldn't use fuckin' bombs, he'd want you to know. It's some renegade element."

The men waited about an hour for DeCicco to leave the club and get in the car.

Pate waited in a car across the street and the others in another car equipped with a police scanner.

Pate pulled up alongside DeCicco's car with the window rolled down, when Pate saw Lucchese soldier Frank Bellino approach the car, thinking that he was John Gotti and detonated the bomb

Casso told the FBI that Pate's car was hit with glass and debris when the explosion went off.

Anthony Casso, the Amuso brothers, and Pate met up minutes later.

Casso said that Pate was bleeding from his ear and the car had damage to the driver's side door.

Casso also said that Pate repainted and cleaned up the car.

Even with Casso's statements, it is unlikely that Pate, or the Amusos, will be charged with the killing of DeCicco because the Federal Government has little evidence other than Casso's version of the story.

But if we take a closer look at the killings of Castellano, Bilotti, and DeCicco we can see the situation in a whole new light.

Nobody kills a Boss without first going to the Commission.

PERIOD!

So for Galante to kill John Gotti, he would also have to go through the Commission first. And this is why I doubt that Gotti was the intended target of the car bombing.

My personal opinion is to save face with the other families Gigante had taken out one of Gotti's men.

An eye for an eye, and call it even.

It was also said that Pate thought John Gotti was he one approaching the car that day.

Many people believe that because the car was remotely set that Pate actually saw the man that many claims that he misidentified as Gotti.

At the time of the bombing, Gotti was a well-known figure in New York City and the surrounding area. And many doubt that Pate did not know that Bellino was not John Gotti.

We will also note that the four other families would have gone after Gotti together. Why just Gigante and the Genovese Crime Family?

And because of this many people feel that DeCicco, and not Gotti were the target that day.

On April 28, the court suspended John Gotti's trial and set August 18, 1986, as the new date for jury selection.

The next day, the government moved to revoke the bail of John and Eugene Gotti, Carneglia, and Rampino from their previous arrest in the March 1985 racketeering case on the ground that they had violated conditions of their release.

Meanwhile, it was believed that Gotti ordered the murder of the vice president and business manager of Local 608 of the United Brotherhood of Carpenters and Joiners, John F. O'Connor who was shot but not killed on May 7, 1986.

Gotti hired the Westies to shoot O'Connor because he had thugs trash a restaurant owned by Philip "Philly" Modica, a Gotti associate.

On the morning of the assault, Mr. O'Connor was waiting for an elevator in the lobby of his office building, 1650 Broadway, at 51st Street when he was shot.

After being shot O'Connor heard the shooter say, "O'Connor, Mr. O'Connor." The shooter was facing him with a gun, his arm outstretched.

O'Connor tried to enter the elevator but slipped to the floor. It was then that he heard and felt a couple of more shots.

O'Connor then got into the elevator, looked back, and saw the gunman put "something" - apparently a gun - in a black bag.

The shooter then walked out of the lobby.

Local 608 member Ivar Michelson was the only other witness to the shooting and would eventually identify a Westies member, Kevin Kelly as the gunman.

A member of the Westies gang, Jimmy McElroy, would later state that

O'Connor was shot by another man, Joseph Schlereth.

No arrest would be made in the shooting until almost three years later.

John Gotti's bail revocation hearing was held before Federal Judge Eugene H. Nickerson, who released Gotti on bail back on March 28, 1985, on a $1,000,000 personal recognizance bond secured by real property.

The Federal prosecutors presented the testimony of a DEA agent who had a confidential informant who was familiar with the members of the Gambino Crime family.

The DEA agent said that Piecyk the key witness in Gotti's assault case had received a "kick in the ass," which the confidential informant took to mean a warning not to testify in court against John Gotti.

Other agents testified that some of their confidential informants' stated that Gotti had become the head of the Gambino Crime Family in the months following the RICO indictment in March 1985.

Gotti submitted two interviews of Piecyk by newspaper and television reporters in his defense.

In both interviews, Piecyk denied being intimidated by Gotti and stated he had been mistreated by the District Attorney's office and the police.

The Federal prosecutors told Judge Nickerson that John Carneglia and Eugene Gotti have demonstrated that they also have intimidated witnesses and will continue to do so if they remained out on bail.

The Federal prosecutors offered tapes and transcripts of four conversations recorded in April 1982 from the listening device that was planted in Angelo Ruggiero's home.

The Federal prosecutors asserted that three of the conversations concern a scheme in which Ruggiero, Carneglia, and Eugene Gotti participated to bribe Jack Conroy who was really an undercover FBI agent who was posing as a telephone repairman for the telephone company.

Their goal was to determine whether there was court-ordered electronic surveillance of their homes or the home of John Gotti.

According to The Federal prosecutors, the fourth conversation concerns a decision on the question of whether to invest $5000 to get information from one of Jack Conroy's, sources who worked at the telephone company, which is notified when phones are being legally tapped.

The bug heard Eugene Gotti say: pay the money "just to get the hook in there."

The Federal prosecutors also told the judge that while on bail, Carneglia and Eugene Gotti may have committed other crimes and gone to meetings and wakes attended by John Gotti and other members of the Gambino Crime Family.

On May 13, 1986, one month after the DeCicco bombing, Judge Nickerson ordered Gotti's bail revoked.

First, Judge Nickerson found that while on bail John Gotti had intimidated Piecyk and that he would most likely do the same to witnesses in the pending RICO trial if he remained out on bail.

Judge Nickerson ruled that Carneglia and Eugene Gotti would be able to remain free on bail until the trial began.

Two days after the order was filed, John Gotti moved to reopen the proceedings to allow Piecyk to testify on his behalf.

Gotti's lawyers presented an affidavit from Piecyk stating that neither John Gotti nor anyone acting at John Gotti's direction had ever threatened him concerning the assault and robbery case.

After viewing the affidavit from Piecyk, Judge Nickerson believed that Piecyk had been "frightened" into changing his mind during Gotti's assault trial and refused to reopen the bail revocation hearings.

From jail, Gotti ordered the murder of Robert DiBernardo. The hit was carried out by Sammy Gravano; both DiBernardo and Ruggiero had been vying to succeed Frank DeCicco as Gotti's underboss until Ruggiero accused DiBernardo of challenging Gotti's leadership.

When Ruggiero had his bail revoked for his behavior in preliminary hearings, a frustrated Gotti instead promoted Joseph Armone as his new underboss to replace DeCicco.

Gotti then sent Armone to Florida to supervise the Gambino Family's activities there.

Jury selection for the racketeering case against John Gotti began again in August 1986, with Gotti standing trial alongside John Carneglia, Nicholas Corozzo, Tony Rampino, Leonard DiMaria, and William "Willie Boy" Johnson, who, despite being exposed as an informant, refused to turn state's evidence against Gotti.

During the jury selection, Piecyk appeared at the Federal Courthouse in Brooklyn.

Piecyk held an impromptu press conference outside the courthouse, after being denied the opportunity to speak in the courtroom.

He told reporters that John Gotti was being treated unfairly by the media, who had portrayed him as a "human monster."

Gotti's RICO trial began on August 27.

The Gambinos were able to compromise the case when George Pape hid his friendship with Westies crime boss known as, Bosko 'Yugo' Radonjić and was placed on Gotti's jury.

Through Radonjić, Pape reached out to Sammy Gravano and agreed to sell his not-guilty vote for $60,000.

Bruce Cutler, Gotti's defense attorney denied the existence of the Gambino family and framed the government's entire effort as a personal vendetta in the trial's opening statements on September 25.

The most serious charges in the RICO indictment died with Paul Castellano and Aniello Dellacroce, leaving Gotti to face lesser charges that had little to do with his current position as the family's boss.

There were also jurisdictional disputes between several state and federal law enforcement agencies. Each law enforcement agency was building its own case against John Gotti.

And unfortunate for the Government's prosecutors, none wanted to share witnesses or information for fear of jeopardizing its own chances for a successful conviction.

With the limited amount of witnesses or information being shared with the Federal prosecutors, the prosecution case relied heavily on testimony by convicted felons.

Bruce Cutler's strategy during the prosecution was to attack the credibility of prosecutor Diane Giacalone's witnesses by discussing their crimes committed before their turning state's evidence.

And each one agreed under defense cross-examination that they hoped their testimony would give them a shorter sentence.

The government's case was unraveling before their very eyes as one informer falsely denied that he ever worked for the FBI. Another testified that Giacalone offered him drugs and her panties to help him when he masturbated while he was in prison in return for his testimony.

John Gotti learned that his close friend Willie Boy Johnson was an informant for the FBI and during the trial, he told him, "I'm gonna give you a pass, and I give you my word no one will bother you," Gotti told Willie Boy. "After we win this case, you won't be able to be in the life again. But you'll get a job, you'll have your family, and you'll be all right."

For Willie Boy Johnson, hearing those words had to be a comfort and relief as any other informant would surely be killed as an act of revenge.

A majority of the jurors were in favor of convicting John Gotti when the jury's deliberations began.

During deliberations, George Pape held out for acquittal until the rest of the jury began to fear their own safety would be in jeopardy.

On March 13, 1987, John Gotti and his codefendants were acquitted after a long and acrimonious trial in which the defense repeatedly yelled crude personal insults at the prosecutors and outshouted the judge's orders.

John Gotti was now free to leave the jail where he was being held awaiting trial.

Gotti's 1987 acquittal was a major upset that further boosted his reputation.

The newspapers dubbed John Gotti "The Teflon Don" in reference to the failure of any charges to "stick."

Five years later, George Pape was convicted of obstruction of justice and sentenced to three years in prison.

Federal prosecutors immediately announced that John Gotti would soon be indicted for a different set of racketeering crimes.

While John Gotti's trial was playing out in Brooklyn in the third week of September 1986 The Commission Trial started and would last for ten weeks in a Manhattan federal courtroom.

The jurors were selected in September on an anonymous basis. They were only identified by numbers and their names were kept secret to protect them from intimidation or interference from any of the defendant's "Family members".

The Commission Trial gained national significance as the first case to focus on the commission of top crime leaders, portrayed by the prosecution as "the board of directors" of the Mafia.

The federal prosecutor's goal was to prove that the defendants conducted the affairs of "the commission of La Cosa Nostra" in a racketeering pattern that included loan-sharking, murders, labor payoffs, and extensive extortion in the concrete industry in New York City.

The key evidence in the trial came from taped conversations of the defendants talking in their cars and social clubs, which were under electronic surveillance.

On November 19, 1986, the jury convicted the defendants of all seventeen racketeering charges, which were in both a conspiracy and twenty related charges of extortion, labor payoffs, and loan-sharking except for Anthony (Bruno) Indelicato the only defendant named in murders "authorized" by the commission.

The jury determined that Indelicato took part in the 1979 slayings of the family's boss, Carmine Galante, and two associates.

After the verdict was read, the judge told the jurors, "You have acted as the true ministers of justice in this case."

The judge revoked the bail of those defendants who had been free during the trial. He ruled that all of them must be held for sentencing because they "pose a danger to the community."

"Nothing stops them," the judge said, adding that they had continued their criminal activities "even in jail."

The convicted Commission Trial defendants were sentenced on January 13, 1987, as follows:

75-year-old Anthony (Fat Tony) Salerno sentenced to 100 years imprisonment and fined $240,000: Salerno was the Boss of The Genovese family and considered the senior member of The Commission with 200 members and hundreds of associates based in Greenwich Village, East Harlem, and on Brooklyn and Jersey waterfronts.

73-year-old Anthony (Tony Ducks) Corallo sentenced to 100 years' imprisonment and fined $240,000: Corallo was the Boss of The

Lucchese family and considered the most powerful crime boss on Long Island with 110 members and an unspecified number of associates based in Brooklyn and the Bronx.

72-year-old Salvatore (Tom Mix) Santoro sentenced to 100 years' imprisonment and fined $250,000: Santoro was the Underboss of the Lucchese Family.

62-year-old Christopher (Christie Tick) Furnari Sentenced to100 years' imprisonment and fined $240,000: Furnari was the Consigliore of the Lucchese family.

53-year-old Carmine (Junior) Persico sentenced to 100 years' imprisonment and fined $240,000 plus 39 years' imprisonment on an earlier racketeering conviction with Gennaro (Gerry Lang) Langella: Persico was the Boss of the Colombo Family, with 115 members and at least 500 associates based in Brooklyn and Staten Island.

47-year-old Gennaro (Gerry Lang) Langella sentenced to 100 years' imprisonment and fined $240,000 plus 65 years' imprisonment on an earlier racketeering conviction with Carmine (Junior) Persico: Langella was the Acting boss and underboss of the Colombo family.

38-year-old Anthony (Bruno) Indelicato sentenced to 40 years' imprisonment and fined $50,000: Indelicato was a Captain in the Bonanno Family, with 195 members and 500 associates in New York, New Jersey, Pennsylvania, Arizona, Florida, and California.

58-year-old Ralph Scopo sentenced to 100 years' imprisonment and fined $240,000: Scopo was a soldier in the Colombo family and president of the Cement Workers District Council from 1977 to 1984.

Because of Scopo's ill health, his case was severed from the racketeering trial of Persico and Langella.

By 1987, the FBI had very little success with electronic surveillance and began to look for locations where it might be best to plant a bug to listen in on John Gotti.

The investigative team picked the Ravenite Social Club at 247 Mulberry Street in Little Italy as the best place to plant a listening device.

The FBI got into the Ravenite rather easily. Unfortunately, because the acoustics of the club was terrible they didn't have much luck picking up any good recordings.

The FBI went back in a few times and moved the bug around and used special audio filters, but even those steps didn't work.

It was at that point that one of the informants the FBI had working for them, informed them that Gotti would sometimes leave the Ravenite through a back door and go into an adjacent hallway of the building where he would talk with some of his captains.

The FBI also learned that Gotti would often leave the hallway and go to an apartment upstairs of a woman named Nettie Cirelli, the widow of family soldier Michael Cirelli.

As it turned out the apartment had also been used by the late Gambino underboss Aniello Dellacroce for his secret meetings.

The FBI now needed to obtain a warrant to plant listening devices in Nettie Cirelli's apartment. And on top of that, they would need an opportunity to plant the bug without her knowing and tipping off Gotti.

On April 29, 1987, Genovese family Boss, 78-year-old Philip Lombardo, also known as "Benny Squint" and "Cockeyed Phil" dies of natural causes in Florida. Vincent Gigante becomes the new official Genovese family Boss.

Also on April 29, a mentally ill 37-year-old Ozone Park, Queens resident named Jeffrey William Ciccone, fired a shot in an apparent attempt to assassinate John Gotti, outside the Bergin Hunt and Fish Club at 101st Avenue and 98th Street in South Ozone Park.

Two witnesses told the police that at about 3:30 p.m. a loud noise, that could have been a gunshot, was heard as Gotti and several companions exited the Bergen Hunt and Fish Club.

The witnesses said that men began pouring out of the club and chased a lone man through the streets and that several men, one of whom wielded a baseball bat, beat and shoved the man into a dark-colored sedan with tinted windows parked about three blocks from the Bergen Club at the intersection of 97th Avenue and 95th Street.

The car then quickly sped away.

There was a trail of blood for 50 feet from the intersection in the direction of the Bergin Hunt and Fish Club.

Tests were made and it was determined that the blood on the street was the same type as Mr. Ciccone.

Gotti denied being shot at and he has told detectives he was unaware of a man being beaten or forced into a car.

Some people quickly concluded that this was an attempted hit ordered by the other Families. However, the organized-crime experts said that the apparent attempt to shoot Gotti appeared to be amateurish and bore no signs of a well-planned gangland slaying.

Ciccone was taken to a Staten Island candy store and tortured and murdered.

The mutilated body of Ciccone was discovered by police officers at 4:30 a.m. in the basement of Paul's Sweet Shoppe at 44 New Dorp Plaza in the New Dorp section of Staten Island after a passer-by reported that the front door of the store was ajar.

A rubber-coated white clothesline was used to tie Mr. Ciccone's hands behind his back and his feet and clothesline was also looped around his neck. He had been shot in the face after he had been stuffed in a mortician's body bag on the floor of the basement.

Five .380-caliber shell casings were found on the floor.

Paul's Sweet Shop is believed to be operated by James LaForte, the son of Joseph LaForte Sr., a recently ousted member of the Gambino family who is disliked by Gotti.

Mr. LaForte and his son, Joseph Jr., have told investigators they did not know why Mr. Ciccone was brought to the store and shot there.

Former soldier Dominic "Fat Dom" Borghese later testified that Gambino family associate Joe Watts shot six bullets into Ciccone's head.

Between August 1987 and January 1988, the FBI recorded a dozen conversations in which Genovese crime family consigliere Louis Manna and other Genovese mobsters discussed murdering John Gotti, Gene Gotti, and a New York contractor named Irwin Schiff.

On August 8, 1987, Schiff was shot in the head while dining at Bravo Sergio, an Upper East Side restaurant he frequented in Manhattan.

Witnesses said that a tall man in a dark suit slipped in the restaurant's side door, walked behind Schiff, and shot him twice in the head with a .38-caliber pistol.

Immediately after the shooting, Schiff's fellow diners, including his blond tablemate, fled from the crime scene before the police arrived.

The FBI overheard Manna advising the hitman to wear a disguise as the target area was fairly open while discussing the murder of John Gotti.

FBI agents warned the Gottis of the reported plot against them.

The murder plot against the Gottis grew out of an underworld "turf war" and was intended to prevent the Gambino crime family from encroaching on the operations of the Genovese family in northern New Jersey.

On December 22, 1987, Gambino Underboss, Joseph Armone, and Gambino consigliere, Joseph N. Gallo was convicted of racketeering conspiracy involving extortion, bribery, and illegal interstate travel to commit bribery.

From 1981 to 1982 to bribe a government official $20,000 to transfer Gallo's son to federal prison, from a New York state prison.

During the trial, Gambino crime family associate George Yudzevich testified against the Gambino underboss in his racketeering trial.

Yudzevich would be found shot to death in California the following May.

Under federal sentencing guidelines, any sentence imposed on the two men would amount to a life sentence at their ages.

With this in mind, the judge released Joseph Gallo on bail before sentencing.

Armone was offered a similar temporary release, but only on the condition that he publicly admits his role in the Gambino Crime Family and renounce his ties to it.

Gotti, however, had banned Gambino Family members from taking plea deals that acknowledged the existence of the family and refused Armone an exception.

Two months later, on February 22, 1988, Joseph Armone was sentenced to 15 years in federal prison and was fined $820,000.

Gallo was sentenced to 10 years in federal prison and ordered to pay fines totaling $380,000.

Gallo became the oldest inmate in federal custody.

After Gallo's conviction, Gotti replaced him with capo Sammy Gravano at consigliere.

On September 24, 1988, in a separate case, Armone was convicted in Florida of extortion, loansharking, and racketeering in Broward County

On February 23, 1992, Joseph Armone died in prison of natural causes. He was buried in the Cemetery of the Resurrection in Staten Island, New York.

Gallo was released from prison in 1995.

Then on September 1, Gallo died of natural causes in Astoria, Queens. He is buried in St. Michaels Cemetery in East Elmhurst, Queens.

On April 4, 1988, Aniello Dellacroce's son, Armond "Buddy" Dellacroce, died from a cerebral hemorrhage caused by severe alcohol cirrhosis.

He was also suffering from the AIDs virus.

He was 32 when he passed away under the fake name "Frank Trainer" in the Pocono Mountains area of Pennsylvania where he had been living as a fugitive for two years.

In an attempt to alter his appearance, Dellacroce had gained over 50 pounds since he had fled New York.

On April 17, Gambino Captain Anthony Gaggi dies of natural causes while being housed at New York's Metropolitan Correctional Center.

On June 29, Genovese crime family consigliere Louis Manna was indicted for conspiring to kill John Gotti and his brother Gene.

The following year, Manna was sentenced to 80 years in federal prison for racketeering and conspiring to murder the two Gottis and Schiff.

Just over 18 months after being acquitted in the trial with John Gotti, any relief or comfort that Willie Boy had all came to an end on August 29.

As a favor to Gotti, Bonanno's family hitmen, Thomas Pitera and Vincent "Kojak" Giattino ambushed Wilfred "Willie Boy" Johnson in front of his Brooklyn home as he walked to his car.

The hitmen fired 19 rounds at him, hitting him twice in the back, once in each thigh, and at least six times in the head.

Before fleeing the area the hitmen dropped jack-like spikes on the street to prevent the possibility of pursuit.

In 1992, Pitera and Giattino were indicted and tried for Willie Boy Johnson's murder.

Giattino was found guilty and Pitera was acquitted but was later convicted of six other murders that he had committed.

Former Gambino capo Michael "Mikey Scars" DiLeonardo later testified that on December 24, 1988, he was led into an apartment belonging to Joe Butch Corrao's mother located on Mulberry Street.

Inside were John Gotti, Jr., Bobby Boriello, Craig DePalma, Dominick "Skinny Dom" Pizzonia, and Nicholas LaSorsa who were going to be officially inducted, into the Gambino Family.

Also present at the meeting were family capo John "Jackie Nose" D'Amico, along with capo Gene Gotti.

Salvatore "Sammy the Bull" Gravano and Pasquale "Patsy" Conte administered the oath to keep Gotti from being accused of showing favoritism to his son.

John Gotti Jr. was soon promoted to capo at the behest of Sammy Gravano, and given him his own crew.

John Gotti Sr. assigned Bobby Boriello to John Gotti Jr.'s crew.

Boriello would soon become the most powerful and closest ally to John Gotti in his crew and was eventually appointed acting capo of the Junior Gotti crew.

Boriello was suspected in several murders, as well as involvement in extortion, loan sharking, and drug trafficking during his early days.

John Gotti was arrested on the evening of January 23, 1989, outside the Ravenite and charged with ordering the 1986 assault of labor union official John O'Connor.

State prosecutors had the testimony of Westies gangster James McElroy and a recording of Gotti discussing O'Connor and saying that his intention was to "bust him up."

Gotti was released on $100,000 bail.

While out on bail, Gotti's relationship with his one-time friend, Angelo Ruggiero was falling apart.

Angelo Ruggiero remained in federal custody after his first heroin trafficking case trial with Gene Gotti and John Carneglia's ended in a mistrial, because of jury tampering.

His bail was still revoked, for the second trial which also resulted in a mistrial, again for suspected jury tampering.

However, for Ruggiero's third trial, in 1989, he was finally released on $1 million bail.

By the summer of 1989, Angelo Ruggiero had terminal lung cancer.

During the last months of Angelo Ruggiero's life, both Underboss Sammy Gravano and Gene Gotti urged John to visit Ruggiero.

Gotti refused because he was angry over Ruggiero's criminal activities being recorded on FBI wiretaps.

In fact, Gotti was so mad that he wanted to have Angelo murdered for allowing himself to be recorded by the FBI.

Underboss Sammy Gravano convinced Gotti that because Angelo was dying of cancer anyway, that it was not even worth it to carry out the hit.

Gotti reluctantly agreed and instead, stripped Angelo of his rank as caporegime of the Bergin crew and severed him from all Gambino Family criminal activities.

When Mrs. Cirelli was on a vacation in Florida over Thanksgiving weekend of 1989, the FBI planted the bug in the apartment over the Ravenite where Gotti held numerous meetings with Locascio, Gravano, and others.

On the recordings, Gotti stated that he had approved or was aware of the killings of Gambino soldiers Louis DiBono, and Louis Milito.

Gotti was also recorded justifying Louis DiBono's 1990 murder in the parking lot of the old World Trade Center. His reason for the killing was because the Gambino captain ignored Gotti's demand for meetings.

"You know why he is dying?" Gotti said. "He is gonna die because he refused to come in when I called. He didn't do nothing else wrong."

Other conversations between Gotti and Locascio would ultimately seal Gotti's fate.

The tapes recorded conversations that showed that Gotti had been concerned about Gravano's acquisition of numerous construction companies. Gotti believed that these acquisitions might become a power base from which Gravano could challenge him.

Gotti was also overheard expressing to Locascio his irritation with Gravano.

This bad mouthing would prove costly to John Gotti later.

On December 5, 1989, 49-year-old Angelo Ruggiero died of cancer in Howard Beach, Queens.

Later, Gene Gotti and John Carneglia were both convicted and sentenced to 50 years in prison.

In January 1990, John Gotti's trial on charges he ordered the murder of carpenters union leader John O'Connor began.

On February 9, 1990, John Gotti is acquitted at trial. It later emerged, however, that FBI bugs had caught Gotti discussing plans to fix the jury as he had in his 1986–87 racketeering case.

This is the third acquittal in five years for the Teflon Don.

In the fall of 1990, the FBI tapes and other evidence allowed the FBI and federal prosecutors in Brooklyn to obtain a racketeering indictment against Gotti, Frank Locascio, who the FBI identified as the underboss of the Gambino family; Sammy Gravano and reputed captain and son of Carlo Gambino, Thomas Gambino.

Gotti set up a 5-man ruling panel to replace the underboss and consigliere positions, in the event that he was arrested and remained in jail awaiting trial. This would allow an imprisoned Boss to have better control of the family.

John Gotti Junior was appointed to this ruling panel along with Nicholas Corozzo, John D'Amico, Louis Vallario, and Peter Gotti. 73-year-old capo James Failla was appointed acting boss by Gotti to run the family.

Bobby Boriello operated John Jr.'s rackets from his Brooklyn social club on Sackett Street.

On the night of December 11, Gambino crime family associates and members arrived at the Ravenite Social club as the FBI watched from an apartment on Mulberry Street.

Gotti had his men show up at the club at least once a week to show respect and to check-in.

John Gotti arrived at the Ravenite Just after 6:00 p.m.

Once Gotti was inside the club the FBI arrest team made their move on the Ravenite.

Gotti, Locascio, and Gravano were arrested at the Ravenite that evening and charged with racketeering and murders.

One of the charges in the indictment against Gotti was that he ordered the execution of Paul Castellano.

John Gotti was again being held without bail awaiting trial.

73-year-old capo James Failla was appointed acting boss by Gotti to run the family on the streets while he awaited trial.

The FBI arrested Thomas Gambino separately in the garment district and was also charged but with lesser offenses and not for any murders.

On April 13, 1991, John Gotti Jr.'s capo Bobby Boriello was shot twice in the head, and five times in the torso outside his home on Bay 29th Street in Bensonhurst, Brooklyn, on orders from Lucchese crime family underboss Anthony Casso.

At the time of his murder, Boriello had been under investigation for running a cocaine trafficking conspiracy, as well as his suspected involvement in the murder of Paul Castellano.

After months of pretrial proceedings, Gravano found out how John Gotti had bad-mouthed him on the Cirelli apartment tapes.

Gravano also knew that if he was convicted he would spend the rest of his life in prison.

Gravano was furious with Gotti after hearing the tapes and decided it was best for him if he turned government witness and help the federal prosecutors in their pursuit to convict the Teflon Don.

On November 13, 1991, as John Gotti sat in jail awaiting his upcoming trial, his underboss Sammy Gravano signs a cooperation agreement with the government.

In 1997 Gravano released a biographical book based on his life titled "*Underboss*".

In the book, Gravano describes an incident in which Locascio, in jail awaiting trial with Gotti and Gravano in 1991, gave him a stolen orange before offering one to John Gotti.

John Gotti became furious and loudly belittled Locascio in front of some of the other inmates.

Gravano said that a humiliated Locascio tearfully vowed to murder Gotti, stating, "The minute I get out, I'm killing this motherfucker."

Gravano says he and Locascio then made a pact to kill John Gotti.

If they were acquitted they knew that Gotti would throw a victory party. And that would give them the perfect opportunity to kill the boss.

Locascio said, "Sammy, two things. I'll bring him to the party myself, and I got to be the shooter."

Before the trial began, federal prosecutors succeeded in having Gotti's lawyer Bruce Cutler removed from the trial.

Judge I. Leo Glasser agreed that secret tapes showed that Cutler and two other attorneys had acted as "house counsels" for the Gambino crime family.

Cutler was disqualified from working on the case since playing the tapes would result in the lawyers having to testify about matters the prosecution intended to introduce as evidence.

The judge ruled that the jury would remain anonymous and be sequestered throughout the trial to avoid any jury tampering by the Gambinos.

And the worst information that the defense received just before the trial was to begin was, that "Sammy Bull" Gravano, Gotti's underboss, would plead guilty and testify as a government witness.

Years later, Gravano would say that John Gotti told him he needed to be the Mafia's "sacrificial lamb" just to save himself.

When the trial began before Judge Leo Glasser in Brooklyn, New York on January 21, 1992, Gotti's lawyer, opened the defense by stating that his client's only crime was the lack of formal education and wasted no time in accusing Gravano of being the rightful object of the prosecution's attention.

During the trial, the prosecutors played hours of secretly taped conversations in which Gotti spoke of murders and other crimes.

Salvatore "Sammy the Bull" Gravano was sworn in to testify against Gotti for nine days, from Monday, March 2 until Friday, March 13.

His testimony included admitting his participation in nineteen murders and implicating John Gotti in ten of them.

Gravano also testified that he and Gotti supervised the slaying of Paul Castellano and that Gotti then succeeded Castellano as the boss of the Gambino crime family.

He added that he in turn became a captain and later the family's underboss.

Gravano finished his testimony against John Gotti by asserting that he became a Government witness and told the truth because of a desire to "turn my life around."

When Gotti's defense lawyer suggested that Gravano's real reason for cooperating with the Government was to obtain a lenient sentence and keep the money he accumulated in a life of crime, he simply replied, "That's not my major concern."

As Gravano left the witness stand Gotti mockingly wiped imaginary tears from his eyes.

After Gravano's testimony videos were shown to back up much of Gravano's claims.

On March 23, the government was resting its case.

The only defense witness John Gotti's lawyers were permitted to call was a tax attorney who claims he advised Gotti not to file tax returns while he was under indictment.

Five other witnesses were ruled ineligible, causing an outburst from attorney Cardinale that resulted in a contempt charge issued by the judge.

John Gotti told the court, "What happened to our defense? I should have put on a little song and dance."

On March 31, Judge Glasser gave the final instructions to the jury. As the day's court session ended, Gotti stood, pointed toward the prosecution table, and called out to the reporters who were present in the courtroom, "the 1919 White Sox," indicating that the prosecutors had fixed the case.

After thirteen hours of deliberations, Gotti was found guilty on all counts on April 2.

Locascio was convicted of all charges, except one count of illegal gambling.

Both men were sentenced June 23 to life in prison without parole and a $250,000 fine.

John Gotti's supporters protested the sentence by overturning cars in the streets outside the Brooklyn courthouse. By the end of the day, seven protesters were arrested on felony riot charges.

Prosecutors say that John Gotti Sr. made his son, John Jr., the acting boss of the family with a committee of captains to assist him.

One benefit that John Gotti Sr. had was the fact that as a family member, John Jr. and his brother Peter were some of the few people allowed to visit him in prison.

It is after these visits that prosecutors believe that Gotti Jr. and Peter relayed John Gotti's orders to the Family from prison.

On September 26, Gravano was sentenced to five years in prison. However, since Gravano had already served four of those years, the sentence amounted to less than one year, and went into the witness protection program.

Gotti surrendered to federal authorities to serve his prison time on December 14, 1992. Almost six years to the day that Paul Castellano was gunned down in front of Spark's Steakhouse on December 16, 1986.

John Gotti was transferred to United States Penitentiary, Marion in southern Illinois.

Ten years later, on June 10, 2002, John Gotti died of throat cancer at the United States Medical Center for Federal Prisoners in Springfield, Missouri.

Just one month before Gotti's death, Joe Bonanno, the last surviving member of the original five bosses, dies of heart failure in Arizona on May 11.

In 1995, Gravano left Witness Protection and relocated to Scottsdale, Arizona.

John Gotti's brother, Peter Gotti, sent a hit team to Arizona to kill Gravano testifying against John Gotti. The hit team was unable to carry out the hit.

In February 2000, Gravano and 47 others were arrested on federal and state drug charges.

On May 25, 2001, Gravano pleaded guilty in New York to federal drug trafficking charges. On June 29, 2001, he pleaded guilty in Phoenix to the state charges.

On September 7, 2002, Gravano was sentenced in New York to 20 years on the federal charges, to run concurrently with the 19-year Arizona sentence.

Gravano spent 17 years in prison and was released early in 2017.

On May 11, 1993, Tommy Gambino was convicted of two counts of racketeering and racketeering conspiracy and sentenced to a five-year prison sentence.

With John Gotti now in prison, Vincent "the Chin" Gigante, boss of the Genovese crime family, was now the most powerful Mafia crime boss in the United States.

In an elaborate act to avoid prosecution Gigante often wandered the streets of Greenwich Village mumbling incoherently to himself in his bathrobe and slippers.

The press soon called him, "The Oddfather".

Gigante's act worked for over ten years and Gigante was determined to be mentally unfit to stand trial.

However, by 1997 he was tried and convicted of racketeering and sentenced to 12 years in prison.

And just like John Gotti, he also died at the United States Medical Center for Federal Prisoners while in prison on December 19, 2005.

Part Six

The Gambino Crime Family After John Gotti

John Gotti Jr.

John Gotti Jr. attempted to do things a little bit different than his father did in the 80s

Remembering how his father's illegal activities had been heard by FBI bugs that were planted in areas where his father held meetings, Gotti Jr. discussed mob business while walking alongside trusted capos down the street of Little Italy.

Gotti Jr tried to portray himself as a legitimate businessman rather than the leader of the most powerful mafia family in the United States.

It was soon learned that several of the Gambino Made men didn't think much of John Jr as a leader.

Many believed that Jr. didn't have the years of street experience to be a ruthless leader and topnotch negotiator like his father. And because of this, the Gambinos lost out on several disputes with the other families.

Vincent "the Chin" Gigante, boss of the Genovese crime family was so unimpressed with Gotti Jr. that the Genovese crime family refused to deal with him.

John Jr. ran the family business throughout the 1990s until a 1997 search of the basement of a property he owned turned up a typed list of the names of the "made" members of the Gambino crime family.

Also found were two handguns, almost $350,000 in cash, and a list of the guests who attended his wedding, along with the dollar amount of their wedding gifts.

Not only did the FBI find information on Gambino Family members but also a list of several men who were inducted into other families in 1991 and 1992.

This list was initially created because the New York Mafia calls for prospective members to be vetted by the other families before being inducted.

However, these lists are destroyed when the member is vetted and the inductions take place.

The discovery of this list enraged John Gotti's father as well as the bosses of the other crime families.

In addition to the list, the FBI discovered transcripts of prison conversations in which Gotti Jr. received advice from his father on how to run the family.

The discovery of this list in Gotti's house earned him the nickname 'dumbfella' in the New York media.

Shortly after the discovery in John Gotti Jr.'s basement, federal authorities indicted him under RICO, charging that he was not only the acting boss of the Gambino Family but received millions of dollars from numerous Gambino rackets.

In 1998, John Gotti Jr. was indicted on charges related to attempts to extort money from the owners and employees of an upscale strip club in Manhattan named Scores.

According to the indictment, in order to stay in business, the nightclub had to pay the Gambinos $1 million over six years.

It was believed that Gotti's share of the money was close to $100,000.

The government offered John Jr. a plea deal to plead guilty to reduced charges of loansharking, bookmaking, and extortion to avoid trial.

Before he could take a deal from the government he wanted to discuss this with his father.

When John Jr. met with his father he was not surprised when he tried to convince him to fight the charges and remain a proud member of the Gambino Mafia family.

However, when Jr explained that he wanted to raise his six children and be a husband to his wife Kimberly, he ultimately relented.

"John, if this is what you want to do, you're your own man," he said. "But they will never leave you alone. The government will never accept it. You think they're going to stop if you plead guilty? They'll just bring another case, and another case."

Shortly after the visit, Jr. pleads guilty and was sentenced in 1999 to 77 months in prison.

Peter Gotti became head of the Gambino crime family after Gotti Jr. was sent to prison and is believed to have formally succeeded his brother shortly before Gotti Sr.'s death in June 2002

Between the years of 1999–2012, Arnold Squitieri held the position of underboss.

However, between 2005 and 2012 he spent in prison. While in prison two Gambino Members Anthony "The Genius" Megale and Domenico "Italian Dom" Cefalù filled in as acting underboss in Squitieri's absence.

Even though John Jr. was released early in 2001, he was found guilty of other charges in 2002 and sentenced again.

He would be in prison when his father died of throat cancer not long after on June 10, 2002.

In June 2002, days before his brother, John's death, Peter Gotti was indicted on federal racketeering charges.

While Peter Gotti awaited trial for extortion and money laundering, the Gambino's leadership allegedly went to administration members Nicholas Corozzo, Joseph Corozzo, and John "Jackie" D'Amico.

On December 22, 2004, Peter was convicted of extortion in the construction industry and for plotting to murder Salvatore "Sammy the Bull" Gravano and sentenced to 25 years in prison.

However, Peter Gotti remained the official boss while in prison, while the day-to-day operation of the family shifted to capos John D'Amico and Nicholas Corozzo.

Because the rest of Gotti's loyalists were either jailed or under indictments Gotti's rivals regained control of the Gambino family.

In the five years between 2004 and 2009, John Gotti Jr. has been a defendant in four racketeering trials.

John Jr. faced crimes ranging from drug trafficking to racketeering and murder.

He was also accused of orchestrating a plan to kill radio host Curtis Sliwa, the founder of the Guardian Angels, for badmouthing his father on the radio.

And just like his father, each one ended in mistrials, giving him the nickname, "Teflon Jr." for evading conviction like his father.

In 2010, the federal prosecutors announced that they are no longer going after John Jr.

He has repeatedly asserted in recent years that he is no longer associated with organized crime.

In 2005, law enforcement recognized Nicholas "Little Nick" Corozzo as the boss of the Gambino crime family.

Corozzo and Leonard "Lenny" DiMaria were released from prison in 2005, after serving ten years for racketeering and loansharking charges in New York and Florida.

Corozzo's brother, Joseph Corozzo, was believed to be the family consigliere.

Arnold "Zeke" Squitieri was the acting underboss until street boss and former ally of John Gotti, Jackie D'Amico named Domenico "Italian Dom" Cefalù the family's underboss.

Cefalù's main responsibility was overseeing the Sicilian faction of the Gambino family.

On Thursday, February 7, 2008, a federal grand jury issued an indictment that led to the arrest of 54 Gambino family members and associates.

This Federal investigation would come to be known as, Operation Old Bridge

Gambino crime family boss Nicholas Corozzo went on the run after he was tipped off by his daughter that her husband and fellow mobster was arrested.

Corozzo stayed on the run for almost four months until he turned himself in to authorities on May 29, 2008.

One of those arrested in the raids was a mobster named Frank Cali, who would become the future boss of the Gambino family.

At the time of his arrest, he was allegedly the "ambassador" in the US for the Inzerillo crime family in Italy.

Most of those arrested ended up pleading guilty and receiving sentences less than three years in prison.

While Gambino Boss, Nicholas "Little Nick" Corozzo, Domenico "Italian Dom" Cefalù, and the upper administration members were in prison, a three-man panel of street bosses Daniel "Danny" Marino, John Gambino, and Bartolomeo Vernace took control of the Gambino family.

Cefalù was released from federal prison in November 2009 after serving two years.

The three-man panel remained in place until July 2011, when Domenico "Italian Dom" Cefalù was been promoted to the official boss of the Gambino crime family, putting an official end to the Gotti regime.

In 2012 Frank Cali was promoted to Underboss.

With Cefalù and Frank Cali's promotion, the Sicilian faction, better known as "Zips", gained control of the Gambino crime family.

In 2015 Frank Cali had taken over as the family's new acting boss after Cefalù had taken a step back and no longer ran the families day to day operations.

Cefalù felt it was better to retire before the feds found a way to indict him.

53-year-old Frank Cali was shot dead outside his home on Staten Island around 9 P.M. on March 13, 2019, by a lone gunman.

The shooting, which was captured on a security camera outside of Cali's home, shows him emerging from his home apparently responding to his Cadillac SUV being rammed into by a pickup truck.

After exiting the home he makes his way down the driveway where he speaks with the individual in the pickup who was wearing a hoodie and a baseball cap.

Cali's assassin picks up the SUV's license plate which had been dislodged in the collision and hands it to Cali.

Cali then goes to the rear of the SUV to place the license plate into a compartment in the rear of the vehicle.

While his back was turned to the pickup truck driver, the driver pulled out a 9-millimeter handgun firing over a dozen shots at Cali.

Six of those shots are believed to have hit Cali as he tries to escape by crawling under his vehicle.

The gunman then stood over top of Cali and fired multiple shots into him in an effort to make certain he was dead before returning to the pickup and quickly driving away.

Frank Cali was rushed to Staten Island University Hospital North just one and a half miles away and was pronounced dead soon after arrival.

The New York law enforcement first believed that John Gotti Sr's brother, Gene Gotti, who was recently released from prison was somehow involved in the killing.

They assumed that 72-year-old Gene Gotti, who was released from federal prison in September 2018 after 29 years behind bars for heroin dealing, was attempting to take control back of the Gambino crime family by eliminating the current boss.

Three days later, a 24-year-old Staten Island resident named Anthony Comello was arrested in New Jersey by U.S. Marshals after the suspect's fingerprints were found on the license plate of Cali's silver Cadillac Escalade SUV led authorities to him and charged with the murder.

Authorities reportedly believe the crime was related to a personal dispute regarding one of Cali's younger nieces rather than any organized crime activity.

However, in a three-and-a-half-hour interrogation with a detective after his arrest, Comello gave conflicting and sometimes bizarre accounts of the shooting.

The allegations against Gene Gotti infuriated his nephew John Gotti Jr, who immediately came out and voiced his opinion about the law enforcement community accusing his uncle of the killing and demanded an apology.

The only response to Gotti's apology demand was:

"Tell Junior we will apologize once his family apologizes to the Castellano, Lino and Johnson families, and all the other families whose relatives they killed and got away with. He should stick to the movie business, or whatever else he's doing to pay the bills."

Following Frank Cali's death, it was reported that Lorenzo Mannino had become the new Boss of the Gambino crime family.

However, as far as the feds are concerned Cefalù is still the boss of the Gambino family.

In 2020 more information would be released to the public regarding Comello and his reasoning behind the killing.

During a court conference at the end of February, Comello launched into a strange, rambling 20-second monologue in which he said his phone had contained information on human sex trafficking and drug smuggling.

He then referenced Russia, Australia, and Ukraine.

He then mentioned an alleged 1950's large-scale CIA program which attempted to manipulate the news media for propaganda purposes named "Operation Mockingbird," without going further into details.

The authorities discovered that he was obsessed with internet conspiracy theories like QAnon and believed he was working to aid President Donald Trump.

Shortly after this court appearance, the media reported that alleged mob-boss killer Anthony Comello has been deemed mentally unfit for trial.

A determination of mental incompetence means that Comello can't aid in his defense and doesn't understand the charges against him.

Comello's lawyer said that the judge ordered Comello to be transferred to a state Office of Mental Health facility for further evaluation.

As far as a motive for the killing, Comello's former lawyer contends that Comello was deluded by conspiracy theories and was defending himself when he shot the victim.

To support this, the defense said that Comello drove to Cali's house to perform a citizen's arrest.

A motion filed in the court by the defense contends Comello believed Cali "held a significant status in a worldwide criminal cabal bent on the destruction of American values and the American way of life."

According to the defense's motion, Comello planned to arrest Cali and deliver him to the military.

The defense also stated that the two men began arguing, and Comello "shot Cali in self-defense" when Cali made a "furtive action" with his hand.

In July 2019, citing failing health, Peter Gotti requested compassionate release under the First Step Act.

His request was denied two months later in September and later requested it again in December, being again denied in January 2020.

In September 2020, the 80-year-old Gotti was housed at the Federal Medical prison in Butner, North Carolina.

The 80-year-old Gotti has a release date of 09/10/2031. On this date, he will be 90 years old.

With Peter Gotti spending his final days in Federal prison, the reign of the Gottis leading the Family may have officially ended.

However, the Gambino Crime Family is still living on stronger than ever.

Printed in the USA
CPSIA information can be obtained
at www.ICGtesting.com
LVHW090154280823
756472LV00006B/59

9 781393 196402